D1111094

Under the Ancestors' Shadow

UNDER THE ANCESTORS' SHADOW

*Kinship, Personality,
and Social Mobility
in China*

BY

FRANCIS L. K. HSU

STANFORD UNIVERSITY PRESS
STANFORD, CALIFORNIA

To Ralph Linton

One of my intellectual ancestors

The preparation of this study was made possible by funds granted by the Viking Fund, Inc. (now Wenner-Gren Foundation for Anthropological Research), a foundation created and endowed at the instance of A. L. Wenner-Gren for scientific, educational, and charitable purposes. The Viking Fund, Inc., is not, however, the author or publisher of this publication, and is not to be understood as approving by virtue of its grant, any of the statements made, or views expressed, therein.

Under the Ancestors' Shadow was originally published in the United States by Columbia University Press in 1948. A British edition was published by Routledge & Kegan Paul Ltd. in 1949. The present edition, which contains a new chapter and a new appendix, was published in paperback by Anchor Books in 1967 and reissued in hardcover and paperback by Stanford University Press in 1971.

Foreword to the 1967 Edition

SINCE publication of this book in 1948, China has undergone a drastic political change which startled the rest of the world. Two kinds of questions are continuously being raised in connection with this momentous development. How could a people with such an ancient tradition of attachment to family and kin so quickly turn Communist? The other is not so much a question as a feeling—now that the Chinese have come under totalitarian control, their lives and ways have been (or will soon be) completely changed.

To the first question the answer is that the common man in China has not been converted to Communism; the Chinese have merely come under the control of a Communist government, in the same sense that they had before this come under the control of a Nationalist government or a Republican government and, centuries ago, a Mongol government or a Manchu government. Communism as an eagerly sought road to salvation and Communism as a superimposed political administration are not the same thing. While all reports indicate that a great deal of popular enthusiasm does indeed exist among the Chinese for their new government, they also clearly say that the new government achieved power through military and political conquest.

In the latter eventuality the political power in control, like all such powers, must necessarily attempt to mold the people under its control to suit its needs. But its long-term success is not a foregone conclusion and will depend upon how far the needs for control on the part of the ruling government can meet the needs for a good, or at least satisfactory, life on the part of a majority of the ordinary people. If the new government, with its revolutionary ideology, tries to break up some of the networks of human relations and to erase some of the age-old cultural values it must provide alternatives. These alternatives, in the long run, must be more or less acceptable to a majority of the Chinese if they are to be absorbed. The many events which occurred in mainland China—establishment of communes, thought reforms, and public confessions (to name but a few) since 1949—show how hard the new government has been trying to create a new psychic foundation for the spread of the new social organization and ideology. The fact that seventeen years after they have come to power the new government has to resort to the often unruly Red Guards is indubitable evidence that the new government has a long way to go before achieving its objectives.

There can be no unequivocal assertion in the positive or negative about how much the Chinese have changed their lives and ways since 1949. All societies and cultures change, even without external pressure, some more slowly than others. Chinese society and culture have, in Western eyes, been changing so slowly that they were often used as the prime example of the unchanging East. But since the middle of the nineteenth century China has never had the freedom of pondering its own way and moving at its own pace. Western (and later Japanese) anxiety to open up China, for whatever purpose, gave China and the Chinese no alternative. There were Chinese leaders who talked about partial change—using Western knowledge for practical ends but adhering to Chinese knowledge as the foundation and structure. There were others who promoted total Westernization. For all Chinese it was not a question of change or no change, but one of how much change.

Many changes have come to China, in any case, since the middle of the nineteenth century: some eagerly sought by the Chinese and others more or less forced on them.

Even without a recital of China's many military defeats, political concessions, and economic shackles at the hands of European powers and Japan, it is not hard to name extensive changes besides such obvious material additions as modern means of transportation, movie houses, race tracks, and Western medicine. Coeducation and romantic love were common in the colleges; foot-binding was on its way out; concubinage, filial piety, and the joint family ideal were being assailed; iconoclasm and the vernacular Chinese were gaining popularity. Even "West Town," the community deep in the mountains of remote southwestern China which forms the subject of this book, was not entirely free from some of these new elements.

True, in 1941–43 the traditionally Chinese attitudes were still so strong in "West Town" that they largely held their own. A local boy returned to West Town after a period of schooling in Hong Kong and one day walked hand in hand with his newlywed bride on the street. Some local man threw a bucketful of human manure over their heads from behind. They had no redress, since they had violated the local taboo against intimacy between the sexes in public, and had to leave town.[1] While I was in the area a deadly cholera epidemic broke out which took over two hundred lives in less than a month. All sorts of traditional measures of defense against the menace were taken, including moral injunctions and public seances and prayer meetings at tremendous cost. At the same time modern health precautions, cholera injections, and efficacious medicines were available free of charge to one and all through the schools and a hospital. But West Towners were not enthusiastic about the new ideas and drugs. The age-old measures remained all-important. Some local people took the new measures and participated in the old. Others frankly refused the intruding help.[2] However, the fact that

[1] I reported this in *Magic and Science in Western Yunnan*, New York: Institute of Pacific Relations, 1943, p. 5.
[2] I reported and analyzed this entire epidemic and measures to cope with it in *Religion, Science and Human Crises*, London: Routledge & Kegan Paul, 1952.

there were local travelers and students who went to the big cities and ports and the fact that some local well-to-do men donated money and effort to build a hospital and schools were indications that West Town was not insulated from the kind of changes which were pressing all China long before the coming of Communism.

There is, of course, no doubt that the changes which have taken place or been envisaged by the new government since 1949 were more drastic and more massive than China had seen so far. I am sure that even West Town has become less isolated and has more actively felt the hands of the government than before. But cultural traditions are tenacious. We must guard against being too hastily impressed by changes that can be brought about in less than two decades in a way of life which has existed and consolidated itself for over twenty centuries. With modern means of propaganda and organization things can undoubtedly be speeded up somewhat. Yet consider the de-Nazification efforts in a decimated Germany and the de-militarization efforts in an atom-bombed Japan. In either case the conquerors had all the cards, and the supposedly oppressed elements of the population actively sought to co-operate. Can we honestly say that these efforts have been great successes and that the emerging Germany and Japan have little or no psychological or cultural linkage with their predecessors? In Germany anti-Semitism has reportedly raised its ugly head once more and former Nazis have reappeared more than once in high places. In Japan the authoritarian and militant Soka Gakai has become so popular and powerful that it recently organized its members into an active political party that is already the third force in the country.

It does not mean that the German or Japanese situation under occupation is identical with that of the Chinese situation after the ascension of Communism. But it does indicate that drastic changes in whichever direction (whether by democratic forces who want more development of the free institutions or by authoritarian forces who want more control) cannot be achieved easily. In each case the subsequent development is intimately tied up with that which existed before. An understanding of the old is essential for an understanding of the new.

Over and above the problem of change, there is great scientific value in knowledge of the basic nature of Chinese society and culture as an end in itself. The Industrial and French Revolutions had profoundly changed the lives of continental Europeans. But that change does not lessen the importance of such a great scholarly work as that of Eileen Power: *The Medieval People*. Without being pretentious, the present book offers a look at the pattern of life of a Chinese rural community before more drastic change overtook it. But we hope to do a little more than that. The new Chapter XII, "Kinship, Personality and Social Mobility in China," provides the reader with a new look at some conclusions of this book in the light of more recent developments under the Kuomintang but especially since the Communist Revolution.

In preparing this book for the new edition I have been greatly aided by my helpers, Mrs. Andrea Sherwin and Mrs. Adele Andelson. I am also grateful to Mrs. W. C. Ts'ien for her help in rewriting the Chinese characters.

F.L.K.H.

October 1966

Contents

xii   *Contents*

List of Illustrations

CHAPTER I

Introduction

WHEN I was about fourteen years old, I overheard a conversation between my father and my oldest brother, who was twenty years my senior. They were talking about the rise and fall of some families with whom they were acquainted and about the circumstances involved. My oldest brother concluded with the following observation: "Wealth is treasure of the nation. Every family can keep it only for a period of time. It must be kept circulating." I do not recall my father's reaction, but since then I have been aware of the rise and fall of families, not only within my limited world of acquaintances but also in other communities about which I knew anything at all.

It is interesting that Dr. Martin Yang, writing about the North China village in which he was brought up, of which he has intimate knowledge, made the following observation:

No family in our village has been able to hold the same amount of land for as long as three or four generations. Usually a family works hard and lives frugally until they can begin to buy land. Members of the second generation continue in the same pattern so that more land is added to the family holdings and it becomes well-to-do. Those of the third generation merely enjoy themselves, spending much but earning little. No new land is bought and gradually it becomes necessary to begin to sell. In the fourth generation more land is sold until ultimately the family sinks into poverty. This cycle takes even less than a hundred years to run its course. The extravagant members die out, and their children begin again to accumulate property. Having suffered, and being fully acquainted with want, they realize the necessity of hard work and self-denial to repair the family fortune. By this time the original big family is gone and in its place there are several small, poor families. Some of these begin to buy land. Thus the same cycle is started again.[1]

As far as the ratio between resources and population is concerned, under given conditions of technology, such an observation falls short of plausibility and even verges on naïveté. For overpopulation is an obvious fact in China. Even where all cultivated land is equally distributed among the farmers, the holding per person is less than half an acre;[2] it seems questionable that "hard work" and "self-denial" alone can cause families to prosper. Yet when one considers all families as being under the same unfavorable conditions, he will have less difficulty in confirming the above observation concerning family vicissitudes.

Furthermore, fluctuations in family fortunes do not pertain only to the peasants. They are also evident among illustrious households of the Empire. Some of these households rose to prominence in a few generations. Most of them degenerated very rapidly and fell to commonplace levels in a few generations. Many of them rose and fell within two generations.

In search of some documentary support, I examined the contents of some books, among them *Native Places and Dates of Birth and Death of Noted Men in Various Dynasties*[3] and *Eminent Chinese of the Ch'ing Period* (A.D. 1644–1912).[4] Through the first of these works, which includes more than twelve thousand entries, I have compared the "native places" of all who possess the same clan names. If two individuals of the same clan name shared the same "native place" and were born from fifteen to sixty years apart, I assume that they were related in kinship and might be father and son or grandfather and grandson. The result

---

[1] Martin Yang, *A Chinese Village*, New York, 1945, p. 132.

[2] G. B. Cressey, *China's Geographic Foundations*, New York, 1934, p. 395.

[3] Chiang Liang-fu, *Li Tai Ming Jen Nien Li Pei Chuan Chung Piao*, Shanghai, 1937.

[4] Arthur W. Hummel, ed., 2 vols., Washington, D.C., 1943.

of the survey was to find a surprisingly small number of individuals who came within the specifications.[5]

The second work gives the biographies of about seven hundred individuals within a single dynasty and much detailed data about their immediate origin, life, and work. My examination of these data shows that intellectual and especially political prominence rarely endured *continuously* for more than two generations in any given family, particularly along the direct lineal line. There are even few cases in which father and son were both eminent enough to be included as two separate entries.[6]

[5] For details see Appendix IV.

[6] In this connection an investigation conducted by K. A. Wittfogel, a leading authority on Chinese history, is most interesting. The procedures used and the broad conclusions reached are as follows: "If we could establish the social position of the fathers and grandfathers of a large number of these officials, especially for the period following the establishment of the examination system (T'ang: A.D. 618–906), we might get a statistical picture of great significance. Under the guidance of our friend and temporary assistant, Wang Yu-chuan, a group of history students was brought together. For the sake of analogy, they went through the biographies of two pre-T'ang dynasties, Han (206 B.C.–220 A.D.) and Chin (265–420 A.D.) as well as the standard collections of biographies of the T'ang (618–906), Sung (960–1279), Yuan (1280–1368), Ming (1368–1644) and Ch'ing (1644–1911) eras, mostly taken from the *Dynastic Histories*. A final study has still to be made, but our preliminary analysis seems to confirm absolutely what the qualitative investigation by Chinese scholars had previously indicated. Some 'fresh blood' may have been absorbed from the lower strata of society by means of the examination system; but on the whole the ruling officialdom reproduced itself socially more or less from its own ranks" (*New Light on Chinese Society*, an investigation of China's socio-economic structure, Institute of Pacific Relations pamphlet, New York, 1938, pp. 11–12; by permission of the institute). Taken superficially, Dr. Wittfogel's findings seem to contradict the thesis which I have just outlined: that families rise and fall within a few generations. A thorough discussion with Dr. Wittfogel has revealed two things. If we represent an individual who was an official by the letter A and one who was unknown by the letter O, Dr. Wittfogel's investigation revealed that the pattern between the generations may either be (I) A–A, or A–A–A, or even A–A–A–A, or (II) A–O–A, or A–O–O–A or even A–O–O–O and O–O–O–A. Sometimes the individuals so represented were not all members of the same lineal line so that, for example, in A–A or in A–O–O–A, the second A may represent the first A's brother's son or his first cousin's great-grandson. Without being able to go into the accumulated data, which await

It may, of course, be objected that these two works only recorded the individuals who reached considerable heights and fail to touch upon others who were in humbler stations. This objection is met by a study of the biographies in district histories, the details of which are given in Appendix IV.

Bearing the limitations of such records in mind, one cannot but be struck by the facts which they do reveal, particularly in a culture in which, up to very recent times, the only important goal of life for the majority of those who were gifted and motivated toward success was to attain a high place in the bureaucracy. When we realize that political prominence did not depend upon the man-land ratio, but very strongly upon influence, especially family influence, the facts revealed by these records become even more striking. As a proverb has it, "If one man has found the path of salvation, even his chickens and dogs enter heaven with him."

Thus, we have a contradictory situation. On the one hand, the inherent tendency of the mechanism of social and political climbing should cause prominent families to continue their prominence indefinitely, particularly along the lineal line. On the other hand, these prominent families tend actually to decline within comparatively short periods of time.

Why do families rise and fall? I looked at some of these families closely. I found that the behavior exhibited by

---

future analysis, Dr. Wittfogel is of the opinion that the occurrence of A–A–A type was about as frequent as that of A–O–O–A type. The second thing which emerged from my discussion with Dr. Wittfogel concerns the question of the degree of prominence which determined that those considered in the investigation were members of the "ruling officialdom." In this there is a wide range. Not only were there fathers and sons who were separated by many degrees in rank, but some were included who were merely scholars without office. Seen in the light of these qualifications, Dr. Wittfogel's findings, we may conclude, when they are thoroughly analyzed and stated, may prove his thesis that the ruling officialdom *as a whole* reproduced itself more or less, but at the same time it may support rather than contradict my present thesis, that families rise and fall, particularly where the lineal line is concerned.

members of the rising families and those of the falling families were sharply contrasted. The climbers tended to be careful, rational, frugal, industrious, and sincere. Those who were declining tended to be vain, impulsive, extravagant, carefree, and arrogant. Then I considered the rise and fall of dynasties and examined some literature which attempted to explain this so-called cycle of Chinese history. The author of the famous historical novel *The Romance of Three Kingdoms* began his great work with this fatalistic observation: "The conditions under heaven are such that, after a long disunity, there will be unity; after a long unity, there will be disunity."[7]

Historians who employ the methods of the social sciences advance, in general, two schools of thought on the subject. One is led by Dr. K. A. Wittfogel, who sees the Chinese society as consisting of three sections: (*a*) the state, or the ruling aristocracy, (*b*) bureaucracy, and those who maintain a symbiotic life with it, and (*c*) the masses, or the peasants. The explanation is that, as time goes on, the second section of society tends to fatten at the expense of the others, thus leading to a general crisis and the fall of the dynasty. In Dr. Wittfogel's own words:

A vicious economic-political circle resulted: accumualtion of private wealth of the new type and accumulation of private possession of land in the hands of officials, "gentry," and great merchants, reduction of land tax, enfeebling of the state, agrarian crisis, internal crisis, external crisis —invasions—state crisis. Although this vicious circle could be periodically smoothed over by the fall and rise of "dynasties," it could never be really overcome.[8]

[7] This passage has been translated differently by C. H. Brewitt-Taylor, as follows: "Empires wax and wane; States cleave asunder and coalesce" (*San Kuo* or *Romance of The Three Kingdoms*, Shanghai, 1925, I, 1. The difference in meaning between this translation and mine is obvious.

[8] K. A. Wittfogel, "The Foundations and Stages of Chinese Economic History," *Zeitschrift für Sozialforschung*, IV, No. 1 (1935), 53. The theory was documented in the English language for the first time by Yu-chuan Wang: "The Rise of Land Tax and the Fall of Dynasties in China," *Pacific Affairs*, IX (June, 1936), 201–220.

The other school of thought, based upon the comparatively more obvious fact of overpopulation, is older and therefore more generally subscribed to. Its conclusion is that after a number of peaceful years the population grew, but the resources, namely, land and technology, remained more or less constant. When overpopulation reached an unbearable point, a period of chaos followed, precipitated by famine, flood, diseases, civil wars, and widespread brigandage. This caused the loss of a large part of the population, which enabled the country to return, once again, to a number of peaceful years under a new dynasty.[9] One writer observed that the more he examined Chinese society, the more he was convinced of the operation of the famous Malthusian population law.[10]

The truth in both lines of thought is undeniable, but following my own trend of thinking I came upon a new factor. I scrutinized the conditions of the ruling house and its bureaucracy and found that the founders of dynasties or their immediate predecessors usually exhibited signs of wisdom and understanding concerning their problems and worked very hard at their governmental tasks; but the losers of dynasties or their immediate predecessors apparently often lacked good judgment and understanding concerning their problems. Some were either licentious and callous or hopelessly weak. As a rule the former had a number of able military and ministerial assistants; the latter received their chief support from eunuchs and members of their harem, and generally turned a deaf ear to, or even killed, any minister who dared to give them unwanted advice. Under such regimes, in spite of general poverty and hardship among the populace, the cost of the imperial household and the bureaucracy which it fostered would steadily increase rather than decrease; the ruler and his

[9] See Ta Chen, *Population in Modern China*, Chicago, 1946, pp. 3–6.
[10] Walter H. Mallory, *China; Land of Famine*, New York, 1926.

favored assistants would either fail to realize the seriousness of the situation or deliberately ignore it.

Thus, while bureaucratic interference with the land tax and overpopulation could be observed near the fall of dynasties, weaknesses of the rulers and their assistants were equally obvious. The weight of the latter factors as contributing causes to the situation must not be minimized.

Seen from this angle, the rise and fall of ordinary families in a small community, of those of officials in high places, and of those of rulers of the empire appear to meet on a common ground. The rising family groups are usually associated with individuals having one series of personality characteristics, while the declining family groups are usually associated with those having a different series of personality characteristics.

Why is it that weak personalities usually compose declining families, while strength characterizes the members of rising families? Early exposure of heirs apparent and of other young princes to harems and eunuchs seems to be at least partially responsible for weakness in the case of the aristocracy. There is, however, no such ready answer in the case of other families. The problem puzzled me for a number of years. Some time ago I came to appreciate a difference in social behavior between the wealthier households and the poorer ones in some parts of China. The wealthier and more scholarly tended to adhere much more than the poor to the socially upheld big-family ideal; this apparently explains the larger households among the rich as a whole as contrasted with the poor as a whole.[11]

Using this difference as a springboard, I proceeded to analyze the culture of West Town. It is here that an answer may be found to the long-puzzling problem—based not so much upon a difference in social behavior between the rich and the poor as upon different consequences of the same social behavior because of economic and status dif-

[11] F. L. K. Hsu, "The Myth of Chinese Family Size," *American Journal of Sociology* XLVIII (May, 1943), 555–562.

ferences. The social behavior here referred to centers around "The Ancestors' Shadow."[12]

Seen in the culture of West Town, the most important factors under the ancestors' shadow which bear on the personality of the individual are two: authority and competition. The first factor consists of the father-son identification and the big-family ideal. The second factor involves a struggle for one or all of three things: (*a*) the glory of common ancestors, (*b*) the glory of a particular lineage within the clan, or (*c*) the position of most illustrious or favorite descendant of the ancestors.

The father-son identification and the big-family ideal support each other. Together they are responsible for a social system which deprives the younger generation of any feeling of independence, while at the same time it enables them to *share* whatever wealth or glory is due to their immediate or remote ancestors. These factors also lay the foundation for an education which is dependent on the past and is intended to shape the young exclusively in the image of the old. This education encourages the young to participate in the adult world much earlier than do the young in Europe and in America.

This identification of the generations and this educational process have the inevitable result that the sons of the rich are as rich as their fathers, and those of the poor are as poor as their fathers. The sons of the rich not only share their fathers' wealth but also enjoy their fathers' power and prestige. The sons of the poor not only share their fathers' poverty but also partake of their fathers' humility or lack of position. Like their fathers, the poor sons have to work hard for whatever they receive. With their fathers they have to struggle for their very existence. The sons of the rich find themselves differently situated. Unlike their

[12] The word "shadow" is used in a figurative sense. As is explained later, the individual has no social existence apart from his forebears. His worth and destiny are not only closely bound up with those of his ancestors but are also regarded as reflections and results of what the past members were and did. Seen from this angle the individual may be said to exist under the shadow of his ancestors.

fathers, who probably have had to labor to reach their present status, they cannot work for what they receive for fear their parents will lose face. It is an integral part of the latter's social position that their sons shall not work. Under such conditions the younger men have no productive way of expressing themselves. Like their fathers now, they have only to ask for what they want. In fact, wealth, power, and prestige are showered on them whether they want them or not.

These differences are expressed most clearly through the second factor which bears on the personality of the individual. Competition as defined by such a culture merely dovetails into and amplifies the factor of authority.

Among both the rich and the poor West Towners competition is very active. But while the poor compete merely for their existence, the rich have gone far beyond that and compete for power and prestige. Here two points of differentiation occur. The poor, being hard pressed by the tasks of making a living, have little time and energy left for anything else and are, therefore, much less ancestor conscious. At any rate, they are not proud to tell their forebears about their present condition. The rich, being comfortably situated, have ample opportunities for leading any kind of life they want to lead. They will enjoy themselves, and one of their main sources of enjoyment will be to polish up the glory of their ancestors or work toward the position of the most illustrious descendants of the kinship group or both.

A second point of differentiation has already been suggested by the first. There is not only rivalry for ancestral favors but also rivalry within the household. The younger members of a poor family not only are little concerned about their remote ancestors but also have less incentive to compete for paternal approval. The older men, being poor, have little material wealth to give them, whereas wealthy fathers can express their pleasure or displeasure in very material ways.

Therefore, while the same father-son identification exists

among the rich and the poor, the difference in their economic conditions has caused the young of the rich and the
young of the poor to develop two different types of personality: the former, a higher degree of *dependence* upon
the old and upon traditional authority, the latter, a higher
degree of *independence* from the old and from traditional
authority. For throughout life children of the poor have to
give for what they take, while those of the rich have to rely
upon what is given to them.

This can be seen to apply not only to people living in
small communities but also to inhabitants of large centers;
not only to those who come of humble circumstances but
also to those prominent in the social scale.

A POINT OF METHODOLOGY

In the following chapters an attempt will be made to
describe and to analyze the cultural settings of these and
other types of personality in West Town. Before proceeding
any further, a few words on methodology are in order. The
term "personality" will be taken to mean "the organized
aggregate of psychological processes and states pertaining
to the individual."[13] It stresses that which is unique in the
individual. On the other hand, the characteristics of such
aggregates may be shared by a number of individuals. In
such a case there emerges a type of "personality configuration." If the elements of a personality configuration
are more or less universal in a culture, we shall call it the
"basic personality configuration." If a personality configuration is shared by the majority of individuals occupying a
particular position in the society, we shall call it the "status
personality configuration."[14] Status personality configura-

[13] Ralph Linton, *Cultural Background of Personality*, New York,
1945, p. 84.
[14] For an exposition of the Linton-Kardiner formulation on the
subject see *ibid.*, pp. 129–130. The terms which they use are "basic
personality type" (or structure) and "status personality type." I have
deliberately used two slightly different terms for one reason. Their

tions are modifications of basic personality configurations in one way or another, but are not opposed to them.

However, it is very difficult to ascertain and to systematize the contents of different types of personality configurations in different cultures and to work them into some taxonomical order. Instead of obtaining a clear picture, we find very little general agreement. It is difficult to establish categories which are universally valid and meaningful. Kretschmer, Nietzsche, Jung, Eduard Spranger, and Freud have, among others, each made valuable contributions.[15] But when I tried to apply some of these systems to the culture under consideration, I found that either many of the facts had to be left out or the categories suggested were without significance to the problem in hand.

I have little doubt that the chief reasons for my failure were my meager knowledge of the sciences of the mind and the fact that I had no psychologist or analyst to collaborate with me in the field.

Recognizing my limitations, I then adopted a different procedure. Instead of approaching the culture with a fixed psychological scheme and fixed contents for the scheme, I let the overt behavior of the people be my guide. Instead of employing psychoanalytic terminology, I resorted to common-sense denominators. In this way my categories and terms may not be too exact, but they are more meaningful for the culture in question. My analyses and conclusions may not penetrate the deepest layers of the mind, but they at least provide all relevant facts of the culture with a proper perspective.

discussion of these entities is primarily psychoanalytic, being concerned with psychological potentialities and their ability to act through the projective system. My present work is primarily sociological, being concerned with institutions and their obvious relations to personality norms exemplified by overt behavior. Using exactly the same terms may confuse the readers. However, in the last analysis, the two sets of terms have an essential area of common ground.

[15] The contributions of these and other scientists on the subject have been admirably summarized and appreciated by Otto Klineberg in his *Social Psychology*, New York, 1940, pp. 427–436.

The procedure is similar to that of Dr. Abram Kardiner[16] in that it allows great flexibility in the characterization of the types and their interpretation. But it differs from that of the latter in several respects. First, Kardiner's works are couched in Freudian terms, while the present study is not. Secondly, while realizing that religion and folklore are not all of any culture, Kardiner nevertheless consistently refers to them whenever he speaks of culture. In one connection he says:

> According as the experiences varied, so did the products of the *projective systems* in folklore and religion. This gave us our first clue, and the same procedure was used on more and more phenomena.
>
> If therefore we again look at the correlation in the previous paragraph, we find that if childhood disciplines constitute one order of institutions then religion and folklore comprise another. We called the former primary and the latter secondary. Also there was something created in the individual by his childhood experiences which formed the basis for the projective systems subsequently used to create folklore and religion.[17]

Although admiring Dr. Kardiner's contribution, I must observe that the development of culture is a complex thing and cannot be fitted into any one simplified formula. Such a simplified formula is least likely to apply to West Town, which has been under the influence of a literary heritage of long standing and of a central government that rigorously and continuously enforced certain nationwide rules of conduct.

However, Dr. Kardiner is not entirely unaware of the weakness of his argument, namely, of trying to explain the basic personality type by the culture and also the culture by the basic personality type. To quote him again:

> The crucial question then becomes: what determines the parental attitude toward children and hence the specific influences to which the child is subject? In general, one can

---

[16] *The Individual and His Society*, New York, 1943, and *The Psychological Frontiers of Society*, New York, 1945.
[17] Kardiner, *The Psychological Frontiers of Society*, pp. 23–24.

say that these parental attitudes are determined by the social organization and the subsistence techniques.[18] Whereas this statement is, strictly speaking, true, we are likely to get many surprises unless we qualify it with several conditions. And these conditions are of the highest importance in relation to cultural change.

If we attempt to define those conditions which qualify the socio-economic determinants of parental attitudes, apparently we immediately run into the problem of social origins. *This is a hopeless task,* and theories at this point are no substitute for demonstrable evidence[19] [italics mine].

Dr. Kardiner winds up his exposition by the following:

What we have been saying is that the operational value of the concept of basic personality is not only to diagnose the factors which mold the personality but also to *furnish some clues* about why these influences are what they are[20] [italics mine].

Two things would have enabled the analyst to avoid oscillating between "a hopeless task" and "some clues." He could have taken the sounder theoretical position of seeing the relation between culture and personality as a spiral as Ralph Linton would have it. According to this view, culture and personality never completely meet at the same points, but follow each other closely.[21] Or, instead of trying to explain at the same time the influences of culture on personality and of personality on culture, he could have obtained better results by concentrating on one side of the picture first. If it is argued that such a procedure artificially breaks up the integral whole of culture and personality, the usual answer is that all scientific efforts create more or less artificial boundary lines between phenomena of the universe, which are essentially one integrated whole. The present work is an attempt to determine the effects of a

[18] Kardiner, "The Concept of Basic Personality Structure as an Operational Tool in the Social Sciences," in Ralph Linton, ed., *The Science of Man in the World Crisis,* New York, 1945, p. 119.
[19] *Ibid.,* p. 119.
[20] *Ibid.,* p. 121.
[21] Personal communication from Dr. Linton.

Chinese culture on the personality—not the effects of the personality on the culture.

Thirdly, in still another respect the present work differs from that of Dr. Kardiner. As a good Freudian, Dr. Kardiner takes the preponderant importance of early training for granted. In fact, the concept of projective system to which he attaches so much importance implies that early training means everything. But personality and culture are both continua. The influence of culture on personality throughout life cannot be lost sight of. As Linton has pointed out:

> While the culture of any society determines the deeper levels of its members' personalities through the particular techniques of child-rearing to which it subjects them, its influence does not end with this. It goes on to shape the rest of their personalities by providing models for their specific responses as well. This latter process continues throughout life.[22]

In the present work the cultural influences on the individual will be traced not only during his infancy but also in his adulthood and old age. Personality will not be regarded merely as the end result of early training, instead, it will be seen in the light of its continued development in and articulation with the culture and its institutions.

THE FIELD

West Town is within a day's journey on foot or horseback from the Burma Road. It is bordered by a lake on one side and a mountain rising to about 14,000 feet above sea level on the other. The general elevation is about 6,700 feet above sea level. The general occupation of the entire area is agriculture, rice being the staple crop. However, trading in various forms is also very common and is the backbone of West Town economy. Trading in this com-

---

[22] Linton, *Cultural Background of Personality*, p. 143; by permission of D. Appleton–Century Co.

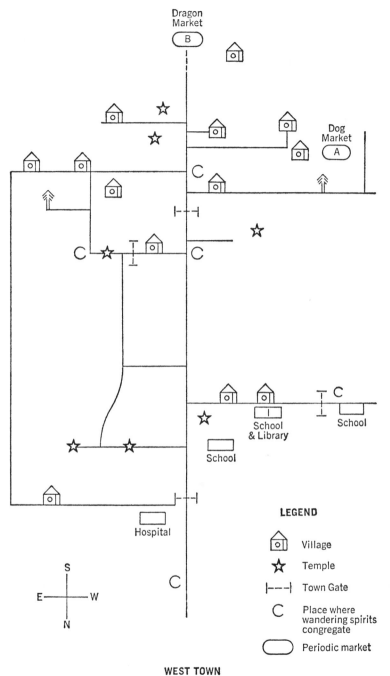

Dragon
Market
B

Dog
Market
A

C

C   C

C

School
& Library

School

C

School

Hospital

LEGEND

Village

Temple

Town Gate

C   Place where
wandering spirits
congregate

Periodic market

S
E——W
N

C

WEST TOWN

FIGURE 1

munity includes both local exchanges in periodic markets and large-scale commercial adventures into the outer world.

West Town is a rural market town. Its first appearance in Chinese history was in the T'ang Dynasty, about a thousand years ago. Today it is under the jurisdiction of a district (*hsien*) government south of it. The local administrative head is a *chen chang* (the headman of a rural town). Theoretically the *chen chang* is elected by the people and then appointed by the magistrate. In fact, he is usually selected by the magistrate with the implicit approval of the people.

The population consists of about 1,000 households and about 8,000 persons. The former are grouped into ten *pao* of about 100 households each. Each *pao* has a headman. Each *pao* is subdivided in ten *chia,* of about 10 households each. Each *chia* has a headman. Both the *pao* headman and the *chia* headman are truer electees of the people than the *chen* headman.

West Town proper is not walled. Its outer appearance is very irregular. There is only one continuous thoroughfare, which leads from the north to the south. The other streets run in east-west direction into it at irregular intervals. Some years ago four gates were erected, one at each end of the main thoroughfare, one at the end of a street which runs into it from the east, and one at the end of a street from the west. In this way a large section of the town is shut from the outlying areas at night, when a town-hired watchman patrols the streets with a gang. However, the town's population is not confined within these gates. Outside are at least nine more or less clearly marked clusters of houses. Each of these clusters is called a village. Within the four gates, each street, or each section of a street, is also designated as a village.

The *chen chang* has charge of the public affairs of the town. Under him is a small police force supported by the town. The racial origin of the inhabitants is a moot question. Generally speaking, both the town and the district seat as well as their satellite villages in the entire area form one of the Min Chia colonies in Yunnan. Yet all the inhabitants of West Town and of eight of the nine near-by villages insist that their origin is Chinese. All have legends about the migration of their ancestors from some central provinces into Yunnan. The most frequently given place for the original habitat of these ancestors is "Nanking," a place which bears, however, little semblance to the present national capital. A few genealogical records assert that their ancestors were from Anwhei province. In this connection the observations of an Englishman, Major H. R. Davis, in the early nineties are most interesting.

The migrations of Chinese into the province have sometimes taken the form of conquering armies, of military colonies, or bands of immigrants sent by the Chinese Government from other parts of the empire. In other cases families or even individuals have come and settled among the non-Chinese tribes as traders or farmers. In all these cases the Chinese immigrants have doubtless intermarried with the original inhabitants, and a race of mixed blood, but of Chinese speech and customs, has thus grown up. After some generations this mixed race would always call themselves Chinamen, and would indignantly scout the idea of a descent from other tribes.

Besides this, as the influence and civilization of the Chinese have spread, the neighbouring tribes have found it convenient to learn to speak the Chinese language, and to adopt to some extent Chinese customs. A time eventually comes when some of them begin to despise their own language, customs, and dress, and to take a pride in adopting Chinese ways. When this idea once gets hold of them, the time is not far distant when they will call themselves Chinamen. A race of Chinese thus grows up who have really no Chinese blood in them.

This process can still be seen going on in Western China. One comes across tribes in all states of transformation. . . . The great majority . . . of the men of the tribes of Western China have so far come under the influence of the Chinese as to adopt their dress. With the women the case is different and the women's dress usually forms the distinctive mark by which tribes can be told apart.

After the adoption of Chinese dress by the men, their next step is the learning of the Chinese language. After

a few more generations perhaps even the women will learn to speak Chinese. This stage once reached, it does not take long for the tribe to become thoroughly Chinese in their ways, and when the women take to Chinese dress and to binding their feet, the transformation is complete. . . .
    I have watched this process going on with Lo-Los, Shans, Las . . . and no doubt it has taken place with nearly every tribe of Western China. The Chinese of this part of the empire must therefore be considered a very mixed race, and the use of the Chinese language can by no means be considered as proof of identity of race with other Chinamen.
    This process of absorption of other races by the Chinese has undoubtedly been going on all over China ever since the Chinese entered the country.[23]

As far as West Town is concerned, the order of acculturation seems to have been somewhat different from that observed by Davis. In West Town both sexes dress like other Chinese and all women past thirty have bound feet, but everybody speaks Min Chia as the mother tongue. In addition, most men and fewer women speak the Yunnanese dialect with a local accent.

Whether we agree with Davis in specific instances and whether West Towners are a mixture of Chinese and earlier inhabitants of the region or are a purer group of earlier inhabitants which has taken to Chinese culture is not important. In general the facts appear to tally with the observations of Davis. West Towners are jealous of their claim to Chinese origin and become annoyed when suggestions to the contrary are made. West Towners emphasize the segregation between the sexes. West Towners heavily guard and value virginity of unmarried women and chastity of married women. West Towners have institutionalized the cult of ancestors to an astonishing extent. Not only the very powerful and wealthy clans but also some ordinary ones establish a separate clan temple. Every family tries hard to ensure good sites for its graveyards ac-

[23] H. R. Davis, *Yunnan, the Link Between India and the Yangtze,* Cambridge, 1909, pp. 367–369; by permission of Cambridge University Press.

cording to geomancy.[24] Old imperial honors granted from Peking have been and are still highly valued. Elsewhere in China the honors displayed by any family are those attained by its own members, sometimes two or three generations earlier. For each honor attained there would be only one plaque over one portal of one family home. In West Town, on the other hand, every honor attained is displayed over the portals of several family homes. Many families display honors attained by some member of the clan who lived ten or more generations ago, in Ming Dynasty or even Yuan Dynasty. When real honors are lacking, imaginary ones are often substituted. These and many other things show that West Towners not only are Chinese in culture but also tend to insist that they are more Chinese in some respects than the Chinese in many other parts of China.

One thing which distinguishes West Town from most rural towns in China is that it contains a disproportionately large number of wealthy families. Some of these families are not merely local celebrities. They are rather outstanding even in the larger provincial cities and Kunming. A few years ago the foremost of these families performed a funeral ceremony that lasted for more than two months and cost about one million national dollars. The salaries of university professors at that time ranged between four to five hundred dollars a month.

Even the lesser families have considerable means. Soon after the fabulous funeral, the wedding of the young master of a small yard goods store in the town cost ten thousand national dollars. The wages of laborers at that time were about two to three dollars per day with board.

This wealth has certainly added vigor to the emphasis on imperial honors, ancestral emoluments, and other tradi-

[24] According to *Webster's Universal Dictionary* geomancy is "a kind of divination by figures or lines, formed by dots or points, originally on the earth and afterward on paper." The word is here used to denote a Chinese system by which a favorable or unfavorable site for burial is determined. The nature of the site is supposed to cause the rise or fall of future descendants of the family group.

tional ways. In recent years it has also been responsible for the establishment of three modern schools, a hospital, and a public library. The meaning of these modern institutions will be made clear in one of the succeeding chapters. Here it suffices to note that the hospital has about twenty beds, one graduate nurse, two doctors of medicine with proper credentials (one was trained in Peiping Union Medical College), a number of assistant nurses, and a nurses' training class. It has arrangements for free medicine and hospitalization for the poor. The schools are: one middle school, one primary school divided into two parts, and one normal school. The three combined had a total enrollment of about 1,400 in 1942. The first and second schools are coeducational. The principal of the middle school was a local man who had studied in Ts'ing Hwa University, Peiping.

In spite of these modern institutions, opium smoking among men over thirty was at the time of this investigation, still prevalent.[25] Not many years ago, before the advent of the power of the Central Government into the province, opium growing was general. Even as late as 1934 fields of opium poppy could be seen anywhere outside the walls of Kunming. This sight is no longer common today, especially in the more accessible parts. In the remoter interior of the province, the author has been told, opium is still being grown. Formerly opium growing and trading were the main source of income of many West Town families. The prohibition of its plantation has caused many small farmers to sigh about the vanished "Golden Age," but it has not prevented the wealthy families from making even greater profit out of the now scarcer supply. This has at least been partly responsible for the wealth of West Town.

There are three general classes of disasters which West Towners fear: diseases and epidemics; drought and too much rain; and banditry and war. Spirits and gods are the

---

[25] Concerning opium smoking and trading in several other areas in the province see H. T. Fei and T. Y. Chang, *Earthbound China*, Chicago, 1945, pp. 103–105, 163, 255–256, 280–282, 288, and 291.

main source of protection from practically all these troubles. The yearly cycle of life in the community consists largely of periodic offerings to the spirits or gods. The following table shows the major annual ritual observances.

RITUAL OBSERVANCES

Lunar month	Day	Occasion
1	1	Spring Festival; offerings to God of Wealth and Goddess Kuan Yin
	9	Birthday of Yu Hwang
	15	Birthday of T'ien Kuan
2	3	Birthday of Wen Ch'ang
	8	Ritual parade of Buddha through the town
	15	Birthday of Lao Chun
	19	Birthday of Kuan Yin
3	3	Birthday of Hauan Ti
	Ch'ing Ming	Visiting ancestral graveyards
	15	Birthday of God of Wealth
	16	Birthday of God of Mountains
	20	Birthday of Goddess Niang Niang
	28	Birthday of Gung Yueh
4	8	Birthday of Tai Tze
	15	Birthday of God of Fire
	20	Birthday of Yuan Shih
5	5	Tuan Wu Festival
6	6	Birthday of the Southern Dipper (Nan Tou)
	24	Birthday of Military Sages
7	7	Birthday of the Northern Dipper (Kuei Hsing)
	14	Ancestor worship
	15	Birthday of God of Earth
	19	Birthday of God of Crops
	23	Birthday of Dragon God
	29	Birthday of God of the Lower World of Spirits

Lunar month	Day	Occasion
8	1	Birthday of Chin Chia
	3	Birthday of Kitchen God
	15	The Moon Festival (Mid-Autumn Festival)
	27	Birthday of Confucius
9	9	Birthday of Tou Mu
10	15	Birthday of God of Water
	(Date varies)	Visiting ancestral graveyards
11	19	Birthday of Sun God
12	8	Birthday of Pa Ch'a
	23	God of Kitchen reports to heaven
	30	New Year's Eve; offerings to various gods

Many of these dates are also observed as ritual occasions in other parts of China, but in West Town instead of being celebrated by informal offerings, most of the occasions listed above involve formal feasting and a large gathering of celebrants. Each is a sort of temple fair, which elsewhere occurs only three or four times a year. Moreover, West Town has other celebrations not listed above. Scattered throughout the entire community are many temples of local patron gods (Pen Chu). Each of these gods governs one area or village, has a surname, a given name, and a birthday. Each of these birthdays is celebrated like the regular ones listed above, except that it concerns only the people of the area which is under the tutelage of that particular patron god.

In addition to the above there are other occasions which call for ritual offerings, such as the birth of a child and even the slaughtering of a pig. Often a family calls in a priest to pray and read the scriptures for a day. This is called a "prayer for peacefulness" and is performed in front of a small altar just outside the family home.

Some of the communal occasions are male affairs; some are female. A number of them are mixed gatherings, where men eat at one side of the temple and women on the other. The graveyard visit in the 3d Moon is one occasion on which men and women of the same household, young and old, visit the graves together. Some of these festivals, such as the Spring Festival, the Ch'ing Ming visit to ancestral graveyards, and the ancestor-worship festival in the 7th Moon, continue for more than one day.

As stated before, there are three general classes of most-feared disasters. With the exception of ancestor worship, the occasions for offerings are to insure good relations with the spirits and gods who might bring about some of these disasters. However, practically all these occasions are so much a part of the life of the community that little thought is given to the particular ends sought during the performance of the offerings. On the other hand, there are a number of special services which are performed only during a crisis. Ways of dealing with a cholera epidemic have been described and analyzed elsewhere.[26] Against the banditry which threatened the safety of the town, against war and possible bombing, against earthquakes (which have taken the lives of hundreds in a region south of West Town), and against other epidemics the methods used were largely similar to those already described as employed during the cholera epidemic. In case of a drought the procedures used differ somewhat. In the spring of 1943, when there was a severe drought, the image of the Dragon God was taken out of his temple and marched in a procession to the source of a spring on top of a mountain north of West Town. The dragon god was flanked in front by a "dry dragon," made of cloth, and behind by a "wet dragon," made of willow branches. The ensemble was kept near the source of the spring for two nights; then the image of the god was reinstalled in his temple. The idea was that there was something wrong with the source of the spring and that the god should be given the opportunity to do something about it in person. This was an elaborate procession,

---

[26] F. L. K. Hsu, *Magic and Science in Western Yunnan*, New York: Institute of Pacific Relations, 1943.

which even the Mohammedans from another village joined in. Normally, West Towners are not on friendly terms with the inhabitants of this Mohammedan village.

Needless to say, any ritual occasion involving some festivity provides amusement for the local people. Even the cholera prayer meeting during the worst period of the epidemic served that purpose to some degree. From this point of view, West Towners have plenty of entertainment. On the other hand, there is no conception of providing recreation in order to increase the efficiency of work. This applies to both sexes. There are no cinemas, no regular theaters or amusement centers in or near West Town. There is a theater of Yunnan drama in the district seat about fourteen miles south of West Town. But since transportation facilities are so meager, most people cannot afford the luxury of such a trip.

However, West Towners do have a certain amount of recreation apart from ritual affairs. In the evening, many shop doors may be found open to welcome neighbours and friends who care to come into the brightly lighted interior for a chat, and little clusters of men stand or squat near some street corner, often near a food stand. There are two or three tea houses, but they are recent additions to West Town life and are not yet popular. Generally they close too early in the evening. The topics discussed at these gatherings range from rumors about national affairs and market prices to local rights and wrongs.

Generally speaking, the younger people prefer the shops, while their elders congregate on the street corners. Therefore prices, war, adventures in Burma and on the Burma Road, and related topics dominate the shop gatherings, while food, local affairs, and reminiscences of the old days dominate the others.

Somewhat different is the gathering which takes place in a small "modern" dispensary located in the market square, usually in the afternoon, which is patronized mainly by the small number of *literati* of the town, including the only surviving *chu jen* (holder of an imperial degree). Other participants in this gathering are the son of one of the wealthiest men in town, recently returned from Hongkong, the *chen chang,* the local chief of police and members of the gentry.

Gambling provides another source of amusement. Until 1943 three gambling dens did a thriving business. They were open nightly and sometimes daily. One was in the home of a police detective; a second was in the home of the headman of a *pao;* the third was located in one of the clan temples. In the first den were gathered middle-aged and younger people who went in for big stakes, which in 1943 often ran into five figures. In the second den were gathered players of all age levels who went in for smaller stakes. In the third were gathered younger people only, and the stakes ran about the same as in the second den. The games played always included *ma chiang* and poker. All visitors, whether they played or not, received free hospitality—food, drink, and a pipe of opium if desired.

Apart from gambling in these dens, West Towners enjoy three days of general license in gambling every year. These begin on the first day of the First Moon and end on the night of the third day. For three days and nights old and young crowd into several shops, which are temporarily turned into open dens, and play, sometimes for tremendous stakes.

From all these sources of amusement women are entirely excluded. They derive their main sources of recreation from the various annual offerings and the periodic markets. Some of these markets take place once in three days; others occur once in six days, twelve days, or annually. The men and women who go to these fairs do so for various motives. Most go to buy or to sell, but many go to find out about prices, to inspect various goods, to meet friends, or occasionally, to enter into intrigues in love affairs. We have mentioned that some of the offering days are purely female affairs and that others are mixed gatherings. On all such occasions women wear their best clothes, make their offerings, and then sit down in circles of five or six in the temple yard to a hearty meal upon the food which has just been offered to the gods.

Before the days of the Burma Road, motor transportation was scarcely known to this region. A trip to Kunming took about two or three weeks each way on foot, horseback, or in man-carried litters. After the opening of the Road the town was soon connected to it by a sort of branch highway. But very few cars or trucks ever traveled on this road. The principal mode of transportation between West Town and the Road remained as before.

However, even before the existence of the Road, West Town had already felt some modernizing influences. The post office was installed a number of years ago. The sons of local families who went away to study or to trade in Peiping, Shanghai, Hongkong, Indo-China, and even Japan and the United States have always brought back some new ideas and ways of life. The hospital and the schools were organized before World War II. Today there are comparatively few males and females under thirty who are opium addicts or have bound feet.

The war has, of course, disturbed the old social routine. First there came conscription, which some families succeeded in dodging; secondly, mail service became more frequent; thirdly, a missionary college took refuge in the community. Most students of the latter institution came from Lower Yangtze provinces, and its faculty members consisted of English and American missionaries as well as Chinese. With these outsiders came freer relations between the sexes, church services, radios, medical care, a new manner of dress, and other innovations.

There were two other churches besides that of the college. One was supported by the American Episcopal Mission, the other by a theological seminary. A third group of people, who described themselves as "The Little Flock," also carried on considerable activity.

However, forces of tradition are still strong. It was still vividly told in 1943 that a young returner from Hongkong, who had walked along the street hand-in-hand with his bride, had been drenched with human excrement poured over their heads. According to the custom of the community such liberty was not allowed, and the young couple had no redress for the rough treatment.

Age-old customs also rule over other spheres of life. For example, public sanitation is completely lacking. Up to 1943 sickly dogs were seen throughout the town, the dung of donkeys, horses and mules was everywhere, and children and even adults stopped to relieve themselves on the main thoroughfare or in any by-way. No one bothered to clean up the streets. About six years ago the missionary college and the local middle school organized a joint campaign of public hygiene. Teachers and students of both institutions carried out a general cleaning up of all the streets and killed about fifty homeless dogs. Quite a number of the local inhabitants supported the effort. At the same time public lectures were given in the main streets by some of the students on the importance and significance of the campaign. For some time thereafter the town was free from obvious heaps of dirt and other signs of uncleanliness. But the old way of life returned gradually, and now few would even recall this campaign.

CHAPTER II

Yin Chai and Yang Chai: Worldly and Other-Worldly Residences

ANYBODY who visits West Town cannot fail to be struck by the aspect and the size of some family homes and by the large number of new homes. West Town is only a small market town in the interior of Yunnan. Its size and location make its appearance all the more striking.

Most family homes are two-storied structures. The walls are usually of brick and stone, plastered with white or yellow lime. The roofs are tiled, and the floors are made of wood or brick. The main portal of the family home (unlike the portals elsewhere in China and even in most parts of Yunnan) is very elaborate. The gateway itself is built of brick, with a foundation of stone, like the rest of the walls, and is about seven or eight feet in height. On this structure elaborate hand-carved woodwork, connecting both lintels of the gateway, is superimposed. Various geometrical or realistic designs are carved on the superstructure, which is usually painted in different colors, according to the carved designs, before being varnished or oiled. Above this wooden structure is a sort of tiled cover with wing-like projections similar to the roof of a Peking palace.

Often a family home has two or three portals, one leading into another. The outermost will have a triple top of brick and tile, with elaborate masonry and small wall paintings, while the next one beyond will have more of the carved woodwork and less of the masonry and wall painting. The third one will be much simpler than the other two.

Hanging over the outermost or over the middle portal

are often one or two plaques showing present or past honors bestowed upon members of the family. These are large varnished black plaques, with golden or pink characters indicating the nature of the honor and the name of the person who acquired it, as well as the date of the achievement. As pointed out before, elsewhere in China the honors thus displayed are those attained by members of the particular family displaying them, sometimes two or three generations earlier. For each honor there would be only one plaque over one portal of one family home. Not so in West Town. Here every honor attained will find itself indicated over the portals of several family homes. Many families display honors attained by a member of the clan who lived ten or more generations ago—and the member who attained this honor might have been a cousin many times removed. In this connection the principle of the-more-the-merrier is also followed. Thus on any one plaque there may be notices of several honors attained by different individuals who lived at different times. This provides the impression that the family has been continually on the side of the great. The desire for family honor is so acute that when real honors are not associated with any known member of the family, imaginary or alleged ones are inscribed on such plaques. There are plaques indicating that the house is the home of a *ta fu* (an official title applicable to various ranks which might be conferred upon the old father of the third assistant in a district government as well as that of a prefect), but mentioning neither the kind of *ta fu* nor the particular person who attained the title. There are plaques on which are four dazzling characters stating that the family was "highly favored and lavishly bestowed upon by the emperor." Such a plaque might show that the family member concerned was merely a student in a government school in the reign of Kwang Hsu. He either passed a preliminary examination or bought his way to such a studentship and could not, therefore, proceed any farther. Such an honor would not be displayed at all elsewhere in China. Another way of showing the same honor in West

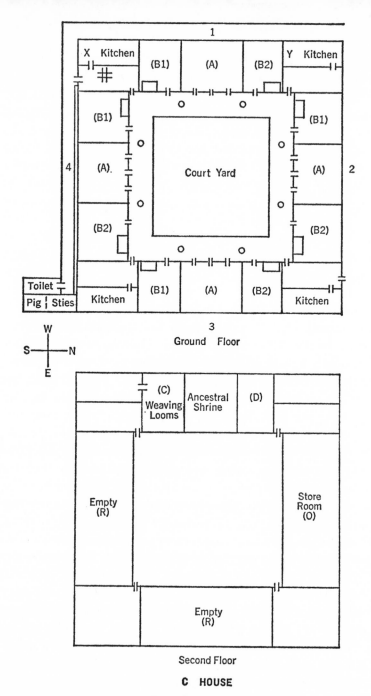

FIGURE 2

The eight small circles surrounding the courtyard are pillars.

Town is to display a plaque on which is written "First step in official ranks" (*chu teng shih chieh*).

Entering the outermost portal, facing east, the visitor would come upon a second one, facing south; the innermost one would face east again. Then he would enter the courtyard. The house may consist of one or two main courtyards, but would certainly comprise more than one minor courtyard. The diagram of the C house represents the typical one-main-courtyard type, while the diagram of the Y house represents the typical two-main-courtyards type. As a rule, there are three rooms on each floor to each of the four sides enclosing a courtyard, which is usually paved with slabs. The rooms on the ground floor are the living quarters of the family. In the diagram of the C house, B indicates bedrooms and A living rooms and ceremonial rooms, having doors that are usually removed during most of the year. The rooms on the second floor are different. Except on the western side, there are seldom any partitions, the space used for the three rooms below merging into one big room on each side. The middle room in the west wing is the room where the ancestral shrine and other shrines are located. Here the family makes its daily offering of incense and one or two dishes of simple food as well as some of its larger periodic sacrifices. For the occasion of the 15th of the 7th Moon, when the most important homage is paid to ancestors, the ancestral shrines are taken down to the room immediately below their usual abode, and there the rituals take place. Room C contains two hand looms, on which some of the females of the family work. Room D is used as a bedroom in emergencies. The big rooms R are left unoccupied. When needed they will be used as store rooms, just as Room C is used at present.

In each courtyard of the Y house the plan of the house is virtually a reproduction of that of the C house, except, of course, that the middle row of rooms connecting the two courtyards opens onto both. In this house none of the rooms on the second floor is used for a bedroom or

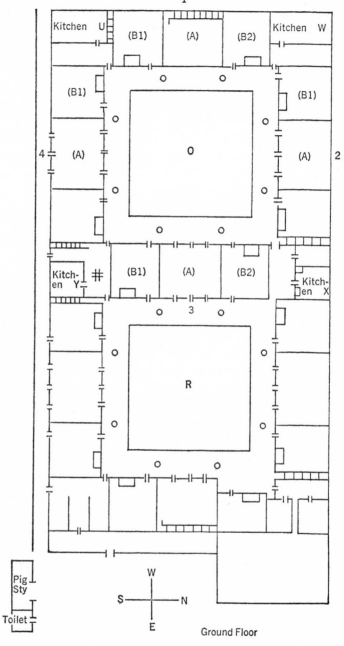

Y HOUSE

FIGURE 3

living room, and none is partitioned. The middle portion on the second floor of Row F is the place for ancestral and other shrines, where all sacrifices and offerings take place. At one end of this large room are two looms, which women of the house operate. The rooms on the second floor of the other sides of the two courtyards are all empty or contain a few articles which the family rarely uses. Empty, also, are all the rooms in courtyard R, except Row S.

The smaller Ch house consists of rooms along two sides of the court; those along the third side are yet to be built. The uses of the various rooms are similar to those in the other two examples given, except that the second floor portion of the western row of the house is partitioned into two rooms, as indicated. The smaller room is a bedroom for two men. Just outside that room, above the staircase, are the shrines.

Some interesting observations may be made on these houses, which apparently represent a very high percentage of all the houses in West Town proper. First, all these houses are too large for the families which built them. Not only single rooms are left empty but also whole rows of rooms remain unused. Second, most of the rooms on the ground floor (they are the most used) are too dark because of the broad covered corridors extending in front of them. The courtyard itself, with houses on four sides, gives very little opportunity for the sun to shine in. Third, the rooms on the ground floor, except when they are located in the middle row of a two-courtyard house, are often badly ventilated and damp when doors are closed; while the rooms on the second floor, though well ventilated, offer little protection against the elements. The tiles are often so badly put together that during the rainy season (from about May to September), occupants of second-floor rooms find it difficult to keep themselves dry.

In sharp contrast to such obvious neglect of the comforts of living are the painstaking effort and thought expended

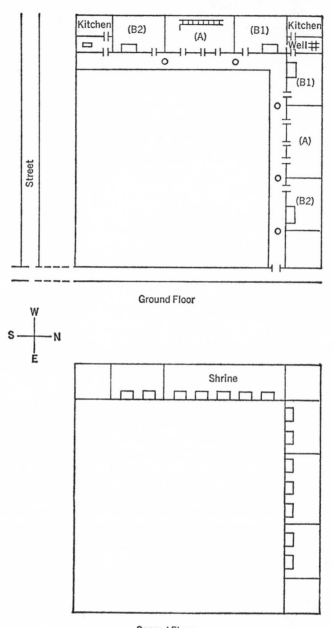

Ground Floor

Second Floor

CH HOUSE

FIGURE 4

on the appearance of these houses. We have just mentioned the elaborate woodwork, masonry, and the plaques on the portals of the family homes. Nor is effort spared in connection with the white-washed walls which enclose the entire house. The walls are as a rule only about two feet lower than the ridge of the house. Near the top of each high wall, on the outside, are small square, rectangular, or circular spaces, bordered by inset tiles. In each space is written a classical poem or a well-known saying, or else in each space is a painting in color, according to the traditional style: flowers, trees, birds, or landscapes. Often the poems and the sayings are inaccurately copied, so that mistakes abound. The upper margins on the inside of the walls are also similarly decorated. In addition the inside of the walls between the outermost and the middle portals to the family homes are more fully decorated. On the middle of the wall directly opposite the middle gateway are usually painted four large characters in black, *Ts'ai yun nan hsien,*[1] while on each of the other two walls are painted large landscapes representing certain peaks of Ts'ang Shan, the mountain west of West Town, or "modern" buildings similar to those frequently seen in Shanghai and Hongkong during the nineteenth century, or modern means of transportation—the train, the steamer, and the aeroplane. On one of the walls of the three houses illustrated I saw four kinds of conveyance represented in one picture: a "modern" five-story building was bordered at the left by the open sea, on which was a steamer. In the sky were two aeroplanes, and in the foreground was a speeding train. In front of the house was a man driving a horse cart. The steamer was about to run aground on the sandy beach; the two aeroplanes were about to crash into each other; while the driver of the cart did not yet seem aware of an imminent collision with the train. The picture, such as it was, represented painstaking local craftsmanship—for every line in the picture was carefully drawn.

[1] Literally, colored clouds are rising in the south. It means that the family is being blessed by good heavenly signs.

In addition to the four walls of a compound there is always another short wall, called a "shadow wall." This is a separate segment of wall, about as high as the others, but standing alone opposite the main portal to the family home. Sometimes a family has two or three such walls, each standing opposite one of the several portals. On such a wall are also usually four large black characters, being either merely a legend, as is the one mentioned above, or an indication that the family is descended from scholarly ancestors (*shu hsiang shih mei*). Such a "shadow wall" makes the enclosure of the family home complete; it "shadows" the openings caused by the portals. The family home is something that must not be exposed in any direction.

Where western influences have not marred their work, West Town craftsmen show a good sense of proportion. Especially fine are the engraving and polishing of windows, house doors, and eaves. West Town windows deserve a special treatise to themselves. I have not discovered two windows which are of the same design. The craftsmen have cleverly worked out all kinds of patterns within the framework of a window—bars, circles, squares, parallelograms, and a multitude of others. The doors are engraved with birds, flowers, and vases, in addition to the simpler patterns of bars and squares. The tips of the tile-supporters at the outer margins of the eaves are often embellished with the same fastidious care.

All this work is time-consuming and costly. Usually a family cannot afford the best work on its house at first. Like the construction of the house itself, the engraving and polishing is done by slow stages. Thus, the Ch house, as shown in one of the diagrams, still lacks a wing, while the Y house has so far only had windows and doors facing courtyard O varnished. One house has an uncompleted garden; one is awaiting the addition of a courtyard; another needs a third row of rooms. West Town houses are in various stages of completion at any given period of time, and work is always in process. With few exceptions the procedure is always according to the same pattern. Like some middle-class English parents who defer their children's education for some years pending the time when they will be able to send them to some public school, West Town families prefer to wait for the day when they can afford more skillful men and better materials for their worldly residences.

The incongruity of paintings having European cultural elements on a traditional wall without other signs of Europeanization shows clearly that such European predilections are merely attempts to enhance the owner's prestige in the traditional way, not to change their traditional scheme. This is why the construction of every new house follows closely in detail all the features of the houses built generations ago, complete with plaques and shadow walls. This is also why the wealthiest family in the community, although they did build a huge modern house near the lake, decorated and furnished in the European fashion and looking like the science hall of some Western university, built also an extra-large family home in the town proper according to the traditional style.

Within this conformity to tradition the houses give evidence of a high degree of competition for superiority. Worldly residences are not so much places to house the individual members in comfort and ease as they are signs of unity and social prestige for the family group as a whole —the dead, the living, and the generations to come. Through unity the prestige attained by any individual member of the household and lineage becomes the prestige of the group as a whole. For this reason the names of the most prominent ancestors are the most ostentatiously displayed. It is in the light of this principle that the following custom may be explained. On the last night of the lunar year, the main portal to every family home is ritually sealed. On the following morning the same portal is ritually opened. The ritual sealing is done in the name of the dead ancestor who held the highest official rank or attained the highest imperial honor ever held or attained by any member of the family. The ritual opening is done by the living member of the family who holds, or has held, the highest honor or official rank attained and held by any living member of the family. Each of these names is written on a piece of red paper, and the two pieces are posted crisscross over the crack between the double doors of the gate. When the gates are opened the next morning these paper hangings are broken in two.

Any struggle for superiority implies that some families or individuals will be left behind. For this reason the families which have achieved superiority must guard against malicious jealousy. A newly built family home is, therefore, an object of envy, not only on the part of the living, but also of ghosts. Approximately three years after the completion of a new house the owner usually celebrates the occasion by entertaining a lot of relatives and friends and by inviting a number of priests to read the scriptures for several days and nights. The priests, by reading the scriptures and by the ritual distribution of paper money and clothes and porridge, aim to propitiate the superior gods and send away all jealous and unsatisfied spirits which may be maliciously disposed toward the house and its owner. Otherwise these jealous spirits might cause the house to catch fire, to collapse, or to be disturbed by strange mysterious noises which will make it uninhabitable.

There are good grounds for jealousy among men too. The poorer people have to live in structures way below the ideal standard. The houses of the poor are usually one-story affairs, with thatched roofs, but no courtyard. The entire house may consist of only one wing, considerably smaller than any one side of the bigger family homes. Some of these houses are found in West Town proper, but they are more numerous in the outlying villages. The little house of a poor family illustrated here was found in Sha Ts'un, a village southwest of West Town. The B rooms are bedrooms, but one of them contains the kitchen as well. A is a smaller room, where the family shrine is located. D is a paved space (or terrace) for leisure, the entertain-

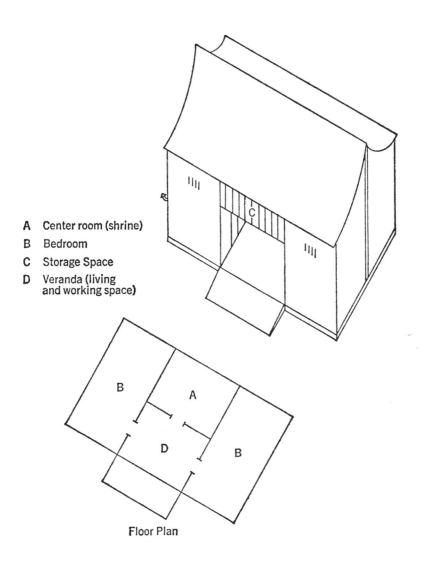

A Center room (shrine)
B Bedroom
C Storage Space
D Veranda (living
   and working space)

Floor Plan

THE HOUSE OF A POOR FAMILY

FIGURE 5

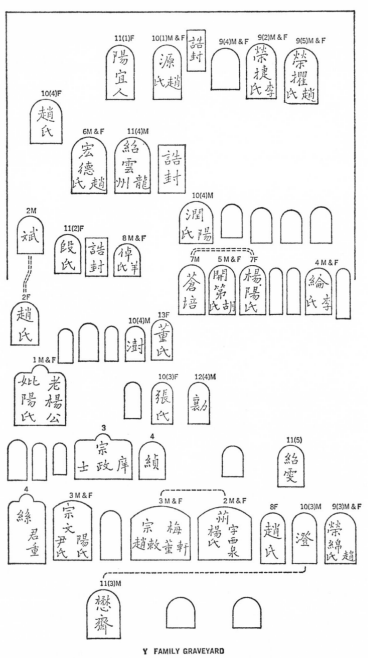

Y FAMILY GRAVEYARD

FIGURE 6

ment of guests, and some work such as sewing, knitting, and the preparation of food. Space C is directly above D. It is used for storage and is supported by boards projecting above the entrance to A. The goods stored are protected from falling by wooden bars. The construction of such a house is usually crude. The walls are not even white washed, to say nothing of being decorated with pictures. There are no plaques. There are no spare rooms. In every respect they bear witness to the harshness of life.

It must be pointed out that between the houses of the comparatively poor and those of the comparatively rich there is no definite demarcation. Gradual gradations lead from one to the other. But at any given point of time the contrast between the extremes is obvious.

GRAVEYARDS

There are three places of residence for members of the family who have passed away—the graveyard (or graveyards), the family shrine, and the clan temple. The graveyard is to house the bodies of dead members of the family; the other two, their spirits.

Naturally, only the richer families can afford to spend much on their graveyards, but a "good" graveyard is the concern of every family, rich or poor. The rich view their graveyards with pride; the poor look upon those of the rich with envy. Every family which has any means has a graveyard of its own. A proper graveyard is just as essential to the family as a proper house. A family which has to entomb its dead in a public graveyard is an object of pity.

A very wealthy family may own a graveyard which

In Figure 7 on the following pages, numbers without parentheses indicate the generation of the buried. Numbers in parentheses indicate the person's lineage. Tablets without numbers are tombs which cannot be identified by the clan. Single broken lines indicate father-son relationship. Double broken lines indicate husband-wife relationship.

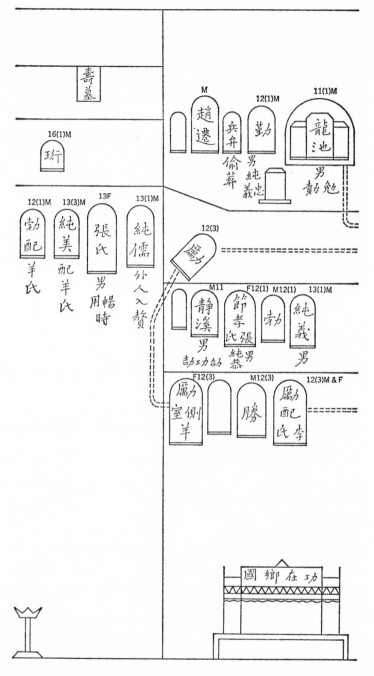

A MORE RECENT GRAVEYARD OF Y FAMILY

FIGURE 7
Above and on facing page.

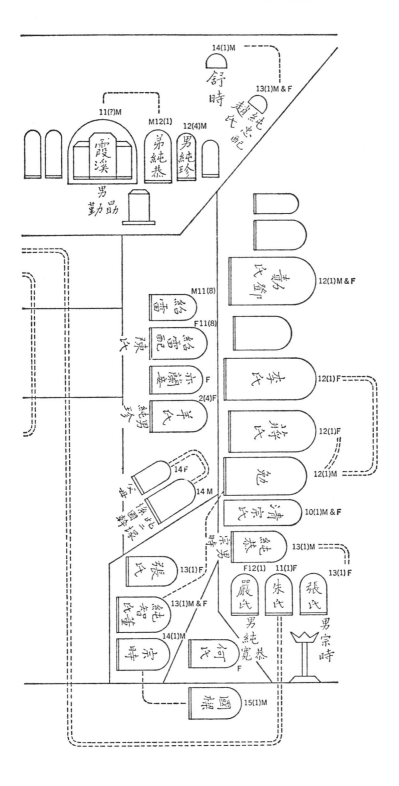

covers a large area. One of the graveyards of the C family, a family distinguished by the fact that one of its ancestors was a cabinet minister in the government at Peking during the early years of the Chinese Republic, lies on the lakeside slope of a mountain between two high points and covers about 35 acres. The slope is terraced, and the oldest traceable ancestors are entombed on the highest terrace. More recent ones are arranged more or less in order on the different terraces. Graveyards are not as a rule surrounded by walls, but each has an entrance arch, with inscriptions identifying the family. Several such arches stand on different levels in this C family graveyard. This indicates that at various times the graveyard had been extended as need arose. The remote ancestors marked only the uppermost part of the slope as their graveyard. As years went by, lower parts had gradually been added. Today there are several irregular groups of tombs beyond the lowest arch.

In principle, entombment should follow a certain order with respect to generation, age, and sex. Seniority in generation and age entails entombment on the upper terraces; if on the same terrace, a senior should be entombed at the left of a junior. A man and his wife should be entombed side by side, the man at the left of the woman. The left-hand side is regarded as the side of higher honor. In practice these principles are rarely observed. In most graveyards not only are tombs miscellaneously arranged but also husbands and wives are often placed at a distance from each other. Sometimes they even lie in two different graveyards. An analysis of the diagrams showing the arrangement of two graveyards of a Y clan, will make the situation clear. This clan is wealthy and possesses a very elegantly written copy of a genealogical record of sixteen generations. There is no reason to suppose that the clan has fallen below the traditionally required standard.

Obviously, in both graveyards the generation principle is almost entirely ignored. Persons of the most remote generations are entombed on ground lower than that used for more recent generations. In some cases they are entombed on the same terrace. In the older of these two graveyards, the tombs of first-generation ancestors, which should have been located in the very highest position are relegated to a terrace far below. Also, older brothers are often entombed at the right instead of at the left of their younger brothers. Some husbands and wives are entombed side by side; others are far apart. Tombs of outstanding male members of the clan are given prominent places in the family graveyards, whereas their wives are sometimes relegated to some other graveyards.[2]

Such violations of the basic principles in the arrangement of tombs is very common. In the smaller graveyard of another family (Ch) are found on one terrace the following tombs:

(9)	(8)	(7)	(6)	(5)	(4)	(3)	(2)	(1)
T'ang grand-mother	Great-grand-mother	Great-grand-father	Grand-father	T'ang great-grand-mother	T'ang great-grand-father	Grand-mother	T'ang third grand-mother	T'ang third grand-father

The kinship terms are the literary terms used by Ego, the informant. Here tombs of grandfather and grandmother are separated by tombs of a higher generation, and the tomb of the great-grandmother is placed at the left instead of the right of that great-grandfather.

In the graveyard of a Y family the most prominent member and his wife are honored with a special temple.

There seem to be several factors which bear on this disregard of the basic principles of the social categories, such as generation, age, and sex. The first one is limitation of space. The cost of land in general has restricted the size of many family graveyards, so that most families own graveyards which contain not more than one or two ter-

---

[2] 11(1)F and 11(2)F are both buried in the older graveyard with their imperial honors (*kao feng*). 10(1)M and F are both buried at the very top of the older graveyard with their honors. 11(1)M and 11(2)M, husbands of 11(1)F and 11(2)F, both occupy the best and most central places in the newer graveyard.

races each. Even when the graveyard is larger, the accumulation of tombs throughout the generations soon makes it overcrowded. This is, perhaps, why often little attention is given the relative positions of tombs. An even more important factor is that members of the clan who have attained high honors deserve special consideration and at the same time bring glory and honor to the graveyard in which they are laid. In the graveyard represented by the diagrams this may be clearly seen. In order to give the older graveyard the benefit of the honors, the descendants evidently found it necessary to entomb the wives of the two most prominent members of the family in that graveyard, rather than with their husbands. This predilection can be seen in almost every graveyard. Individual achievements have become the all-important factor and may supersede all other principles of rank in the arrangement of tombs.

Another closely-related factor is the practice of individual competition. Not only whole graveyards but also individual tombs are arranged according to geomancy. Geomancy, or the art of "wind and water," may be applied to the location of a house, a graveyard, a tomb, a city wall, or to any place inhabited by living or dead human beings. In connection with the graveyard, they are based on the idea that the prosperity of the descendants depends upon the places where their ancestors rest in peace. In West Town, as in other localities around the Tali area, geomancy requires, generally, that every normal family graveyard must be on the lakeside slope of the mountain. In addition to this general rule there are numerous detailed prescriptions which it is not possible to describe in full here. Obviously many graveyards must be above or below one another. Strictly speaking, if within one family graveyard the higher terraces definitely represent a better or senior or more prosperous position, then according to geomantic thinking the family graveyard which happens to be directly above another has taken the lucky wind out of the other family graveyard's sail. Strangely enough this does not follow.

What does follow in this case is competition within the same graveyard. In West Town there are not only many cases of "stealthy entombment" (i.e., a poor man deliberately entombs a deceased family member in a highly situated family's graveyard, so as to share the good geomantic effects of the prosperous family) but also struggles between members of the same clan for a "better" location for their own immediate ancestors in the same graveyard. The idea seems to be that the "better" the parents are situated the better their immeditae descendants will succeed in their worldly affairs. Not infrequently a geomancy reader will point out that a certain graveyard expands (Fa) a certain branch of the clan. The location of each tomb is considered individually by the geomancy reader to obtain the best geomantic "advantage" of the entire graveyard.

The fourth factor bearing on the arrangement of graveyards is that sometimes after a sudden drop of the family fortune there has been a relaxation of effort concerning the resting place for the dead. Then some ancestral tombs are obscured by dust and weeds. If some future members of the clan become prosperous and attempt to rebuild the ancestral graveyard, as they usually do, they discover tombs of very remote ancestors beside and on ground below tombs of members who lived and died at a much later period.

A man's duty toward his deceased ancestors does not stop when he has provided a graveyard with good "wind and water." He has to do his best to decorate the tombs. The higher-class tombs are very costly. As a rule they are built of solid blocks of granite, with a huge upright stone tablet in front of each, under a sort of circular roof. At the top of this tablet are engraved general words of remembrance of all the family ancestors. The rest of the tablet is divided into three parts. The central column indicates the title, name, sex, and age of the deceased. In the right-hand column or columns are the titles and names of the person who composed the inscriptions on the entire tablet, as well as that of the calligrapher. The left-hand columns show the names of the buried person's immediate descendants,

as well as the date of the erection of the tombstone (Pei).
As many titles as possible are inscribed on this tablet. If the
deceased person had not earned any title for himself or
herself, then fake titles are used. There are two ways of
doing this: one is to inscribe *hwang ts'ing tai cheng yi shih*

皇 清 待 贈 逸 士

for a man, or *ju jen*

孺 人

for a woman, meaning that the deceased was just waiting
for the Ts'ing emperor to grant some honor; the other way
is to place *huang en yu lai*

皇 清 優 賚

at the top of the tablet, meaning that the emperor had been
very generous in his favors to this person, and inscriptions
below to the effect that the entombed was given the title
either of *ts'e shu ju jen*

慈 淑 孺 人

for a woman, or *ts'un chueh yi sou*

諄 懇 逸 叟

for a man, by the whole village. *Ts'e shu ju jen* means
"a kindly and virtuous old lady" and *ts'un chueh yi sou*
means "a good and honest old hermit." The titles of the
persons who composed and wrote the inscriptions on the
tablet are, as a rule, higher than that of the deceased; these
titles also increase the family glory. The names of descendants inscribed on the lefthand side of the tablet may be
born or unborn. Often they include two or three generations, and when anyone inquires, he is told which are the
names of actual descendants and which are merely names to
be given to the future descendants in case there are any.

The cost of a granite tomb was in the summer of 1943

about $30,000 national dollars. Many families cannot bear the cost in any one year. They have to construct the tombs gradually, in much the same manner as they build up their worldly residences. Here again, like the choice of a good geomantic site, one's attention is paid first to one's own lineal ancestors—parents and father's parents. I could enumerate any number of graveyards, similar to the one of the Ch family, already illustrated, in which some tombs are elaborately constructed, while others side by side are but heaps of earth or pebbles. Upon closer examination I usually found that in the better tombs rested the dead whose immediate descendants were wealthy and prosperous. In the case of the Ch family, the present head of the family told me that the two most elaborate tombs (Nos. 3 and 6 in the diagram) in his family graveyard were those of his father's parents (his father was still living and his mother was buried in another graveyard) and that he and his father had been wanting to elaborate tombs 7 and 8 (which are his father's father's parents' tombs and were built of second-grade granite) as soon as they could manage it financially.

It is also common for coffins and even tombs to be prepared in advance for aged parents. In most cases such empty tombs cannot be differentiated from other tombs. They are made of granite slabs, with a fully inscribed tablet at the head. When the time comes for the loaded coffin to be placed within, the slabs covering the back part of the tomb are removed to accommodate it and are then replaced. During one of their regular visits to the ancestral graveyards, some member of the family will put a small red sign on the tombs of near relatives. On a tomb not yet in use the red sign will read "Blessing" or "Longevity" instead of "Everlasting Rest," or some such sentiment, which it is usual to put on the tombs containing the deceased ancestors. Living parents accept this as a matter of course, with pleasure and satisfaction. I have seen an old man standing beside his own tomb and conversing with guests on a *ch'ing ming* day.

Some of the stone tablets before the tombs are painted in colors. Young people often take great pains to oil the tablets of their parents or their father's parents. Like the worldly residence, a fine graveyard is a source of pride. On one of the regular visiting days the head of the family is prone to show his guests around and describe how after a struggle he finally succeeded in securing such a graveyard having very good "wind and water."

FAMILY SHRINES AND CLAN TEMPLES

Family shrines and clan temples serve the same purpose, except that in principle the former house the spirits of past ancestors within *wu fu* (that is, descendants of common great-great-grandparents), while the latter house all spirits of the wider clan which are not in any family shrine. In practice, however, the demarcation is not so clear. There are family shrines containing tablets of very ancient ancestors; others contain only a few lineal ancestors. Some families have no clan temples, and in that case they put the names of all known ancestors in the family shrine.

There is a family shrine in every household, rich or poor. It is usually situated in the part of the house that faces west. It is always in the middle room of the second floor, on a specially built wooden platform. The name of each ancestor is written on a wooden tablet, together with his or her age at death. Other characters on the tablet show the date and hour of the person's birth, as well as the direction according to geomancy of his or her tomb. These tablets are either housed in single wooden pavilions or in double husband-wife pavilions. The tablets of dear ones are often specially decorated with colored silk. These tablets are arranged in order. In front of them are always offerings of dishes of food, incense tripods, candlesticks, and a vase of fresh or artificial flowers.

As a rule these tablets do not stand alone. Beside them are often an image of Confucius and tablets of Kuan Kung (god of war and wealth), Buddha, or other gods. Any offering of incense or food to the ancestors is inevitably shared by the deities.

A clan temple is usually built by the free contributions of members of the clan—the richer ones contributing more than the poorer ones. As the cost of such a building is considerable, only a clan with wealthy families can afford it. One clan temple is known to have been built by a single donation from one man.

The clan temple has no plastered images as in the ordinary temple. All male ancestors of the clan who are not in household shrines and their wives are represented by tablets. In West Town proper there are altogether twelve clan temples, five of which share the surname Y, and two share the surname Ch. No two of the other five temples share the same surname. All these temples are built of some durable material—brick, stone, or pine wood—and are usually painted and varnished throughout. A typical example is illustrated on page 52.

The central hall (A) houses the ancestors and is a lofty one-story building, with a large and well-paved front veranda. A broad staircase leads to the level of the courtyard. The two large houses at the sides of the inclosure (B and C) are of two stories and are usually unoccupied, except when a caretaker lives in some small section of one of them. These houses may be rented out to tenants, but otherwise they are only used for longer or shorter periods on occasions of worship, clan conference, gambling party, or when the genealogical records are being edited. The two small houses on each side of the main hall (D and E) are kitchens for use on the last-mentioned ritual or social occasions. F is a large shadow wall, like the ones found in any family home, and G and H are two small doors leading to the outer courtyard. The inner courtyard is usually paved with slabs or bricks, but the outer one is usually unpaved, except for two paved paths leading to the main gateway (J). The two courtyards are about equal in size. The main gateway is as impressive a structure as the gateway to any large family home and is similar to it. On the upper and inner part of the structure, on either side of the entry way, is a large piece of marble, on which is inscribed the names of all ancestors who attained any degree of prominence in the official or scholarly world, together with the dynasties in which they lived and their achievements.

The importance given to individual achievements is seen

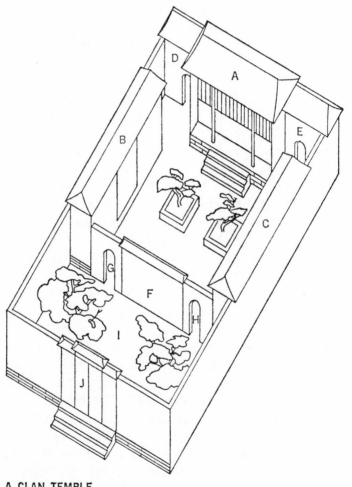

A CLAN TEMPLE

FIGURE 8

most clearly in the arrangement of ancestral tablets. The central hall contains three shrines, each of which is terraced. Usually the name of each ancestor is represented on a large tablet which is placed in one of the three shrines. But without exception only the names of ancestors who attained imperial honors or official prominence are included in the central shrine, occasionally their wives as well. The most ancient ancestor, the so-called *shih chu,* or primary ancestor, who invariably was of some official prominence, is placed in the center of this shrine. As a rule all tablets in this shrine are varnished in red with inscriptions in gold. The two side shrines contain all male ancestors and their wives who are not in any family shrine. Tablets in all three shrines are arranged in order of seniority and of generation.

Our survey of the worldly and the spiritual residences of the community shows clearly their complete submission to ancestral authority, on the one hand, and their struggle for and recognition of individual and family superiority, on the other.

CHAPTER III

Life and Work under the Ancestral Roof

THE distribution of living quarters in family homes will provide us with useful clues to the understanding of the behavior which regulates life and work under the ancestral roof. Several basic features may be observed. First, the old father or mother lives in the wing of the house occupied by the eldest son, which is usually the west wing. Secondly, in the normal course of events, some rooms seem to be overcrowded, while large sections of the house remain unoccupied. Rarely do the members of any family live on the second floor. Thirdly, except for children and husbands and wives, the two sexes are generally separated. Only one exception to this rule was observed.[1] The fourth feature is that the members of each individual family within the household usually occupy rooms in the same wing or in two wings adjacent to each other. Except for slight variations,[2] the above features are characteristic of all dwellings. This shows that the distribution is determined by rules of social appropriateness, not by considerations of personal preference, comfort, or hygiene. These rules emphasize the importance of generation, sex, and seniority, on the one hand, and of lineage, on the other.

A glance at the interior of the rooms will merely reinforce the impression that personal preference, comfort, and hygiene are disregarded. Rooms A in the diagrams are usually living rooms. Even in the richest house these rooms

---

[1] In a C household a seventy-year-old grandfather lived in the same room with his eighteen-year-old granddaughter before her marriage.

[2] See Appendix I.

fall far short of American standards. There is always a long rectangular table placed against the wall opposite the several doors which constitute most of the opposite wall. In front of this long table is a square table. Beside the square table and along both walls are several square chairs or broad benches seven or eight feet long. On the wall facing the doors are usually hung one large scroll in the center, inscribed with a large character meaning "Longevity" or "Blessing," and a couplet on each side of it. The couplet may have been presented to the family by friends or relatives when the house was first completed or when one of the younger members was married. Other walls have similar embellishments. On the long table there may be a clock or a large framed slab of marble ground in a scenic design, with a tubular vase on each side of it. Between the frame and the marble will be inserted a few calling cards left by men of social standing. The impressive titles on these cards will bear witness to the fact that the family has some connection with more important person-ages. On the large square table are such articles as teapots and cups. The benches and chairs are usually without covers or cushions.

The bedrooms are as a rule cluttered with too many boxes, chests, tables, and beds, in no definite pattern. The second floors, whether partitioned into rooms or not, are, apart from the family shrines, unsightly. They are usually untidy, some containing a haphazard collection of weaving looms, large and small baskets, dried vegetables, unused carrier chairs, and pots and pans, while others are empty or merely contain some hay. Dust is usually thick. When the rooms are used on special occasions for worship, such as the 15th of the Seventh Moon, they are swept and dusted by the women of the house.

RELATIONSHIP IN THE FAMILY HOME

The principles underlying the kinship system are lineage, generation, sex, and seniority. The fact that relationship terms are correlated with the kinship system has long been established. It is less well-known that terms of reference are closer to the actual kinship structure than terms of address.[3] The diagrams on pages 58–61 give the relationship terms used in West Town.

The terms of address express the kinship structure clearly enough, but the terms of reference put a number of relationships in greater relief. For example, Ego has no terms of address for younger brothers and their wives, but refers to them as T'ai and T'ai Fuoo, respectively. In the same way, Ego may address the husband of his father's sister's daughter by name if the husband is younger than himself, or by the term applicable to his father's sister's son. Ego may refer to the same person, however, by the term Biao Mei Beng Bao.

The principles expressed in these relationship terms are lineage, generation, sex, and seniority. In terms of the generally acknowledged ideal, the kinship structure is as follows. The basis of kinship is patriliny, and the most important relationship is that of father and son. The father has authority of life and death over the son, and the son has to revere and support his parents. Mourning and worship after the death of the parents are integral parts of the son's responsibility.

All other relationships in the family group are regarded as extensions of the father-son relationship or subordinate or supplementary to it. No matter what the biologist has to say, the mother-son relationship in West Town is based upon the fact of reproduction as much as it is the extension

[3] F. L. K. Hsu, "The Differential Functions of Relationship Terms," *American Anthropologist*, XLIV, No. 2 (April–June, 1942), 248–256.

of the father-son relationship. The biological fact is not ignored. In West Town it is customary for a son to wear mourning two years for his father, but three years for his mother.[4] The reason for this longer mourning period is said to be that the mother has had more trouble in caring for the children. But apart from this, the mother derives the attributes of her position in the lineage from the father. The pattern in mother-son relationship is essentially similar to that of the father-son relationship, except that the mother has less authority. Furthermore, there appears to be no ideal formulation as there is in the case of the father-son relationship.

The husband-wife relationship is strictly held to be supplementary and subordinate to the parents-son relationship. As will be seen, a marriage is made in the name of the parents taking a daughter-in-law, not in the name of the son taking a wife. There is to be no observable expression of erotic life between any couple. As a matter of fact, newlyweds are supposed to sleep in the same bed for only seven days. After that they occupy different beds, but in the same room. In public they are to appear indifferent toward each other. At the death of his parents a man is expected to show such deep sorrow as to be barely short of suicide. At the death of his wife a man is expected to show some grief, but never enough to make him forget his filial duties. If there is a quarrel between his parents and his wife, a man has no alternative but to take the side of the older people against his wife. A woman's first duties are to her husband's parents; only secondarily is she responsible for her husband. She is expected to submit to her husband, as she submits to her parents-in-law and her father. He may beat her, but she may not beat him. In return, both her husband and her father-in-law are responsible for her support.

The relationship between brothers is supplementary, but not subordinate, to that of the father and son. In fact,

[4] See Chapter VII.

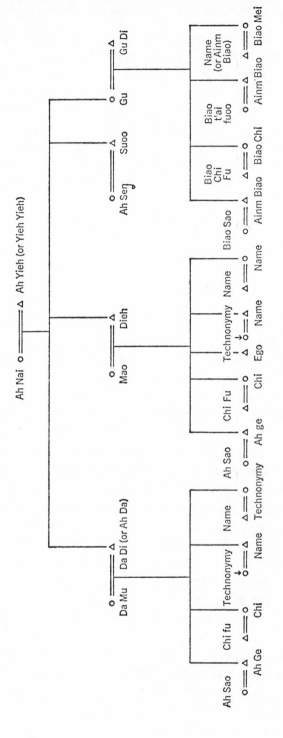

TERMS OF ADDRESS ON FATHER'S SIDE

FIGURE 9

If Ego has a son or a daughter, he will sometimes be addressed as Ning of So and So (name of Ego's child). Husband and wife have no terms of address for each other.

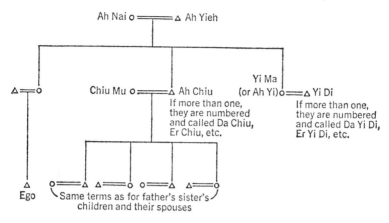

TERMS OF ADDRESS ON MOTHER'S SIDE

FIGURE 10

harmony among brothers is greatly desired in order to maintain and enhance the father-son relationship. There is much emphasis on the idea that "brothers are from the same source." They are expected to help each other—even to support each other when necessary. Older brothers have some authority over younger ones, and younger ones have to defer to their older brothers, especially if their father is not living. The more harmony there is between brothers, the happier their parents will be.

As mentioned before, a woman's first duties are to her parents-in-law. She serves them and mourns over their death just as their son would do. But in the day-to-day life father-in-law and daughter-in-law relationship amounts almost to avoidance; they do not even converse with each other freely. On the other hand, the mother-in-law and daughter-in-law relationship follows, in a broad way that of mother and daughter.

One hears much less about the parents-daughter relationship in the community than one does about the parents-son relationship. In broad outline the former is similar to the latter. The mourning obligation of children to their parents is the same regardless of sex. This obligation remains un-

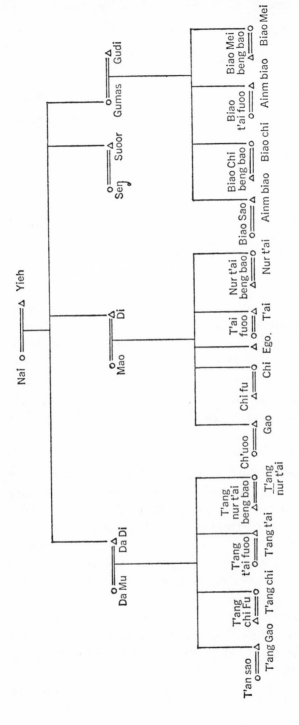

TERMS OF REFERENCE ON FATHER'S SIDE

FIGURE 11

All terms have the prefix Nge, meaning "my." A man refers to his wife as Nge Nao Vuer Ni; a woman refers to her husband as Nge Hao Duair or Nge Bao Ni. A son is referred to as Ze Ni; a son's wife, as Ze Vuer Ni.

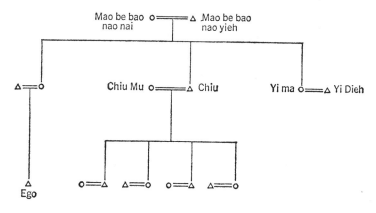

TERMS OF REFERENCE ON MOTHER'S SIDE

FIGURE 12

All terms have the prefix Nge, meaning "my."

altered after a daughter's marriage. A woman has to submit to her parents' authority just as does her brother.

Socially, however, a woman is expected to be closer to her mother than to her father. As a matter of fact it would be definitely regarded as unusual if she should appear to be otherwise. This is evidently related to the question of practical necessity, since a mother would have much more to teach the younger woman.

More important would seem to be the principle of sex segregation. This principle works out in two ways: on the one hand, there is a social ban against any close association between persons of different sexes, and, on the other hand, a woman's association with her own parents in a patrilineal and patrilocal society is of little importance. A woman's relationship with her own parents thus tends to be informal. After marriage, her contacts with her father becomes negligible.

The relationship between brothers and sisters is, similarly, less well defined and socially emphasized than that between brothers. The principle of sex segregation makes it imperative that brothers and sisters do not associate with each other closely, but when authority is in question the male is the dominant party. Furthermore, older brothers tend to exert much more authority over their younger sisters than over their younger brothers.

In spite of the fact that in terms of biological nearness there is no difference between fraternity and sorority, the relationship between sisters is informal and without socially defined content. Their relationship is a matter of personal adjustment rather than of kinship.

Between sisters-in-law (namely, between wives of two brothers) the socially desired relationship is one of harmony and cooperation, as between brothers.

A woman and her husband's older brother avoid each other, after the father-in-law and daughter-in-law pattern. Between a woman and her husband's younger brother there is greater freedom and often joking. This relation is unique in the community.

Between more remote kinfolk the relationship follows the model of that within the basic family. For example, the relationship of a man and his father's brother follows the father-son pattern. The relationship between cousins of the same sex follows the brotherly pattern. The intensity of each relationship (duties and privileges) is in direct proportion to the socially prescribed nearness of the particular individuals in the kinship structure. The relationship pattern between husband and wife is the only one which has no extension in the wider kinship sphere.

Actual life, however, may differ considerably from these socially upheld norms. The differences are, naturally, more apparent in the more well-defined relationships than in others. The often-emphasized version of the father-son relationship in China is the ideal one outlined above. But this one-sided arrangement is not true in general in any part of China known to the author. It certainly is untypical of the West Town families. The father has great authority over the son, but his authority is subject to the fact that socially a father and his son are part of each other. The older man cannot abuse his power without injury to himself. The son is obliged to please and support his father, but the latter is also the provider for the son at all times. He owes it to his ancestors to see that his sons are suitably married. A lazy father who leaves his son hungry will have no respectable place in the community, and a shiftless father who squanders the family resources is likely to encounter socially encouraged resistance from his adult sons.

In other words, the father-son relationship cannot be described by anything short of the psychological term "identification." For whatever the one is, the other is; and whatever the one has, the other has. The generally accepted pattern of behavior between father and son, far from being a negative one of authority and submission, or of exploitation and support, is much better described by a more positive literary saying, "The father is kindly toward his son, and the son filial toward his father." As soon as the sons have married and have had children, the West Town father consults them and defers to their opinion almost as frequently as they do to his.

The husband-wife relationship may deviate from the ideal picture in several ways. Wives should unconditionally obey their husbands. Many cases support this norm. Yet the wife has means of bringing her husband around to her wishes if she is determined to do so. In case of a quarrel with her husband, many a woman's first resort is, like that of the American wife, to go home to mother. But she may choose to use her "evil" force, not her charm, to defeat her husband. Not long before I went to West Town the following incident occurred. A man was so addicted to gambling that he was always found at a certain den. His wife, in desperation, went to the den one night while the gamblers, including her husband, were at their hottest. She made a big row with her husband then and there.

Quarrels among gamblers were not uncommon. As soon as such quarrels were patched up, the whole affair was at an end. But if a man and woman quarreled in someone else's home, the owner of the latter was doomed. It was one of the worst omens possible. In this case the owner not only permanently banned the husband from his den but also resorted to the use of witchcraft for revenge.

A second way of deviating from the socially upheld norm occurs when matrilocal marriage takes place. Here the husband, in many cases, not only fails to exert his full authority over his wife, but may be completely under the thumb of his wife's mother, who by custom is his mother. In Chapter IV the usage of matrilocal marriage is described. Here an actual case will illustrate the point in question. A couple by the name of Chao had an only daughter. They ran a grocery store. The daughter was married to a "married-in" son-in-law, a young man from a Tung family, and had given birth to a son and a daughter. The young husband and wife were very happy together. The young man worked very hard for the store. But the wife's mother constantly insisted that he was eating "free rice" and nagged him in one way or another. She forced him to go away from home and to make some money by trading. On the morning of his departure his wife was very tearful, while his mother-in-law shouted and was angry as usual. A few months later he returned home, stricken by malignant malaria and died shortly afterwards.

The matrilocally married husband's position is not unlike that of the daughter-in-law in most parts of China, where the mother-in-law and the daughter-in-law relationship is rife with suspicion, hatred, and implicit or open quarrels. I have a copy of Arensberg's book on Ireland and was amused to find that Ireland has the following proverb:

> Bean mhic is máthair chéile,
> Mar chat agus luch ar aghaidh a céile
>
> Mother-in-law and daughter-in-law like
> cat and mouse together.[5]

This proverb finds, however, no support in West Town. West Town daughters-in-law work very hard. But so do

[5] Conrad M. Arensberg and S. T. Kimball: *Family and Community in Ireland*, Cambridge, Mass., 1940, pp. 92–93.

their mothers-in-law, living in the same house. Often these older women work hard, not because of necessity, but because they prefer to. West Town mothers-in-law do not wait for their daughters-in-law, as do mothers-in-law in most other parts of China, to bring them food, make clothes for them, and wait on them hand and foot. They work hard whether they have daughters-in-law or not. They do not believe in the idea of *hsiang fu* (enjoy life) at the expense of their daughters-in-law, as do elderly women of other parts of China. The relation between West Town mothers and their sons' wives is definitely cordial and without significant tension.

LIVELIHOOD ACTIVITIES

A livelihood may be made in four spheres: home, field, market, and shop. Homework largely belongs to women. It consists of laundering clothes, cooking, sewing, and attending to babies, but these are not exclusively feminine activities except laundering clothes. I have seen men cooking, attending to babies, and even sewing a little, but I have never observed a single instance of a man laundering anything. Normally a woman will wash only her own clothes and those of her husband and children. If her mother-in-law is dead, she will have to take care of her father-in-law's and her husband's unmarried brothers' laundry as well. If the family can afford it, her husband will persuade his father to take a second wife. So strong is the association of laundry work with these relationships that there is no way for an outsider to get his clothes washed if he is not married to some woman in the locality.

Customs concerning work in the field are much less rigid. Men do the comparatively heavier jobs, such as carrying the crops from the fields to the homes or spreading fertilizer. Women do the planting, gathering, weeding, and threshing. But either men or women may do any work that is most convenient at the moment. Furthermore, any family which can afford it will depend upon hired labor—male or female.

The most popular line of work in the community is, however, trading. There are several kinds of evidence for this. A tabulation of the occupations of male members over fifteen years of age in fifty-one households from the local census records is given below.

Trading or shopkeeping	58
Farm work	23
Educational work (all except two are pupils in school)	14
Government work (public offices)	7
Military occupations	7
No work	8
Handicraft	6
Medical practice	1
Police force	1
Total	125

The fifty-one households represented are all located in one police area of the town. But a sample study of 42 households scattered in different areas of the town confirms the importance of commerce or trading. In the forty-two households were found 120 males over fifteen years of age. Of these, 69 (or over 50 percent) admittedly engaged in such activities.[6]

[6] In Kai Hsien Kung village (Kiangsu Province) there were 360 households. Of these only 6 persons were silk spinners, 10 were retail traders, 4 ran agent boats, 25 were engaged in crafts and professional services, such as carpentry, tailoring, and midwifery. Together they make only 45 households, or about 12 percent of the total (see H. T. Fei: *Peasant Life in China*, London, 1939, pp. 139–140). One also gets the impression from Fei that most of the 12 percent engaged in retail trade and crafts and professional services were males. Ta Chen has given much more detailed data on the subject. According to Chen's compilation and investigation persons of both sexes engaged in commerce occupy 4.5 percent of the total population in Kiang Ying (Kiangsu Province); 11.5 percent in Kiang Ning (Kiangsu Province); 7.31 percent in Lan Hsi (Chekiang Province); 1.77 percent in Cheng Kung and 11.72 percent in Kunming Lake Region (both Yunnan Province); and 8.11 in three *hsien* in Szechwan Province. The percentages of males engaged in commerce

The importance of commerce is also shown by the number of shops. It is estimated that there are about 250 to 300 shops in West Town. The vast majority of these shops are owned and operated by West Towners. This means, in a community with 1,000 households, or about 8,000 individuals, one shop for every three or four households or 20 to 30 individuals.[7] The proportion is not surprising, but while some of these shops are small family affairs, others are on a large scale, with a large number of employees, some of whom often travel among widely scattered branches of the same establishment.

Commercial activities may be carried on in a shop or directly between homes and markets, or between West Town and outside points. There is no fixed formula. If the family owns a shop, the activities are more or less continuous. Otherwise the activities may be intermittent. Whether a trader goes to the periodic markets or to Hsiakuan or to Kunming on a particular commercial trip is often entirely dictated by opportunities for profit. For this reason some men whose formal occupations are noncommercial are almost certain to be occasionally traders as well. In this category we must include the farmers, the craftsmen, and even most of the adolescents in school. It is clear that the importance of commercial activities is much greater than the actual number of established shops would indicate.

The most interesting thing about West Town and the entire southwest is the popularity of trading among women.

---

for these respective areas are: 7.12, 15.43, 13.04, 2.34 and 15.04, and 9.72. If we include the number of individuals engaged in manufacturing, the percentages are double the ones quoted above in every case, but not much more (see Ta Chen, *Population in Modern China*, Chicago, 1946, p. 116).

[7] In Phoenix Village (Kwangtung province) there were 21 shops among a population of 650. Of the 21 shops, 15 were owned and operated by outsiders. There were only one priest and one fortune teller. Of the twenty-one shops, 13 sold food and pork, 2 medicine, 1 opium, 1 was a barber, 1 dry goods, 1 paper, 1 coffin, and 1 dye. (See Daniel Harrison Kulp: *Country Life in South China*, New York, 1925, pp. 36, 90, 94.)

In this connection there is a much greater difference between formal records and actuality.

A tabulation of the female members over fifteen years of age in the same fifty-one households referred to above is given below.

Spinning and weaving	48
No work	19
Taking care of family	7
Pupils	5
Government work	1
Medical practice	1
Midwifery	1
Farm work	1
Unknown	4
Total	86[8]

In the sample study previously referred to of 42 households scattered in different areas of the town shows the same predominance of spinning and weaving among women.

Most females do their spinning and weaving at home. The yarn a woman handles may be supplied by a small local factory. For washing and preparing it for weaving she will be paid by the factory on a piece basis. In some cases she is under contract with the factory to weave the yarn into cloth, for which she will be paid also on a piece basis. This arrangement bears remarkable resemblance to the system known as the Merchant Employer System which was found to exist extensively in Kao Yang District, Hopei Province. It was found that more than 80 percent

[8] The percentages of females working in manufacturing industries in the previously quoted six areas are: 0.48 percent (Kiang Ying); 1.66 percent (Kiang Ning); 0.14 percent (Lan Hsi); 3.57 percent and 8.77 percent (Cheng Kung and Kunming Lake region); and 56.3 (three *hsien* in Szechwan). The percentages of females in commercial positions in the same areas are: 1.27 percent (Kiang Ying); 0.10 percent (Kiang Ning); 0.38 percent (Lan Hsi); 1.22 percent and 7.00 percent (Cheng Kung and Kunming Lake region); 3.89 percent (three *hsien* in Szechwan), see Ta Chen, *op. cit.*, p. 116.

of Kao Yang farm families participated in this institution in 1933, and the merchant employers, who supplied the villagers with looms as well as yarn, found markets for the finished products in most parts of China and even abroad (Singapore).[9] West Town employers' business was on a much more limited scale. The factories, of which I found two in the town proper, one of them located in a temple, are small. Each has about ten hand looms of the kind which women use at home, and each has less than twenty workers.

This picture of more than 50 percent of West Town women as wage-earning spinners and weavers is, however, misleading. Most of them carry on such work as a part of their own enterprises. They buy the yarn, wash and dry it, weave it into cloth on family owned looms, send the finished product to a professional dyer, and take the cloth to the market themselves for sale. The periodic markets are a wonderful institution, especially for the women of West Town. The following typical schedule shows how a woman may adapt her life to this institution. This woman is the mother of four sons, three of whom are married.

16th of 8th Moon: West Town Market
   She buys yarn, washes and dries it at home, then starts weaving.
17th and 18th of the same month: Teng Chuan Market
   She sends her eldest son to inquire about the price of various commodities, including cloth and yarn. Her son may sell on her behalf the cloth woven with yarn bought on the 6th of the same month.
19th: West Town Market
   She goes to the market to inquire about prices. Buys more yarn or cloth if prices are favorable.
20th: Dragon Market
   Cloth woven from yarn bought on the 16th of the month

[9] For a complete description of the system in Kao Yang see C. Wu, *A Study of Merchant Employer System in Kao Yang* (in Chinese), Tientsin, Published by Nankai Institute of Economics, 1934.

is ready for the dyeing process. She sends it to the dyer. She goes to the market and sells some cloth woven from the yarn bought on the 10th of the month in West Town Market.

22d: West Town Market

Buys more yarn for cloth if prices are favorable. She will certainly buy some if the sale in the Dragon Market has been good.

23d and 24th: Teng Chuan Market

She gives the cloth woven from yarn bought on the 19th to her dyer. She sends her son to this market to sell the cloth from yarn bought on the 13th and 14th of the month.

25th: West Town Market

She buys more yarn.

26th: Dog Market

She sells cloth woven from yarn bought on the 16th (West Town Market) of this month.

This is a woman who has adequate capital and can do her business continuously. Those who are not so fortunate have to wait until they have sold out one lot of cloth before they can buy more yarn to weave into more cloth. There is another method which older women prefer. The profit is less, but there is much less work involved. Many an older woman buys white cloth in one market—for example, the West Town Market—then dyes it herself or pays a professional dyer to do the job, and sells it in a different market, usually the Dragon or the Dog Markets. The dyeing process takes about four to six days.

The average earning of some of the women may be deduced in the following manner: In August, 1943, coarse yarn cost about $400 (this and other figures below are in Chinese currency) per catty (sixteen ounces), and fine yarn cost about $700 per catty. It takes seven ounces of each kind of yarn to weave into a *chia* (a "piece," which is a local unit for measuring cloth, about twenty to twenty-two feet long and one foot, two inches wide).[10] Each "piece," if not dyed, will fetch about $550 on the market. Since it takes about one work day to weave a "piece," the net income per day was about $60. The wage of a laborer in the fields during the corresponding period was about $100 per day.

West Town women also carry on other types of trading. They sell vegetables, matches, seeds, pots and pans, rice and beans, cakes and noodles—almost any commodity to be found in the markets. There are always more women than men participating in any market. It would be no great exaggeration to say that every West Town woman is connected with some sort of trade.

In the management of shops, too, women have a considerable part. Some shops are managed informally in the best cooperative spirit. An example of this is a cake shop. The family which owns it has five members: mother, son, daughter-in-law, and two grandchildren under three years of age. The mother does all the mixing and preparation of the dough, and the son, all the baking and sale of the cakes. The daughter-in-law cares for the children and cooks for the whole family; she comes into the shop to help with the work only when there is a rush.

Other shops are owned by families in which the husbands do not bother about anything but the net income. A striking, but by no means unusual, example is the gambler husband mentioned in one of the preceding chapters. After the row at the gambler's den the husband beat his wife bitterly. Some time later the husband was said to be even more careless about his family and the shop than before. The current belief was that this was caused by the gambling den keeper, who took revenge by applying a kind of witchcraft charm against the husband, called *tze you hsi*. This charm was performed by a witch from a village on the east shore of the lake. Anyhow, the wife became more than ever the manager of the home as well as the shop.

[10] Each local foot is slightly longer than the foot in America.

She had four children, the oldest was 15 and the youngest still feeding at her breast. The husband continued to gamble.

We have thus a picture in which the work of the male is, in the final analysis, remarkably similar to that of the female. There are, to be sure, certain observable quantitative differences. First, in general women work much harder than do men. Women usually get up fairly early in the morning, work like beasts of burden throughout the day, and go to bed fairly early in the evening; while the men get up very late in the morning, talk and drink tea and/or smoke opium throughout the better part of the day, and go to bed much later than their wives and mothers. A large proportion of the males in West Town smoke opium, but hard as I tried, I could not find any female addict. Secondly, the radiuses of operation in trading are much larger for men than for women. Men take longer expeditions—to Hsiakuan, Chien Chuan, or other points. A remarkable number of West Town males go to Burma, Indo-China, Hongkong, Shanghai, and other ports for purposes of trade. Some of them make big "killings." Some West Town men are top ranking citizens in the business circles of the provincial capital. The women, on the other hand, make more trading "sorties," so to speak, but confine themselves to much shorter distances. At most, some of them operate within a radius of about five to fifteen miles. Their transactions are usually on a smaller scale than those of their husbands.

Thirdly, the bigger shops are organized on a more formal basis than smaller ones. When they are so organized, women have no part in them. The very small family shops usually occupy some part of the family home. The larger establishments are, as a rule, located in separate premises. There are at least two outstanding West Town firms which in terms of size can measure up to some of the biggest establishments in Tientsin or Shanghai. These firms have branches in many cities, including Kunming, Shanghai, Hongkong, Rangoon, Haifong, and even points farther south. Since the closing of the last motorable land route to Burma in 1941, both have maintained representatives in Calcutta, India to make contacts with the outside world and prepare for the day when the sea lanes would be open again.

These firms are under the direction of managers and submanagers, assisted by clerks, workers, technicians, salesmen, accountants, and apprentices. They manufacture, invest, import and export, and carry on any enterprise which appears to be profitable. Although some of the workers may be family members, or relatives, these larger establishments also employ other West Towners and outsiders. For women to work in them would mean, therefore, the violation of the principle of sex segregation, which is one of the important factors in social organization.

In spite of these differences a man and his wife may be seen managing a food stand together, running a small shop, going to market together, or participating in work on the farm. Either men or women may perform certain duties according to their convenience. The only work rigidly assigned to females is laundry. The only work performed exclusively by men is making out genealogical records and the ritual propitiation of the gods during an emergency, such as an epidemic. On such occasions even the cooking for the priests is done by men.

Thus, as far as West Town is concerned the term "stronger sex" has more social than physical significance. Men are supposed to be authoritarian toward their wives. They must show that they can lick their wives in any quarrel. Otherwise they will be a laughingstock in the eyes of the public. In terms of work the difference is not great. In fact, some women have been seen to carry things on their backs over a distance of many miles. In this respect women of poor families usually work harder than those of rich ones. On the main highway on market day or when there is a temple fair one would probably be able to count three women to one man, all carrying loads on their backs such as baskets full of vegetables, walnuts, sweet potatoes, or large bundles of bamboo poles, or even tables and chests of drawers. Most of such women would have natural feet, and they would be inhabitants of outlying villages, whom West Towners regard as poor "tribes people."

CHAPTER IV

Continuing the Incense Smoke

THE DESIRE for male descendants is intense. In local usage this is to insure the continuation of the smoke from the incense at ancestral shrines. To perpetuate this smoke insures the continuation of the family line. There are two ways of acquiring male descendants: adoption and marriage. But adoption, even of near kin, though sometimes practiced, is not favored. Any elderly man who is sonless feels very unhappy. He is also pitied by others. Like the elderly American who does not want to be reminded of his age, the sonless West Towner is very much offended when reminded of his wife's barrenness. He cannot afford to be powerful or wealthy; the more powerful or wealthy he gets, the more he will be an object of envy as well as of pity and the more he will feel that others are laughing at him. The sonless man knows well who will laugh last, for a sonless man is like a tree without roots. The time when he is enfeebled by advancing years will also be the time when his power and wealth will be taken away from him. He can adopt his brother's son or the son of his cousin on the father's side, but everyone knows that an adopted heir is not as good as a genuine one. The adopted son will never treat the adopted father like his own father. For a woman it is even more serious to be without a son. Most West Towners are aware of cases such as that of z (Yi family, Appendix I). z was married when she was 23, and her husband left for Japan three months later. He died in Japan one year later; she never even saw his coffin. His family was well-to-do, so she stayed with them—and adopted the second son of her husband's older brother. z is now about thirty-seven, and the boy, a middle school student in Kunming, is nineteen. All is well on paper, but for z the situation is disheartening, for she can have neither the sentimental satisfaction nor even the formal respect which is due a mother. When the boy comes home he neither addresses her as a mother nor comes to live in her wing of the house or to eat with her. He simply goes to his own mother and ignores z.

z and the boy both realize that however poorly he treats her there is no other person to inherit her share of the family property. The law of the Republic says a person has complete freedom in willing his property. But the custom says that the property of a sonless person goes to the son of his brother (if adopted) or to all sons of his brothers (if no formal adoption took place), and custom is still the deciding factor in West Town behavior.

The discomfort of an heirless person extends beyond his or her worldly existence. After death his or her spirit will suffer the fate of a vagabond, crushed by poverty and misery, and will be entirely dependent upon charity. This will be discussed in Chapter VI.

Just as the illnesses of children are attributed to spiritual causes, the incidence of pregnancy and the sex of the newborn child are regarded in a similar light. There are a number of customary ways of supplicating for sons.

(1) On the eighth of the First Moon an Incense Fire Fair takes place in Tang Mei Temple, just beyond the Dog Market (see figure 1, page 15). The center of interest on this occasion is the Goddess of Fertility (literally Goddess of Sons and Grandsons). Her image is surrounded by those of male babies and children of all kinds. On this day sonless couples will take with them some incense and candles to pay homage to this goddess. Each couple will insert the incense and the candles in the burner and in a pair of the many candlesticks on the table in front of the goddess, respectively, and they will take home from the same table some incense and candles. By so doing the couple has increased their chances of the arrival of a son.

(2) On the seventeenth of the Second Moon, a big temple fair takes place in Wei Pao Shan Temple in Meng Hwa (about ninety miles southwest of West Town). A number of people from West Town go to that fair to pray for sons.

(3) On the third of the Third Moon a fair in honor of Tai Tze (prince) takes place in Pao Ho Temple near Wan Chiao (about seven miles south of West Town). The image of Tai Tze is a tiny wooden one. Male and female participants in this fair throw coins at this image. Sons will be born to those whose coins hit the image. A woman who throws coins at the image may feel somewhat bashful and may cover part of her face with her hat. They leave immediately after hitting the image.

(4) On the eighth of the Fourth Moon another fair in honor of Tai Tze (prince) takes place in West Town itself and in many other villages where the temples have an image of this spirit. The same procedure will insure the birth of sons to those who have been successful.

(5) On the twenty-fifth of the Sixth Moon is a festival called Torch Festival, which is held in all parts of Yunnan. There are several legends connected with this festival, which we cannot relate here. On that evening every year, people of the community make up several huge torches with bamboo and straw fifteen or twenty feet in height, and stand them in various parts of the town. At the tip of each torch there is a small paper *tou* (a boxlike structure in imitation of the container used to measure rice and other cereals). Toward dusk a crowd of men, women, and children gathers below each torch. One man climbs about halfway up the torch with the aid of a ladder and lights it there. All cheer. As the fire blazes and breaks the torch in two, the *tou* at the tip will fall. Anyone who catches the *tou* before it touches the ground will enjoy the arrival of a son the following year; most of the aspirants are newlyweds. Some wealthy families even hire young men to catch it. Sometimes the catching of the *tou* has resulted in bloody fights. The family which catches the *tou* will be responsible for

the cost of the torch the following year in that neighborhood.

(6) About one and one half miles west of the town there is a temple called Sheng Yuan Temple. The most worshiped deity in this temple is a small, two-feet high, image of Ah Tai (the grand lady). She has bound feet, and pious women always provide her with more pairs of shoes than she can possibly wear. A woman who is anxious to become pregnant will go to this temple and steal one of the shoes from the image. She takes it home and burns the laces into ashes and swallows the ashes. After that she makes a new pair of shoes and takes them to the Ah Tai. On the first of the Ninth Moon all those who have had sons born to them pay homage to this goddess in gratitude. Others go to her to pray for such satisfaction. At the time of the investigation the image was wearing only one shoe.

PREFERRED AND DISFAVORED TYPES OF MATING

Marriage in West Town is, as in other parts of traditional China, a family affair. Matchmaking is prompted, as a rule, by the family's need for descendants and the parents' desire for grandchildren, especially grandsons. There is a good deal of marriage among relatives, but there are limits and rules. Theoretically marriage between all blood relatives is forbidden. An effort to enforce this rule may be clearly seen in some genealogical records, where all records concerning matrilocal marriages give specific information as to the name and location of the family of origin (in case an outsider married into the clan), or the family of adoption (in case a clan member married into another clan). This was done expressly "to avoid mistaken but unintentional marriages among blood kin in the future." In fact, not all blood relatives are barred from marriage. Marriage between two families of the same surname is not forbidden. An examination of the genealogical record, or the present composition of any family makes this point amply clear. A T family record shows four wives bearing T as their surname before marriage; a Y family record shows sixteen wives bearing Y as their surnames before marriage; a Ch family record shows three wives bearing Ch as their surnames before marriage, and so forth. That this custom is still prevalent is borne out by an examination of the present composition of any family in West Town. On the other hand, two persons bearing the same surname must not marry if they are of the same clan, or *chung*, even if their relationship is not traceable within *wu fu*.[1] On this point all my informants agreed. In a place where contacts are close and genealogical records carefully kept, this is not hard to avoid.

Within this limit several features of West Town marriages are of interest. First, the records of present or past relatives of all families examined show a consistent tendency for marriages to be made between persons of the same two surnames. The previously mentioned Ch clan record indicates, for example, that in seventeen generations the clan had taken women who bore the surname Y before marriage. This fact alone may not indicate that these women all came from one clan, for there are more than ten Y clans in West Town which are not related. The following two kinds of data from a Ch family record are, however, significant: (1) In one case three out of five brothers by the same mother, in two cases all three brothers by the same mother, in seven cases both brothers by the same parents, in six cases two of three brothers by the same parents, in three cases three of four brothers by the same parents, and in one case all four brothers by the same parents were married to women bearing Y as their surname before marriage. (2) A study of the lineal ancestors of some of those who have taken wives from a Y clan shows that in one case this relation lasted six generations, either

[1] *Wu fu* literally means five degrees of mourning. It includes nine generations lineally (four above and four below ego). Collaterally it includes ego's siblings and cousins up to the third. For a diagrammatic representation of the concept see F. L. K. Hsu, "The Problem of Incest Tabu in a North China Village," *American Anthropologist,* XLII (January–March, 1940), 124.

two thirds or three fourths of the brothers of any generation marrying wives bearing that surname. In two other cases the same situation lasted for nine generations. In one or two instances the grandfather and the grandsons married spouses bearing Y as their maiden surname, while the father had married a spouse bearing a different surname. But in most cases the relation was continuous. Such facts at least would seem to suggest that many of the women who were related as mother-in-law and daughter-in-law or grandmother-in-law and granddaughter-in-law must have come from the same Y clans.

An examination of the T family record makes this conclusion inevitable. One hundred and seventy-two members of this clan married wives bearing the surname Y, twenty-two married wives bearing the surname Yi, sixty-five married wives bearing the surname Ch, and forty-eight married wives bearing the surname L. Now we may have some doubts concerning the origin of the women bearing the surname Y, of which surname there are more than ten different clans in the community, but many of the women bearing the surname Yi and L must have come from the same clans, respectively, because there are only one L clan and one Yi clan in West Town.

Secondly, between two clans only one form of marriage is encouraged, a second form is tolerated, while others are forbidden. The most favored forms are marriage between father's sister's son and mother's brother's daughter (a kind of cross-cousin marriage), and marriage of two sisters from one family to two brothers of another family. When father's sister's son and mother's brother's daughter are not available, father's first or second female cousin's son and mother's first or second male cousin's daughter will be preferred. The following example is fairly typical.

As is shown in the diagram, in the third generation two female cousins married two brothers and in the fourth generation a2w is going to marry her father's sister's "son." The fact that her father's sister died and that her future

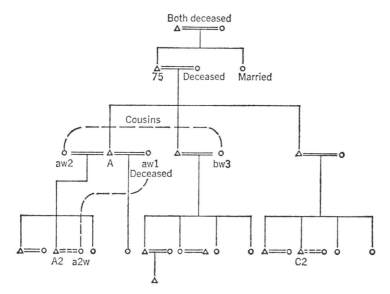

MATRIMONIAL RELATIONSHIPS OF C FAMILY

FIGURE 13

aw1 was a2w's father's sister. Although aw1 is deceased and her place has been taken by aw2, the marriage-to-be between a2w and A2 is still technically considered to be in accordance with the preferred pattern. Double broken lines signify betrothal.

mother-in-law is another woman makes no difference in the preference.

I have not been able to ascertain the actual frequency of occurrence of this type of mating, but all informants agreed that it is a very large number. One reliable informant even put it as high as 70 percent of all marriages in West Town. This may be an overestimation, as is shown by the fact that although a family may have some marriages according to this preference, it usually has several others which were contracted freely and without any regard for it. However, two things may be mentioned at this point: first, this type of mating is preferred not only in West Town but also in Yunnan and other parts of China about which I possess information, such as Kwangtung, Kiangsu, Hupei, Hopei, and Manchuria. Secondly, very often two sisters or two paternal female cousins marry two brothers or two paternal male cousins in the same family. This mating is in the same spirit as the father's-sister's-son and the mother's-brother's-daughter marriage and must be added to the total number of cases of preferred type of cross-cousin marriage.

Marriage is tolerated between a boy or a girl and his or her mother's sister's daughter or son, respectively. West Towners admit that such marriages exist, but say that they are rare.

It must not be supposed that the approved and tolerated forms of marriage are rigid prescriptions. In fact, many marriages are more or less variations on the same themes. The matrimonial relationships between the following three families show that instead of marriage between children of two sisters there could be one between mother's sister's nephew-in-law and aunt-in-law's sister's daughter; instead of marriage between father's sister's son and mother's brother's daughter, there could be one between father's female cousin's son and mother's male cousin's daughter.

Disapproved are marriages of the father's sister's daughter to the mother's brother's son, and any "exchange marriage," such as that of a brother and a sister (or two cousins of different sexes) of one family to a sister and a brother (or two cousins of different sexes) of another family. For it is obvious that exchange marriages, if carried on in more than one generation, would automatically become the disapproved type of cross-cousin marriage.

About this type of marriage West Towners unanimously expressed disapproval and most of them even denied that it was practiced at all. But facts contradict this denial. In the following diagram the two women $y1$ and $y2$, who were married into the Ch family, were from the same Y clan which took their husbands' sisters in marriage.

Furthermore, a study of the same Ch family records shows twenty marriages with T women; while a study of T family records shows sixty-five marriages with Ch women. A review of other family records shows similar

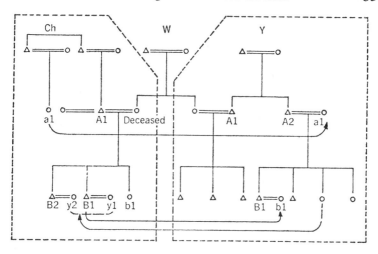

MATRIMONIAL RELATIONSHIPS OF THREE FAMILIES

FIGURE 14

B1 of Y family is the mother's sister's husband's brother's son of b1 (his wife, or mother's sister's nephew-in-law). With relation to a marriage in the previous generation (that between a1 and A2), the B1b1 marriage is also one between father's female cousin's son and mother's male cousin's daughter, a marriage following the pattern of the approved type of cross-cousin marriage (father's sister's son and mother's brother's daughter). y1 and y2 were from the Y clan and were first cousins on the father's side.

relationship. It is, of course, impossible to decide, without further data, whether these marriages were actually exchange marriages. It is possible that a number of the Ch or T women thus married came from some other locality. But it seems impossible that all these women were outsiders. What is more, the two Ch clans and the one T clan in West Town are known to have been matrimonially related for a number of generations. Consequently, there must have been some exchange marriages in the long run; that is, there is no rule against *A* woman from entering *B* clan merely because one of the *B* women has previously been married into the *A* clan, provided the kinship relation between the two families in both clans are not so close as to make the mating immediately recognizable as an exchange marriage on the father's-son's-daughter and mother's-brother's-son pattern.

West Towners give several explicit reasons for these preferences regarding marriages, but these reasons we cannot go into here. I have dealt with this whole question elsewhere.[2]

BETROTHALS AND WEDDINGS

Besides marriages of the preferred and tolerated types, there are, of course, a large number of marriages contracted between families which are either not closely related or not related at all. For such marriages the part of go-between is of great importance. She must carry the proposal to the girl's family and ask for the young lady's "eight characters" (the year, month, day of the month, and hour of the boy's birth and of the girl's birth) and later conduct the negotiations concerning the gifts. If the girl's family hands out the "eight characters," this is a sign of preliminary consent. Thereupon the eight characters are sent to the diviners by the boy's family, to find out whether the boy and the girl are suited to each other. The go-between has to be familiar enough with both families to answer queries of each family about the other, but she is usually a relative or friend of the girl's family. The go-between is usually a woman, but may be a man; he or she may be a professional or an amateur. When the go-between has satisfied the girl's family about the proposal, the diviners' part comes in. Diviners are important to all marriages. Diviners are usually men, but occasionally they are women. Most of them are blind. To find out whether the match is suitable the diviners use a method which is popular everywhere in China—examination of the "eight characters."

[2] F. L. K. Hsu, "Observations on Cross-Cousin Marriage in China," *American Anthropologist*, n.s., XLVII (January–March, 1945), 83–103.

This system of divination is explained in a general way by Henri Dore in his monumental work, *Recherches sur les superstitions chinoises*.[3] It is a system similar to the European horoscope, which tells, among other things, the "suitability" of matches. The diviner receives a fee, which in 1941 was $200 per match.

Even if the mating is in the preferred category, a go-between and some consultation of the diviner are indispensable, because otherwise the marriage hints of elopement and because there will be no one to mediate in case of trouble or dissatisfaction. But for such matings the go-between may be any relative. If the family is really determined to put the match through, they can always consult several diviners, whose reports are bound to conflict with each other. Not that the families concerned take the system of divination lightly, but they can always find something wrong with the diviner if he does not give the desired answer.

Once the match is found to be "suitable," a date is set for the betrothal. No formal ceremony takes place on this occasion. The boy's mother goes to the girl's family and hands over some presents and a small amount of money together with a folder of red paper with the names of the betrothed written therein. This is the beginning of the formal admission of the relationship by marriage, or *chi chieh nao kuai hsi,* as West Towners call it. The essential presents on this occasion, wrapped in red paper, as far as I could ascertain in 1943 were generally as follows: (1) Six or more pairs of sugar lumps (one pair weighs about two pounds); (2) Two or more packets of water-pipe tobacco (two packets weigh about one and one half pounds); (3) Two bottles of white wine (about two pints); (4) Some pounds of miscellaneous sweetmeats (walnut sweet, pine-seed sweet, etc.); (5) About $1,000 (1942–43).[4]

[3] For some misinformation on it see J. G. Cormack, *Chinese Birthday, Wedding, Funeral and Other Customs,* Peking, 1923, pp. 35–36.
[4] In 1942–43 the nonofficial exchange rate between the United States and Chinese dollars was about U.S. $1.00 = CN $60.00.

The whole thing would cost about $2,000. A sort of banquet was arranged by the girl's family for the boy's mother and any other relatives who might accompany her and for the go-between. On the same day the boy's family also put on a sort of celebration, while the sugar and the tobacco were given freely to relatives and family members. Some wealthy families might invite outside guests on this occasion as for weddings.

This marks only the beginning of gift-making by the boy's family to the girl's family. There are at least two more gifts of money and many more gifts in kind. Sometime after the betrothal the boy's family sends to the girl's family, together with some articles in jade and silver or gold, a sum of money much larger than that given upon betrothal—perhaps ten times as large (it would be almost $10,000 for an average family in 1943). The articles are the girl's ornaments: one pair of jade bracelets (worth about $1,000 to $2,000 CN in 1943), one or two pairs of earrings, one or two hairpins (if silver, worth about $200–$300 in 1943; if gold, $1,000–$2,000 in 1943), etc. This is called the Hsiao Ting, meaning minor betrothal. Just before the wedding another amount was given, this time even larger than the second amount, sometimes three or four times as much (about $30,000 or $40,000 in 1943). This gift in money is accompanied by a large quantity of pork (sometimes amounting to half a pig), four kinds of miscellaneous food, and some dress material for the girl.

The size of the money gift in this case is first specified by the girl's family and then communicated to the boy's family by the go-between. When there is bargaining, as there usually is, the go-between visits first one family and then the other until an agreement is reached. The money given by the boy's family is given supposedly to make up the girl's dowry. Usually a large part of it does go into the girl's dowry, but only the generous family gives what is left over to the girl for her own use after marriage. The granddaughter of a C family married into a Y family. The latter paid $36,000 CN as the last installment. The girl's family maintained that they must add much more to that sum to make up the dowry. Many other people said that the girl's family made good profit out of it.

During the first year of betrothal the boy's family makes two gifts in kind, which are of little economic value, but are given however poor the families concerned. On the fifteenth of the Eighth Moon (the Mid-Autumn Festival) the boy's family sends to the girl's family a huge round cake of wheat flour. This cake is white, sweet, and decorated with red flower designs on the top. Its diameter usually measures three feet, and it weighs about twenty pounds. On the seventh of the Ninth Moon the boy's family sends to the other family a similar huge round cake of wheat flour, this one mixed with *kao liang* (sorghum) flour to give the cake a yellowish red color, with similar designs and flowers atop. These cakes may be dispatched by servants, and it is not necessary to send a visitor from the boy's family. In some cases another huge white cake is sent just before the wedding, but not generally. These cakes, like the tobacco and the sugar sent on the occasion of betrothal, are again freely distributed to the girl's relatives. If the betrothal lasts more than one year, these formalities may or may not be repeated.

West Towners prefer early betrothals—at the age of seven, eight, or nine years. This is likely so specially in the case of a preferred mating. But there is no formal rule about it, and betrothals at sixteen, seventeen, or eighteen years of age are by no means rare. Great disparity of age between husbands and wives is not considered normal. In spite of the intense desire for progeny, they do not believe in early marriage. The lowest age approved for marriage in West Town would seem to be seventeen for males and sixteen for females, while the majority of boys and girls marry two, three, or four years later than that. I know of one case of marriage in which the girl was fourteen and her husband about seventeen, but it was generally acknowledged that this was because the boy's family was badly in need of help. His father was almost blind, and his mother old and feeble. He worked as a laborer in a match factory in Tali. Generally speaking, betrothals may last from one or two years (if the betrothed are of marriageable age) to five, six, or even ten years (if the betrothed are children). In most other parts of China there will be during the years of betrothal ceremonial and social exchanges of gifts and visits between the two families, but certainly neither the boy nor the girl will go to the other's home, nor can they see or meet each other. Not so in West Town. Here from the day of betrothal the boy and the girl assume active roles with regard to the future spouse's family.

As may be expected, the boy's duty toward the family of his future father-in-law is less than that of the girl toward the family of her future husband. Even so, he participates in all important ceremonial and social functions that take place in the girl's family. In recent years his picture may be hung on the living-room wall with other family pictures. If his future father-in-law or mother-in-law should die, the girl's family informs him by sending him a new melon-shaped cap and a pair of sugar lumps (the latter similar to those sent to the girl's family at the time of betrothal). He comes to the home of the deceased with tokens of condolence (two or three bowls of rice, some paper money for the dead, and some actual money) and a special prayer written out on a sheet of yellow paper. He kneels in front of the corpse and reads the prayer (or somebody else reads it for him), kowtows, and then burns the prayer with the paper money. He then goes into mourning like the sons of the deceased.

The first visit of a girl to her future home with the boy's family, when she is always entertained by a feast, may take place on a similar occasion, that is, the death of one of her future parents-in-law (when she must participate in the mourning as though she were an actual daughter-in-law), or it may take place about the first *Ching Ming*, the day in the third lunar month on and near which ritual visits to ancestral graveyards take place. This festive period lasts about two weeks, and within that period practically all members of all families, except the very old and infirm, make one or two group visits to the ancestral graveyards. A girl is usually invited by her fiancé's family and participates in these visits just as do the other family members. She comes to the house several days before the date of *Ching Ming* and returns to the house of her parents some days later. During this time, if her future husband's father or mother or both are dead, she wears mourning for them just as her fiancé does until she goes back to her parents' home. Some young men observe the same formalities in the homes of their future wives during this period, but this is not, however, required.

After the first visit the young girl often comes to the boy's family. She must come not only on special ritual and ceremonial occasions, such as funerals, weddings, or the lunar New Year, but also if her future parents-in-law are ill. She may also simply spend an indefinite period of time with her future husband's family like a married daughter, periodically going home to visit her own parents. In some cases the young girl stays for a very long time, even more than six months.

The relation of the girl a2w with her future husband's family (see diagram on p. 81) illustrates this best. Her fiancé is a graduate of the local lower middle school, works in an alcohol factory in Kunming, and is away from home most of the year. They have been engaged to each other since childhood, but about two years ago he told his own mother (unrelated to the girl by blood) that if the girl remained illiterate he would definitely break the engagement. The girl's family ignored this threat, but his mother is a teacher in the local primary school, and she did not want a broken engagement in her family, which would probably have caused trouble with the family of her husband's first wife. She took charge of the young girl and sent her to the primary school where she teaches. This future daughter-in-law came into her future husband's family to live for two months, three months, and five or six months at a time. Before careful inquiry I took it for granted that she was a regular member of the family. She participated in practically all the family's life and work, sleeping, working, eating, and occasionally going to market with the other family members as a matter of course, except that when her fiancé came home she usually went back to her parents' home. There is, however, no obligation to avoid each other. They may not assume any terms of familiarity, or converse with each other intimately, or eat together. But there is absolutely no bar against an occasional exchange of words, and they go to visit ancestral graveyards in the same group. The other fiancée of this family (that of C2 in Generation IV), who was recently betrothed, comes to her prospective husband's family less frequently and stays for shorter periods. Some West Towners said that girls who were engaged in childhood could come to their future homes to participate in its life and work very closely, while girls who became engaged when "grown up" only made the regular visits on definite ritual or ceremonial occasions. Others said that this was not necessarily so, and quoted cases to prove their point. There is no absolute demarcation between the behavior of a child and that of what West Towners call a "grown up," and it seems to depend upon the girl's ability to "get along well" in her future husband's home whether she stays there for longer or for shorter periods. Consequently, the longer the duration of betrothal, the more familiar the future daughter-in-law becomes with the life and work of the family in which she is to establish her rightful place in life.

This being so, and especially because of the West Towners' preference for child betrothals, it is evident that for most West Town girls marriage is a gradual process and the wedding does not mark such a tremendous psychological, social, or even physical change for them as it would have done had they before that event been entirely excluded from the life and work of their future homes. This point has significant bearings on West Town family life.

Betrothal, until very recently, used to be absolutely binding for both sexes. Once betrothed, it was impossible to break away from it. Men, of course, could resort to concubinage as an escape, but they had to take in the first betrothed as the wife without exception. With the influences of the schools and the outside world, standards are changing. The young man who threatened to break his engagement unless his fiancée became literate is one case in point. There are at least three cases to my knowledge in which the engagement was broken or tentatively broken. A second-year pupil in the local junior middle school was by family arrangement engaged to be married during the eighth lunar month of 1941, but she eloped with someone else and went to Kunming. There was a great uproar. Finally, since the girl "could not be found," her parents returned all the presents and money which they had received as a result of her betrothal.

Another case was that of a local girl of the T clan who went to school in Kunming. She had been since childhood engaged to her father's female cousin's son. Her fiancé went to school for one or two years and was a shop assistant in Hsia Kuan. While in Kunming the girl began to be friendly with boys, and that "spoiled" her reputation in West Town. Her family promptly brought her back and kept her at home. She began to go out with a student of the college who had taken refuge in West Town. One day the two were out strolling in the fields, when three men armed with revolvers stopped them and threatened to cut off their noses (this being the traditional punishment for adultery in West Town) because their behavior corrupted the good customs of the land. Quickly a group of spectators gathered, including some students from the same college, who would have interfered on behalf of the victims if violence had been resorted to. Although their noses were saved, they were bound and sent to the local police; the latter turned them over to the magistrate's office south of West Town, which transferred them to the District Court, which promptly dismissed them for lack of any legal charge. It transpired that the three armed men were either friends of the girl's fiancé or his hirelings, who were known rascals and who had had an eye on the money that they might be able to squeeze out of the victims. Moreover, the girl's widowed mother had agreed to her companionship with the college boy. Even so, local opinion was definitely divided on the affair. The engagement was broken, and whatever money and other presents had come from her fiancé's home were returned. Today the girl is in Kunming, happily married to the same student, who now has the degree of Bachelor of Arts.

The third case occurred in Er Yuan, north of West Town, and is on record in Tali District Court. I have quoted this case in detail elsewhere,[5] and shall only mention here that it involved a young man who was murdered by his fiancée and her older sister. His fiancée was in love with a middle school student and considered that to murder the man to whom she was betrothed since childhood was the only way of withdrawing her obligation to marry him.

All three cases, in spite of their variations, show the real strength of West Town betrothal. The two girls who finally got away with the men of their own choosing cannot go back to live in West Town today.

At the end of a long or short betrothal the wedding takes place. The wedding, unlike the betrothal, is a very formal affair. In it certain rites and ceremonials are essential. The year of the wedding is generally determined by the boy's family. Certain factors, such as the death of the boy's mother, may hasten it; but the girl's parents have the right of delaying it if they need their daughter's help in the house, or advancing it if they feel that the saving of rice is more important. The date and hour when the wedding is to take place are exclusively chosen by the boy's family, upon the advice of a diviner. The latter not only decides the date and the hour of the wedding ceremony but also specifies the exact moment of entry of the sedan chair into the house gate, the direction which the bride is to face when first entering and sitting in her room, and so forth. All these

[5] See F. L. K. Hsu, "Some Problems of Chinese Law in Operation Today," *Far Eastern Quarterly*, May, 1944, pp. 217–218.

have to do with the future success of the married life and the blessedness of the family as a whole.

The whole of the wedding ceremony is picturesque, but it is quite unnecessary for purposes of the present volume to do more than outline it here. On the day before the wedding, the girl's dowry is sent to the boy's home. All articles in the dowry are carried on the shoulders of hired laborers in a procession through the streets. If the two homes are near each other, the general practice is to have the procession cover a long, circuitous route, so that more people may have an opportunity of looking at it. The following is a list of the articles which made up the dowry of a C girl, who married into a Y family, and in my opinion it is fairly typical of the middle class dowries.

2 leather chests
3 tables with drawers and cabinets
2 red lacquered square stools
2 smaller square stools, also red lacquered
2 bottles of cold cream
4 tins of face powder
2 little tins of rouge, for application on chins
2 bottles of glycerine
1 Chinese writing ink container
2 glass plate stands (for containing fruit)
Several sticks of writing brushes
8 drinking glasses
2 western writing pens
Several pencils
2 tins of local face powder
3 long gowns
   1 of wool material
   1 of red silk
   1 of yellow silk
About 15 suits of cotton cloth
6 pairs of shoes[6]

[6] A girl never receives land or a house as her dowry.

The larger articles, such as chests and tables, were each carried singly, while the smaller ones, such as bottles of cold cream and shoes, were carried on trays in two's or four's so that a procession containing the above listed number of articles would be quite a long affair. Such a procession was accompanied by a band, drummers, and ushers.

The second important thing about the wedding is the red sedan chair and the ritual offerings. The sedan chair is a specially decorated object with many embroidered designs and shuttered glass windows on four sides. Most of the designs suggest the early birth of sons. This red chair and usually one or two blue ones are hired by the boy's family and sent to the other family to receive the bride. The bridegroom rides in one of the blue chairs, and his father's sister or cousin or his father's brother's wife rides in the other blue chair. They go in procession with a band and come back in procession with the bride in the red chair. Before leaving her home the bride shows reluctance, and sometimes she and her mother shed tears. The sedan chairs and her expression of reluctance are the prerogatives of a woman in her first wedding and therefore very important to her honor and her pride.

When the chairs arrive in the bridegroom's home, three ritual offerings are made: the couple first pay homage to Gods of Heaven and Earth, then to the Kitchen God,[7] and then to ancestors. At each altar offerings of food, fruit, and flowers were laid before the actual rituals were begun. The bridegroom inserts fresh incense sticks into the bowls before kowtowing side by side with his bride. These rites are necessary to give spiritual validation to the marriage. Then the couple is led by an elderly woman, usually of the

---

[7] The Kitchen God in West Town is usually worshiped in the temples of the local patron gods. In such a temple the Kitchen God is represented by a large tablet situated on a side shrine. Unlike North China, in West Town there is not a small shrine to him in every family kitchen. Here, if he is worshiped in the family homes at all he has a special tablet, about the size of an ordinary tablet for an ancestor, in the family shrine.

same clan, to pay respect (by kowtowing) to the boy's parents, uncles, aunts, the older brothers and sisters-in-law, and any other senior relatives present. This is the formal introduction of the bride into the house and clan, and is the social validation of the marriage.

The other important features of the wedding are the feasting and the jubilation. Before the event, notices are sent to relatives and friends, both by the boy's family and the girl's family—sometimes separately, sometimes jointly—for feasting and jubilation take place in both families. As a rule the notices are given in the name of the parents who are "marrying off their daughters" and "taking wives for their sons," as the notice cards run. In recent years strange notices have been seen in West Town, because of modern influence. The wedding announcement card of the second son of a Ch family was inscribed as follows:

> This is to announce that on the 25th, 26th, and 27th of the tenth lunar month—I myself am going to get married. There will be wedding feasts, for which your honorable presence is requested.
>
> > Your younger brother (ceremonially speaking)
> > Ch —— —— bows.
>
> The tables will be set at our house in West Town Village.

This family keeps a small store where they sell cloth and imported goods. The third son attends the local junior middle school. The second son, the bridegroom, attended primary school for a few years and sometimes wears a modern Sun Yat-Sen suit. He likes to associate with students of the missionary college, to many of whom one of the wedding invitations was sent. He does not realize the inconsistency of his card, that the "moderns" never use dates according to the lunar calendar, that while they determine their own marriages, their invitations are always in the name of their parents (as are those of the Europeans), and that on such formal cards they never put the ceremonial words signifying "your younger brother," which adds a personal note to the card.

The festive spirit is higher in the boy's family, where the

large number of guests give greater signs of jubilation. The girl's family generally invites guests to two feasts—one on the morning of the wedding day, the other on the day of the bride and groom's return visit, namely, the fifth day after the wedding. The boy's family generally feasts for two or three days, and the wedding ceremony takes place on the last of the feasting days. A guest going to either the boy's or the girl's family takes with him or her a small gift of money, wrapped in red paper. In 1941 the usual amount was about $10.00; in 1943, about $100.00 or $200.00. The closer relatives and friends give more. In the boy's family the feasting is always a continuous affair. The courtyard, or courtyards, is covered by an awning. The guests—men, women, and children from West Town proper and from some of the outlying villages—arrive at all hours in the two or three days. They are received by members of the family and shown to rooms in different parts of the house to rest. The setting and clearing of tables are continuous processes. This is one of the occasions when children and adults can stuff themselves as much and as frequently as they please. The situation may be described as general license in eating. The hosts have to show their willingness by being unreasonably generous with their food. The guests can for once forget any consideration of economy. Some early arrivals eat for two or three days. Men and women sit by themselves and eat at different tables. Relatives or friends from distant villages may not return home until several days after the event. Those who cannot attend these celebrations in person forward their gifts by someone else, who will feast in their behalf.

There is a good deal of general merrymaking in addition to the feasts. In most families storytellers are employed to entertain the guests throughout the day. Some families also borrow a gramophone and some records, which may be too old to sound like anything but log-sawing. As a rule, talent is encouraged, so that under the same awning a professional singer with his three-stringed plucking instrument, the gramophone, and two or three Chinese violins are likely to be performing at the same time. Nobody listens carefully; they talk, they feast, they yell. Applause is given, not according to the quality of the performance, but because of the person who is performing.

On the wedding day the main interest is provided by the bride. Everybody, except the elderly males, wants to have a peep at her; she sits practically motionless all day long, except when told to partake of food ceremonially with the bridegroom. At dusk the fervor centering around the bride runs even higher. The younger people, male and female, crowd into the bride and bridegroom's new room and make fun of them. The couple are compelled to perform stunts, to make gestures of intimacy, and so forth. And the merriment infects everyone present. It lasts until about midnight, and then the guests disperse after yet another meal, consisting of noodles, preserved sweets, peanuts, and tea.

Virginity in a girl is valued. If a girl were known to have been mixed up in any clandestine affair, her only chance of marriage would be to go to some distant village or to Kunming, where no one would know her history. Ordinarily, the behavior of most boys and girls in the community is common knowledge to any family that cares to find out. If, however, a girl's lost honor is discovered after the wedding bells are rung, then practically no one will turn her out and make the fact known. The family's honor as a whole is too important to be risked. The husband may dislike her or he may proceed to take a concubine, but she will be formally and socially his wife and his parents' daughter-in-law.

For an ordinary family (boy's family) all the expenses involved in a wedding, including feasting, but excluding money and articles given to the girl's family before the wedding, would amount to about $10,000 in the early part of 1942. This sum was actually spent by the family of the young man who sent out the "modern" invitation quoted above. Wealthier families easily spend much more. For the woman's family, the cost is far lower than that of the man's. For any family, to marry the daughter off is much less important than to get the son a wife. Besides, the girl's family can usually make use of what has been left over, after making up a dowry, from the gifts in money during the girl's betrothal.

On the day after the wedding the bridegroom's married sister or sister-in-law, or both, pay a visit to the temple of the local patron god, to make ritual offerings similar to those performed after the birth of a child.

MATRILOCAL MARRIAGE

In some circumstances the girl's family may decide to take into their home a son-in-law instead of marrying their daughter into another family. Such a marriage is called *zou mei* (or Ju Chuei in Chinese, which term the local people also use). The majority of families contracting such a marriage do so because they have no sons and do not wish to adopt a nephew from the same clan. There are only rare exceptions.[8]

Elsewhere in China this type of marriage is comparatively rare and is always looked upon as degrading to the male. A man who has married into his wife's family will not be able to raise his voice in the community. Both he and his wife's family are usually poor and of low social status. Not so in West Town. Here, although no exact figures are available, it is estimated that more than one third of all marriages are of the *zou mei* type. Some West Towners put the proportion as high as above 50 percent. Although people say that only a poor fellow would marry into the family of his wife, yet they talk about it freely and give information regarding married-in cases in their own families without reserve. A study of the kinship relations of many of the wealthy and important families in the town shows that such marriages are indeed common. One of the

[8] An old man Y (B. L.) has four sons and one daughter. The latter is married to a *zou mei* husband because the old father liked her very much. Her case did not cause any family trouble.

two wealthiest families in West Town acknowledges that its fortune was begun by a *zou mei* member. His sons built a special temple for him on the hill, and West Towners used to look up to him as the leading member of the community. He died a few years ago.

West Towners generally say that *zou mei* marriages are never arranged when the men and women are adults. They are arranged when the boys are younger than twelve years of age, sometimes only five or six. They say that if a man is an adult and still shows no sign of achievement whatever, no girl's parents will care to take him in at all. On the other hand, if such a man had means of his own, either through work or inheritance, he would not care to go and take somebody else's family name. One informant even compared *zou mei* marriages to selling one's family name. Seen in the light of family adjustment, this is perfectly understandable. Marriage of the patrilocal type stresses the necessity of a gradual transition for the girl, so marriage of the matrilocal type stresses the necessity of a gradual transition for the boy. If the incoming son-in-law were already grown up, his habits, ideas, and sentiments would already have been formed, and a sudden change of environment would certainly make his new family life difficult. It is also easy to see why when adult *zou mei* marriages do occur they occur generally in one of the two following ways: (1) an able assistant in a shop may be made son-in-law in the family of his proprietor; (2) two families who have known each other for a long time may decide upon a matrilocal marriage between themselves. Both situations evidently foster factors favorable to the success of future adjustment between the incoming son-in-law and the girl's family.

A matrilocal marriage is arranged like any other marriage. There is the usual consultation of diviners and the usual employment of a go-between. But only one lot of gifts of betrothal consisting of some sugar lumps and pipe tobacco (but not bracelets and other bodily ornaments) change hands, and these are sent from the girl's family to the boy's family. No money is included in the gifts. A date is then set for the transfer of the boy. This date is chosen by a diviner, just as for a wedding, but unlike a wedding, the families are not concerned with the hour of the boy's entry into his new home. The boy, dressed in his best, is led to his new home by his older brother or an uncle. They both walk to his bride's dwelling. Upon arrival, he first pays respect to his new "parents" and then worships before the family shrine. However, he and his fiancée do not meet each other on this occasion. Then the ceremony is considered complete. There is some slight feasting in both families. From this moment the boy takes on the surname of his father-in-law and assumes a new forename, which has one character or a radical in common with his patrilineal cousins in the

ORTHODOX MARRIAGE

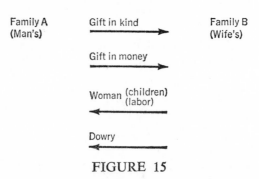

FIGURE 15

new clan. From this moment he acquires full membership in his father-in-law's family, but he does not have any intimate relations with his future wife until sometime later, when a wedding ceremony, like that already described, formally marries them.

The important thing to be observed is that while the matrilocal type of marriage is evidently prevalent, it lasts for only one generation. In the next generation the usage automatically reverts to the patrilineal and patrilocal pattern. *Zou mei* marriages are merely a supplementary arrangement in the interest of the basic pattern, but it gives the individual and his family certain advantages which would be absent in other circumstances.

The preceding diagram illustrates the position of patrilocal marriage. In a patrilocal marriage most of the gifts come back to the man's family in the form of dowry. There is something left over, and part of the surplus is consumed in feasts. The economic advantage of the gifts to the wife's family is negligible, and the wife's family loses a working hand, while the man's family gains one, together with some part of the money it paid out and the possibility of getting more working hands (children).

In a matrilocal marriage (as illustrated in the diagram below) the initial advantage of the wife's family is great, for the few gifts do not compensate the husband's family for the loss of a man and his descendants. But his family does benefit, for since it is poorer than the wife's family, the son who has married-out will have a better chance in life with his new family's property. Secondly, if the matrilocally married man has more than one son, one of them must return to his father's clan and continue his

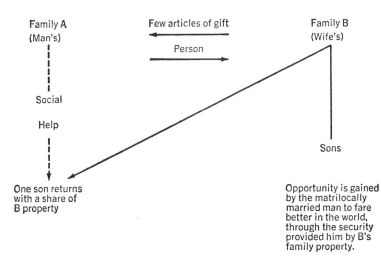

MATRILOCAL MARRIAGE

Family A (Man's)   Few articles of gift   Family B (Wife's)

Person

Social

Help

Sons

One son returns with a share of B property

Opportunity is gained by the matrilocally married man to fare better in the world, through the security provided him by B's family property.

FIGURE 16

line. This son is fortunate, because he starts life with a share of property from his father's family by marriage and also a share of whatever his father's family by origin possesses. Thirdly, the married-out man, having fared better, will actually give as much help to the son who has returned to his blood relatives as to the sons who remain with him, thus enabling the family of his origin and the returned son to prosper. This was what actually occurred to the two clans Ye and Y. Less than thirty years ago Ye clan was barely well-to-do and Y clan was very poor. A man from Y clan entered Ye clan by way of *zou mei* marriage. With the help of the Ye property, this man made a fortune; the Ye family is now one of the two richest families in town. He then helped the Y family as much as he could, with the result that the Y clan, though not yet comparable to the Ye in wealth, is also one of the richest families in town.

The advantages of a *zou mei* marriage may also work out indirectly.

ZOU MEI MARRIAGE

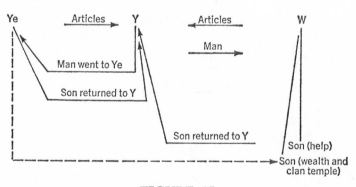

FIGURE 17

In this case two men from Y family entered W and Ye families, respectively, by way of *zou mei* marriages. The W's were shoemakers in a small way. Two sons were born to this union. When this marriage took place the Y's were very poor. Later the Ya family became wealthy with the help of Ye; the Y's then helped the second of the W sons to become prosperous. This second son returned to the Y clan to continue his father's line. He built a large clan temple for the W clan and gave his older brother a fairly impressive business fortune and a large house. In this way the custom of matrilocal marriage sometimes provides the poorer individual with greater security and opportunities in life. The prevalence of this custom in West Town is undoubtedly partially, if not wholly, in effect because of its results.

REMARRIAGE AND CONCUBINAGE

There is not a single old spinster or bachelor in the community. Every man or woman gets married sooner or later. Since marriage is arranged by the family and the need for descendants is so great, this is natural.

Theoretically, both widows and widowers may remarry. In fact, however, more widowers than widows do so. A widower often marries a widow. It is hard for a man to get an unmarried girl for a second wife, except when he is wealthy. Partially as a result of this, the incidence of widows who remarry is high. One informant says that three-tenths of all widows remarry. I have not been able to check up on this point, but West Towners do not deny that widows remarry as they disavow divorces. Under no circumstances can a widow marry a bachelor. The second marriage of a man to a virgin girl involves just as much of a wedding ceremony as did his first marriage; but the second marriage of a woman is a very modest affair. She is not even entitled to a ride in a sedan chair. The prospective husband's father's brother's wife or his brother's wife goes to the widow's house and escorts her home on foot. In some cases she is taken to her new home in the small hours of the morning before everyone is up, and sometimes late at night after most people have gone to bed. The darkness of the streets protects her from being waylaid by any member of her parents' family. The latter, if successful in intercepting the widow, will insist on taking her back, because they "could not allow one of their women to spoil the family honor by shamelessly marrying a second time." The woman's dead husband's family usually receives payment for her remarriage. Often her parents' family can be pacified by a share of the "bride price."

In her second marriage a woman is a dishonored object. The marriage may touch off the wrath of the gods as well as the spirit of her departed husband. It was generally believed by my informants that if a woman had a son, or even a daughter, she should not try to remarry. She should get her daughter a matrilocally married husband. In this way continuation of the family line and her own comfort in the other world would be insured. But a very poor widow usually tries to get married again.

When a widower remarries, he is merely being dutiful or satisfying a necessity. If no heir survived his first wife, his duty to his ancestors makes remarriage imperative. If he has sons, the necessity for someone to wash, cook for, and otherwise take care of him and his children makes such a step unavoidable.

This logic lends ample support to the custom of concubinage. As noted earlier, betrothal is so binding that it is usually impossible for either party to get out of it. A consummated marriage becomes even harder to dissolve. This applies to both sexes. But while a woman cannot be divorced by her husband unless she has committed some very obvious misbehavior, such as adultery, a man, dissatisfied with his wife, may desert her and formally marry again or take a concubine. His wife can do little to prevent it, and she can never find another man to marry her. To marry a woman whose husband is alive is the greatest ill omen one can bring upon himself. In such circumstances a woman can devote herself to prayer in temples, weaving, and trading on the various markets, or if she has children she may devote herself to caring for them.

The case of the second daughter-in-law in a Ch family

will illustrate this point. She was young and good looking, and had adopted modern styles for her hair and dress. Her husband's family was well-to-do. She gave birth to one son, who died. For some reason the husband did not like her and had married someone in Kunming. At the time of investigation she was still unaware of his second marriage, though other family members knew what was going on. In commenting on this case one informant concluded: "She couldn't do anything about it even if she knew the facts. The age-old mentality is just like that."

Concubines are taken by wealthy persons, generally ostensibly to acquire sons. Many informants are very explicit on this point. Y.C.Y., for example, has a wife and a concubine. Neither has given birth to a child. He expressed to me the following sentiments: "I married a concubine to get a son. . . . This is really a troublesome question. It [the problem of an heir] has delayed and messed up all my plans for developing my business outside West Town. I have to stay at home all the time."

Yet a review of the eleven cases of concubinage I have collected will show that more than half of them have nothing to do with the popularly professed reason.[9] In six out of eleven cases the wife had given birth to sons. In the remaining five cases the concubines were taken because the wives were barren.

There are two possibilities: one, that these eleven cases of concubinage are not representative of the community as a whole, for the actual incidence of concubinage is, according to my estimates, about 150 among the population of eight thousand.[10] Also, it is possible that the majority of

[9] See Appendix II.

[10] This figure is obtained in the following manner: The genealogical records of five clans were studied for total number of marriages contracted in each clan. The number of concubines in each clan is counted. The ratios for these clans are as follows: (*a*) T clan: total number of couples recorded, 421; number of concubines, 22. (*b*) Ch clan: total number of couples recorded, 328; number of concubines, 17. (*c*) Y clan: total number of couples recorded, 54; number of concubines, 6. (*d*) W clan: total number of couples recorded, 188; number of concubines, 14. (*e*) Ye clan: total number

these 150 concubines were taken in the interest of continuing the family line and that the six cases (shown in
Appendix II) of concubines taken for other reasons are
exceptions. The other possibility is that concubinage is a
much more general pattern than the family organization
and that the idea of resorting to concubinage as a means
of continuing the family line developed merely as a ration-
alization.

The two possibilities are not, however, in conflict. Concubinage occurs in India and in a large number of other
societies where the family organization often bears little
resemblance to that found in West Town. Concubinage in
these societies is often associated with acquisition or expression of prestige, or with polyerotic tendencies of the
male. Given the usage, it can be easily rationalized in a
culture in which continuation of the family line is of ut-
most importance.

---

of couples recorded, 277; number of concubines, 3. The ratios for
these clans are: T, 5%; Ch, 5%; Y, 11%; W, 7%; Ye, 1%. But
the Ye record is very incomplete, and the Ch and W records do not
distinguish between step wives married after the death of the first
and concubines. The Y clan is much too small for a good sample.
The T record is the most reliable. However, forty-three households
were studied for family composition. These households contain 144
wives and 7 concubines, giving a ratio of 4.8%, which coincides with
the T ratio. Now West Town contains about 1,000 households with
probably 3,000 wives. Five percent of this number is 150 concubines.

CHAPTER V

Propagation of the Ancestral Line

THERE ARE three basic points of reference in the institution of marriage as it appears in West Town. The first is that it is a means for prolongation of the patrilineal family line. Where this line is in danger of becoming extinct, matrilineal and matrilocal marriages are contracted freely. The sanction of ancestors is an integral part of the marriage.

The second point of reference follows the first: marriage is male-centered. The emphasis is not upon partnership between the man and his wife, but upon woman's duty to her husband and especially her parents-in-law. The woman is obliged to produce sons, which are her indispensable contribution to matrimony. In addition, one of the cardinal virtues of the woman is obedience to her husband and her parents-in-law. With such an emphasis, there is no room for romantic union. Prescribed mating is prevalent, and a girl's early betrothal as well as familiarity with the man's family are encouraged to ensure harmony in the household. Horoscope and gods are important safeguards to success in marriage. Concubinage is regarded as normal.

The third point of reference is the well-known double standard of morality. The very obvious evidence for this is found in connection with remarriage and adultery. Remarriage for a widower is normal; for a widow it spells dishonor. Infidelity for the man is not extraordinary; for the woman, it amounts to social suicide. Under this double standard foot binding seemed a reasonable addition to differences between the sexes.

These points of reference are perfectly in keeping with the elementary aspects of the kinship system, which we have described in Chapter III. Briefly, the system is based upon a theory of blood, and follows the principles of lineage, generation, sex, and seniority. The father-son relationship is the core and all other relationships are either its extensions, supplements, or held to be subordinate to it. Every part in the system either supports, or is a result of, the over-all emphasis on the continuation of the father-son line.

THE BIG-FAMILY IDEAL

The continuity of the father-son line may be ensured either by systematic dispersal of younger male members of the family by limiting inheritance to the eldest son or by emphasizing the integrity of the ancestral property and encouraging unity among all family members as a single group. The former is the usage of primogeniture; the latter is the "big-family ideal."

Primogeniture has often been mistaken as a necessary part of the big-family ideal. In fact, they are quite exclusive of each other. Primogeniture means that all but the eldest son disperse; the big family ideal dictates that all sons must stay under the same roof and that, at least theoretically, all sons have a more or less equal right to the ancestral property.

In West Town the socially upheld usage is the big-family ideal, which emphasizes unity in the household, not primogeniture. Unity is promoted by parent-arranged marriages, following consultation of the horoscope, preferential mating, early betrothal—not romantic attachment. This unity is to be arrived at not so much by a better adjustment of the many personalities involved as by a gradual inculcation in the individual of his or her place in the kinship hierarchy. This unity is enhanced by strong rules against adultery within the household.[1] This unity is also promoted by a common family home as well as by a graveyard which will be adequate for many generations. It is further buttressed by worship of the same ancestors and by unity in the clan. The most tangible signs of the latter are clan or ancestral temples and genealogical records.

Under this unity, sons do not attain social maturity until the death of their father. Whatever property the father has automatically becomes the property of his sons. The father does not have to make a will, for there is no alternative to this customary will. Whatever power and prestige the father has is automatically shared by his sons. Even if he should not wish it, people would look upon the youngsters in no other light. This unity also explains certain facts which at first sight seem incompatible with the social structure. We have seen the intense desire for sons. Yet in West Town, as well as in other parts of Yunnan, there is a practice which must by any definition be considered as birth control. Husbands and wives sleep in the same room as long as their sons are not married. After the latter's marriage, some parents continue to sleep in the same room; others do not. After the birth of a grandchild, it is definitely more desirable for the older couple to live in different rooms; it would be considered disgraceful for the older woman to become pregnant after such an event.

A review of the family cases investigated shows that with few exceptions old couples whose married sons have children live separately. In a Ch family, which keeps two small dry goods stores, the parents have four sons, only one of whom was not married at the time of this investigation. The old father sleeps in the shop on one side of the street, while the old mother sleeps in the one on the opposite side of the street. The third son told me that his parents adopted this arrangement a number of years ago. In another Ch

---

[1] This question has been discussed elsewhere. See F. L. K. Hsu: "The Problem of Incest Tabu in a North China Village," *American Anthropologist*, XLII, No. 1 (January–March, 1940), pp. 122–135.

family the old mother died some time ago, and the sons got the old father another wife. The latter is about the age of the youngest of the daughters-in-law, yet the old father sleeps in the bachelor room on the second floor all the time. The eldest son also sleeps in this room sometimes, but does not avoid having normal sexual relations with his wife.

In both of the above cases the old men are past sixty years of age, but the practice is not restricted to people of such advanced age. In a C family a woman of forty died in 1943. She was pregnant. To avoid the birth of a child after her son had been married, she resorted to primitive methods of abortion and died as a result.

In discussing this matter West Towners uniformly gave me the following reasons: "It looks embarrassing for a couple to sleep together after their son is married," or "It is shameful for a woman to get pregnant after her daughter-in-law has already entered the house."

Why, it may be asked, in view of the intense desire for sons, do birth control practices such as these develop? The answer is that such measures underscore the unity of the family as a group. The function of continuation of the ancestral line is vested in the father before the son is married and transferred to the son after that event.

This fact is especially clear when we realize that West Towners who do not observe this rule are old men who took young concubines for reasons totally unrelated to the question of family continuation.[2]

There is more evidence for this emphasis on unity of the family group in some census data. The whole community is divided equally, according to the number of households, into ten *pao*.[3] Each *pao* contains ten *chia*, and each *chia*, about ten households. The record of the fourth *pao* has been analyzed, and the results are given below.

The total number of households in this *pao* is 100 and

---

[2] Two such cases came to my knowledge; in both cases the sons are wealthy and prosperous (Cases 4 and 5, Appendix III).

[3] For the local organization see Chapter I.

the total number of persons reported is 860. The average size of the household is 8.60 persons. The size distribution of these households is as follows.

THE FOURTH PAO

Number of persons per household	Number of households
2	1
3	4
4	4
5	12
6	6
7	20
8	14
9	9
10	5
11	5
12	5
13	5
14	2
15	1
16	2
17	1
18	1
19	2
23	1
Total	100

Some very interesting features stand out from these tables. First, only males are socially acceptable as family heads. The sole exception is in the case of a widow who has a son and a daughter, 9 and 12 years of age, respectively. Secondly, there are two uncles (father's brothers) younger than the father, but no uncle older than the father living under the same roof. In the same way, there are more younger than older brothers of the family head living under the same roof. These facts indicate that the family head is usually chosen on the basis of seniority in any generation. The oldest brothers are the natural family heads. Thirdly, compared with a total of fifty-two brothers of the family heads living in these families, the total of only eight sisters of the family heads is very small, and all are, furthermore, younger than the head of the family. For the same reason, there are more grandsons under these roofs than granddaughters. These facts suggest that practically all women marry, and that as far as this *pao* is concerned, patrilocal marriages dominate. Fourthly, sons and daughters of family heads are in the majority in all families. Parents and children are the core of any family.

The kinship distribution in these households is as follows (the relationship terms are those used by family head).

KINSHIP DISTRIBUTION IN THE FOURTH PAO

Male	*Number*	*Female*	*Number*
Family head	99	Family head	1
Father	7	Wife	91
Grandfather	1	Concubine	3
Father's younger		Mother	35
brother	2	Grandmother	3
Older brother	4	Wife of father's	
Younger brother	35	younger brother	10
Brother's son	69	Wife of father's older	
Son	147	brother	3
Grandson	47	Older brother's wife	12
Great-grandson	2	Younger brother's wife	31
Father's brother's son		Wife of older cousin	5
(cousin older than		Wife of younger cousin	7
family head)	4	Brother's daughter	45
Father's brother's son		Younger sister	8
(cousin younger		Daughter	94
than family head)	9	Daughter-in-law	41
Sons-in-law		Granddaughter	32
(married-in)	2	Granddaughter-in-law	1
		Wife of brother's son	10
Male total	428	Female total	432

Grand total 860

The most important features of these two tables are, however, the average size of the family and its composition. The average size is 8.60 persons; in composition not only are 47 grandsons and 32 granddaughters distributed among 28 families, 39 brothers distributed among 28 families (thirty of them married), 43 brothers' wives distributed among 34 families (four of them widowed), and a large number of brothers' sons and their wives and children but also 13 male first cousins (father's brother's sons) are distributed among 8 families, 12 of whom are with wives and children.

Compared with the results obtained for China as a whole, these families are much larger (5.3 vs. 8.6), and their composition is much wider in scope.[4] Elsewhere in China, as soon as sons are married, the family unit becomes unstable, so that a smaller proportion of the families have married brothers living in the same household, and a still smaller proportion of them include married first cousins. The big-family system is an ideal aspired to, but not reached by the great majority of Chinese families outside of West Town.

DIVISION UNDER THE SAME ROOF

Is it true, then, that the ideal of a big family has been realized in West Town more than in any other area investigated? That was the question in my mind after completing the analysis of the census data.

Specific information was then obtained in 42 households in different parts of the community, covering a total number of 394 individuals. The distribution ranges from 2 persons per household to 32, and the average is 9.38 persons

---

[4] For a summary of a number of findings on the subject, see C. M. Chiao, *Rural Population and Vital Statistics for Selected Areas of China, 1929–31*, Shanghai, 1934, and L. S. C. Smythe, "The Composition of the Chinese Family," *Nanking University Journal*, V, No. 2 (1935), and also F. L. K. Hsu, "The Myth of Chinese Family Size," *American Journal of Sociology*, XLVIII (May, 1943), 555–562.

per household.[5] This average figure is even larger than that obtained from the census, but agrees with the other figure in being much higher than that obtained for all China.

A closer scrutiny of the life and arrangement of these households reveals, however, a different story. Each of these households is a separate unit socially and ritually, but may be several units in economic arrangement. In other words, most of these households are divided under the same roof.

Elsewhere in China, when a household is divided, it is divided completely. The property will be parceled equally between the brothers (a slightly larger portion being allotted to the eldest). If both parents are living, they will receive a share of the property equal to that of the sons. If only one parent is living, he or she will receive a smaller share than that of each of the sons and will be billeted with one of the sons. If the size of the property is very small, the living parent may not receive a share, but will live and eat with each son's family in turn for a certain period of time, let us say a month. But the property is managed exclusively by whoever owns it, beginning with the day the family is formally divided, when a ceremony takes place. If one brother has to borrow money from another, or the father from one of the sons, it is like borrowing from outsiders.

Elsewhere in China, too, when a family is divided, each new group is registered on the police register as a separate household; each new household has its own family altar, where its members worship; each new household sends its own ceremonial gifts in case of weddings, funerals, and births among relatives or friends common to all members of the undivided family; in other words, each new household is regarded as a completely separate unit. If the family is well-to-do, the separate units will certainly move out to new residences. If the family is not, the separate units will occupy different parts of the old house. The latter will be

5 See Appendix III.

partitioned and rewalled to give the several units the appearance of private households. As time goes on, the several units tend to move away to other houses until only one of the units remains.

This picture is decidedly untrue of West Town. Here the households, though larger in appearance than in most parts of China, rarely remain undivided. Many households are divided as soon as the sons are married. If there is only one son in the house, this may not happen. But when one or more of the sons have children, the family will definitely be divided along the individual family line.

The division may or may not be heralded by a ceremony, which ancestors will be invoked to witness. The landed property and the shops are usually divided equally among the sons. In some cases the oldest son demands a somewhat larger share. If the land and the shops are not divided, they will be jointly managed, but the crops and the profits will be equally shared among the several units each year. Each son and his immediate family will occupy and own one or more wings of the house. Each unit has its own kitchen. The eldest son will have the west wing. The parents, if living, may reside in the west wing with the eldest son, or each of them may live with a different son. They may eat with each son's family in turn, or always separately with two of the sons and their families. The sons provide them with petty cash and clothing. If the old father smokes opium, that too will be supplied by the younger persons.

The division of the household may be preceded and precipitated by quarrels, open or hidden. If it is a formal division, offerings will be made at the family altar, and relatives will each send some gift (usually a pair of sugar lumps similar to the ones given during an engagement ceremony) to each of the new units. All such relatives will be entertained at tea or dinner.

In some cases a share of the property is reserved for the aged parents' burial. This property may be used by the older people during their lifetime and is much smaller than the share of any son. The monthly allowance given to the parents may be agreed upon in advance, or it may not. The amounts given by the sons may not be equal.

Senior members of the clan are invited to witness a formal division. They are to see, with the male members of the family, that the property is equally divided into units. They are to mitigate any strained relationship. There will be a "document of division," which specifies the property of the family and the manner of its division and is signed by all parties concerned before witnesses.

Here division ends. The family altar remains in the west wing of the house. Before that altar all family members worship their common ancestors and family gods as they have always done, although each unit will make its own offering on all except a few occasions, to be noted. Each new unit will reside in that wing or wings of the house which it owns, without expecting to move away or to set up another altar. With regard to community affairs, whether religious or social, the larger household remains one unit. In any community prayer meeting there will be one contribution from the family, invariably given in the name of the old father or, if he is dead, of the eldest brother. For any occasions such as marriages, funerals, or births among relatives or friends, there may be one gift only from the larger household in the name of the old father, or there may be separate gifts, if the old father is dead. On festivals and New Year's days the separate units may entertain relatives at dinner separately, in turn (one unit each year), or all units may do it together. If both parents are living, the latter custom usually prevails.

Theoretically, the old father can enjoy nearly as much authority over the sons as he ever did; in fact, the younger people may quietly push him aside. The emphasized ideal is for the sons to listen to the older man just as much as they ever did, but the actual picture seems to depend upon the strength and quality of his personality. In a Ch family the old father appears to have greater authority over the sons than do some other fathers. He keeps the keys to all important family chests, but he had to stop indulging in séances upon complaint from his sons. In a C family, on the other hand, the old man enjoyed much less authority, even on the superficial level. During a quarrel with the family's tenants, the old father first conceded to the demands of the latter, but his grown-up grandsons (in the absence of their fathers) countermanded his promise completely and imposed their own decisions. On the next morning, the old man even made some gesture against the tenants.

Applying this pattern as the criterion for classification, it has been found that the forty-two households with 394 persons and an average size of 9.38 have actually to be divided into 72 families with an average size of 5.47 persons. The last figure comes strikingly close to the figure for all China.[6]

The whole pattern of division under the same roof may best be illustrated by a few specific cases. The first is a Yi family (see Appendix I). The family has four branches, represented in the diagram by the letters W, X, Y, Z. About ten years ago Y went to Kunming and closed up, on behalf of the family, a few small shops belonging to the family. After coming back to West Town, he and his wife bought a small stove and a frying pan and started to cook some of their own meals. Evidently Y had pocketed some of the common fund in his trust, and he and his wife had decided to have better food than that served from the common kitchen. Other members of the family clamored for division. They requested some elderly members of the clan to come as witnesses and helpers in the event, but most of them declined the honor, saying "Your type of family is hard to deal with and divide" (meaning that the members would be quarrelsome). As a result, the land was not divided, but the members lived apart and ate separately. Since the elders of the clan had refused to come, a few of the married daughters senior in generation to the heads

[6] See Appendix III.

of the four branches were invited. These women helped to divide the family belongings, including kitchen utensils. A mason was hired on that day to build three new kitchen stoves with mud bricks. The family's common land was in charge of Y, since X lived in Kunming with his concubine and her children, and W lived in Kunming with his wife. Y was the only male of this generation living at home. The land owned in common is now tilled by tenants who are unrelated to the family. The tenants turn in about half of the crops to the family, dividing them into four approximately equal portions. Each unit takes one portion.

In addition to the property in West Town, the family as a whole also owns some land and houses in Tali and Hsia-kuan, as well as some shops in Kunming. W and X, who live in Kunming with some members of their families, manage and take the profits from the shops in Kunming, while Y manages and receives the returns from the land and the houses in the two nearby localities. W's share of the crops at home belongs to his mother, the old concubine. z being an illiterate woman and having only an adopted son, who is not loyal to her, has no means of getting at the property out of town. She only grumbles to her friends and relatives about it, and they console her with the suggestion that she will never need more than she is receiving. She is kept in ignorance of the returns from these other sources and information about them.

On festival days the three branches W, X, and Y take turns entertaining relatives at dinner. The others say that since z is alone, she does not need to entertain separately. She only helps with the work during such entertainments. Each branch of the family makes ritual offerings at the common family altar, and on the 15th of the Seventh Moon the whole family worships ancestors together.

The second illustration is taken from a Ch house given in the same appendix. The family was divided a few years ago after an open quarrel. They agreed to divide, but there was no formal ceremony of division. There were three sons, X, Y, and Z, and an old father, L. X, as eldest son said that although he was entitled to a larger share of the property, he did not want it. He and Z each took charge of half of the family's land and used the income. Y is in Mandalay, Burma, married to a Burmese woman, and is in business on his own. He does not ask that any money be sent him from home. But members of the family said that when and if he returned he should receive part of the land from X and Z.

The old father, L, does not have charge of any property. His sons supply him and his wife with clothes and with pocket money. He is also adequately supplied with opium. He and his young wife take turns eating with the family of each son for one month at a time. L and X, though each officially is supposed to live in a bedroom with his wife, actually more often live together in a bachelor room on the second floor.

The two units worship together and send ceremonial gifts and community contributions as one family. The sons ostensibly show obedience toward the father, although one of them complained to me that his father was too lazy. He even told me that his father nearly squandered the whole of the family's property before he and his brothers grew old enough to work.

A third illustration is provided by a Na family. The composition of the family is as follows: Old father (70), old mother (65), oldest son (40), with wife and four children, second son (30), with wife and children, and third son (16), with a newly married wife. All the men of the family are horse dealers. The second son (30) and his immediate family live by themselves in the same house. The other two brothers live together. The old parents live together in one room, but the father eats with the eldest son's family, while the mother eats with the second son.

There are two exceptions in the forty-two cases studied. One family was composed as follows: old mother (75), first son (60), with his wife, second son (55), with his wife, four children of the latter (all sons, to be referred to as A, B, C, and D), with wives of A and B. Here we have an undivided family of three generations all eating together. Even so, the family was not undivided in all respects. The first son (60) had a shop of his own in Kunming, the income from which was his own. The second son (55) was exceptionally wealthy. He had several shops in Kunming and elsewhere in which leather goods and herb medicine were sold. Young man A helped his father in business, but young man B did free-lance trading in Kunming on his own. They all contributed freely to the family expenses. There are three possible explanations about the relatively undivided state of this family. First, the two sons (60 and 55) were both wealthy, and the second (55) was unusually generous. Secondly, the first son (60) had no heir and might be hoping to take one of his younger brother's sons as heir. Thirdly, A and B, though married, had no children. Generally family division occurs after the birth of children.

Another exceptional case was a family which had two small dry goods stores. The family was composed of father (65), mother (64), daughter-in-law (widow), with her son, second son and his immediate family (wife and three children), third son and his newly married wife, and fourth son. This family lived in two wings of a small house. The widow and her son lived on the second floor of one wing; the third son and his bride lived on the ground floor of the same wing; the second son and his family lived on the ground floor of the other wing. The aged father slept in the main shop about half a mile away. The aged mother slept in a small shop of her own just opposite the main one. The fourth son slept in the main shop regularly. The third son, though he was supposed to share a room with his wife at home, slept in the main shop most of the time.

The family worshiped together, sent ceremonial gifts together, and ate together as far as possible. Usually the women and children ate together at home, and the aged mother and the men ate together in the main shop. Food was cooked at home by the women and brought to the shop by one of the sons or one of the wives. If one of the sons happened to be home at mealtime, he ate with the women and children.

The family owned a small amount of land which was rented out to tenants. This property was not divided, nor was the main shop. Even the profit from the main shop was not definitely divided. The family members took approximately what they wanted and helped with the work of the shop whenever they could. The second son did a lot of independent trading between the different markets. Only the aged mother's business seemed to be her own. She managed her own store and kept her own stock and money. When one of her sons made a sale for her, he kept an account of it and turned the money over to her later. In Chapter III we have described her work at some length.

Both the sons, with whom I conversed many times, strongly denied that the family was divided. They told me that their mother only wanted to see how much she could make and how much the main shop could make. However, in the course of at least one of the conversations they admitted that their mother wanted to make some money for her own burial.

That division under the same roof is the normal thing is further supported by the fact that, unlike people in other parts of China, West Towners are completely unemotional about family division. They never think it undesirable or try to deny its necessity. Some of the local comments are typical: "Few families with three generations can eat from the same kitchen; they can't get along together"; "Men do not mind it (living together), but women have small hearts (meaning they will quarrel over small things)"; "It is troublesome to have too many people eat from the same kitchen"; etc.

Thus, West Town has a pattern of family life which is little known in other parts of China. Elsewhere, the average size of households is surprisingly small, because most families of several generations cannot get along under the same roof and because when they divide they break up completely. West Town has developed a pattern which, while maintaining the existence of the joint household, also allows freedom for the individual family. This pattern has important effects on family relationship. Early division of a family group removes an important source of family friction, allows greater expression of the erotic aspect of marital relationship, and greater scope for individual competition, and thus enables a household to maintain a high degree of social and ceremonial unity in accordance with the big-family ideal. Division under the same roof reconciles, in other words, ancestral authority with individual competition.

THE CLAN AND ITS SOLIDARITY

"Clan" is here used in the sense of a unilateral descent group. In West Town such a group is patrilineal; that is, it traces its origin to a common male ancestor. Theoretically, the longer the line of ancestry, the wider will be the extent of the clan, and the more ardent the fervor toward the common ancestry, the greater will be the solidarity among members of the clan. In fact, however, while the former is generally true, the latter is definitely not the case. The household is, as we have seen, characterized by a clever device of division under the same roof which reconciles ancestral authority with individual competition. The resulting organization is one in which the external aspects are much more impressive than the inner relationships. West Town clans closely resemble West Town households; they have plenty of external emoluments, but they lack inner solidarity.

Since family names are identical with clan names, it would seem reasonable to use the number of the former for an indication of the number of the latter. Unfortunately, several unrelated clans may have the same name. On the other hand, only a portion of the census data is available. The one hundred families covered by the census data and the forty-three families covered separately give twenty-three family names. But there are more than twenty-three family names in West Town. A review of four exhaustive genealogical records, including two of the largest clans, shows that the women of these clans bore forty-three other family names before marriage, making the total of known family names sixty-five.

It is impossible to determine whether or not all these women married into the four clans were from West Town, although, judging from the fact that an amazingly high percentage of marriages are local matches, many of them must have come from the same community. The most interesting thing about these data is the frequency of a certain number of family names. The most frequent names from the several sources are given in a comparative table below.

1. *T record:* Y (172), Ch (65), L (48), Yi (22), Ho (16), Tuan (15), Tu (13), W (11), Ch'en (7), and miscellaneous.
2. *Ye record:* Y (103), C (36), Ch (31), L (20), Yi (18), T (13), Ch'en (7), and miscellaneous.
3. *Ch record:* Y (146), C (20), L (20), T (20), Yi (22), Tsao (16), Tuan (15), Ho (8), Ye (8), W (6), Kao (6), and miscellaneous.
4. *Y record* (small clan): Ch (14), Y (16), C (8), T (3), Yi (4), L (5), Yong (4), Ho (3), and miscellaneous.
5. *Census data:* Y (56), Ch (8), Yi (7), T (6), W (4), Tuan (4), Hsu (3), Kao (2), C (2), and Chou, T'an, Tu, Huang, Wu, Sun, Yen, Ting (one each).
6. *Separate data* (43 families): Y (11), Ch (11), Yi (5), C (4), Li (2), Ho, Su, Tu, Na, Yung, T, and Tuan (one each). Three family names not known.

The numbers in parentheses in the clan records refer to the number of instances in which women of the given family name have been married into the clan which has the record. The numbers in parentheses in census data and separate data refer to the number of families of the given family name. In the case of the clan records the word "miscellaneous" refers to those names which appear in the given record less frequently than the smallest number of instances given here for that particular family name.

The clan names Y, Ch, and Yi appear in large numbers in every list. The names C and L each appear in five lists. The names Ho and Tuan appear in lists Nos. 1, 3, 4, and 6. The name W appears in 1, 3, and 5. The name Ye appears in 2, 3, and 5. The name Tu appears in 1, 5, and 6.

These data agree with estimates by local people. Their estimates varied somewhat, but agreed on the following:

Name of clan	Number of clans by this name in the community	Approximate number of joint households in each clan
Yi	1	100
T	1	100
C	1	100
Ye	1	30
W	1	30
Ch	4	150 (in all; one has 70–80 households, another has 40 households)
Y	10	300 (in all; one has only 3 or 4 households, another has about 40 households)
Kao	1	10
Total	20	820

The only important difference between this table and the previous list concerns the clan name L. The name L appears in five clan records in considerable numbers, but people said that there were very few households in the community with this name. They mainly came from outside. Since there are about 1,000 households in the community, the inevitable conclusion would seem to be that more than 80 percent of them belong to these twenty clans.

There are twelve ancestral temples which belong to the following clans: T (1), Yi (1), Ye (1), W (1), Ch (2), and Y (5). The L clan has no temple in the community. In Chapter II we have seen the structure and arrangement of these temples, and in Chapter VII we shall see some rituals performed in them. Here it will suffice to recall that these temples are a sizable expression of interclan competition.

The bases for a clan's prestige and power in the community are official connections and money. When official connections are high, there is usually money. When money is plentiful, official connections will be sought. Size comes in for only secondary consideration. Thus, the three clans Ye, T, and Yi are commonly regarded as the "big clans." T has both size and money. Yi has size and considerable money. Ye has more money than either of them, but is the smallest. All three have connections with the bureaucracy.

With the exception of these clans, the question as to who is ahead of whom becomes debatable. The Ch people, who have a living Chu Jen (an imperial degree) among them, regard their clan as the next in importance. The people of one of the Y clans regard theirs as being one grade higher than the Chs. The C clan was once powerful, when it had a member who was the prime minister in the Peking Government during the early twenties. This clan has now lost its vigor; it has little money and hardly any existing official connection, but still is large enough to qualify as a "big clan."

These and lesser clans compete with each other for prestige and power all the time, sometimes openly. They compete with each other in ritual and ceremonial showings during such events as death or marriage. The occasion is celebrated in individual families, but members of the same clan share the splendor. They compete with each other in working out the genealogical records. This involves prolonged research and writing up, which cost considerable sums of money. Renewed efforts to enlarge and retouch the records usually begin when some members of the clan have become prosperous. A considerable number of the scholars of the clan join together and use rooms in the ancestral temple as offices. Each clan prides itself on the authenticity, antiquity, and inclusiveness of its records. Members of two of the less wealthy clans glowed with pleasure when I asked them if they had seen a record of the Ye clan (one of the leading clans of the community). They said that the Ye people could not have done any "research" on their ancestry, because they did not have many facts about it. Actually, the Ye clan have a modest genealogical record, but not as extensive and pompous as befits that of a leading clan of the community. Since they started their fortune comparatively recently, they did not have any previous records comparable to those of other clans. Here the word "facts" includes everything which would add to the grandeur of the clan.

These clans also vie with each other with regard to graveyards and ancestral temples, which are living monuments of the greatness of a clan. They always desire something unusual which the other clans do not have. In recent years new devices have gone into these traditional usages. The Ye people built a special temple in the graveyard in honor of their recently deceased parents. The Ws and one of the Ys, who are the *nouveaux riches* of the community, built their ancestral temples in the modern style.

The clans vie with each other also in the matter of contributions to local causes. In any local prayer meeting, whether against an epidemic or banditry, the two top-ranking clans always contribute more or less equal amounts. In the building of the hospital and the three schools, these two clans also watched each other closely. We shall see later how in connection with the middle school the two top-ranking families each insisted on marking out its own part clearly. That such contributions are primarily made to enhance clan and family prestige may be seen in the fact that during the 1942 cholera epidemic the families which made the modern hospital possible were also the highest contributors to the prayer meetings. The hospital sent out trained nurses to persuade reluctant West Towners to take modern precautions, including inoculations. At the same time the priests also performed their ritual dances on many specially constructed platforms to induce reluctant gods to retract the epidemic-causing devils which they had released to punish the sinning people.

I have heard of, but have not been able to verify, instances in which the clans engage in an occasional open duel. One incident concerned the purchase by a member of one clan of a piece of public property to improve his house, and its opposition led by members of two other clans. Another occurrence was the case of the girl of T clan who became friendly with a college student. The details of the case were given in Chapter IV. It is to be recalled that no real harm was done to the girl and her lover by the mob, but many informants told me with great impressiveness that the armed band was hired by the Ye clan. The idea behind the action was that, whatever the outcome, the affair itself would have caused some damage to the T clan. Other informants insisted that the armed band was composed of friends of the girl's local fiancé, who merely wanted to protect the interest of the absent boy. I think the latter version was closer to the truth.

However that may be, the fact that West Towners used the story as an instance of clannish strife is significant. It shows that among them the idea of such strife is prevalent. But two factors prevent conflicts from becoming serious. One is that most of the clans are related by marriage. Yi is related to Ye. Ye is related to T. Yi is related to one of the Chs. Ch is related to Yi. Ye is related to two of the Ys. One of the latter is related to the Ws. Moreover, these relations are very recent and clearly traceable. In some instances the relations concern the present generations, prominent in the clans' affairs.

The second and more important factor in shaping inter-clan relationship is the lack of organization and solidarity within each clan. One would expect that a clan based upon the authority of the father over his sons and inter- and intra-generation unity would have a clan council. But none of the twenty clans studied has any such council. Many clans have no authorized head. There are no regular officials appointed to take care of the clan temples. Some matters, such as building additions to the temple or fresh efforts to study the genealogical records, are decided upon by those who can pay. Other matters, such as securing funds for ritual offerings and determining the amounts of donation to be collected for such occasions,[7] are decided upon in a more or less democratic way at an open meeting of family representatives or, if such a meeting is not possible, by posting bills in the ancestral temple and inviting opinions. Democratic decisions are desirable, but they are not in line with the particular type of family organization found in West Town.

Again, one would expect these clans to have means for disciplining undutiful and erring members. But none of these clans has such a provision so far as I was able to discover. Elders deny the existence of such provision. In the important matter of sexual offense, either plain adultery or incest, there is no evidence to show that the clan, as such, takes any action against it. Informants did not even give any ideal picture involving the clan's authority. Some of them said that a culprit would be punished by his or her parents or closely related elderly members of the family or clan. One informant said that the culprit would be punished by elderly persons within the Wu Fu. Another said that everybody looked after his own family affairs. This informant told me that there were three ways of dealing with a girl who has committed sexual offense: (1) the parents or older brother could beat her and then shut her up in the house; (2) they could have her secretly married to a man in some distant locality; (3) they could report the case to the police and have the adulterer arrested. However, in fact, he continued, few parents would report the deed to the police and damage their own reputation. The clan members as well as other people in town would gossip if they heard about it, but the primary responsibility of punish-

---

[7] As far as can be ascertained, most clans do not have collectively owned land as source of income. One of the top clans, T, has 9.9 *mow* of land in the clan's name.

ment rested with the parents and other closely related members of the immediate kinship group.

Three cases occurred during the investigation which would come under the category of sexual offense. In one case an engaged male ran away with a girl who was betrothed to some one else. The girl's older brother took action and secured the young man's arrest and conviction in a Kunming court. The second was the one referred to in connection with inter-clan competition. It was, as we have seen, friends of the "wronged" party who took action and punished the intruder. In still another instance, a man and a woman were discovered sleeping together in some empty building. They were discovered by passers-by and beaten.

Lastly, one would expect that within each clan fellow members would generously help each other and take each other's troubles to heart. This may not be the case at all. The family which is responsible for the elevated position of the Ye clan has been most helpful to not only members of his own clan but also to relatives by marriage and other unrelated West Towners. One informant said that about seven tenths of the new houses built in recent years are traceable to Ye influence. The family which is responsible for the elevated position of the T clan, on the other hand, though just as mindful of the elevated position of its clan as are the Ye people, is not so generous. Some West Towners complained that this family preferred to make a good showing outside West Town, such as trying to be in the good graces of personalities high up on the official ladder and contributing ostentatiously to national causes, but was harsh on fellow clansmen and relatives. Such complaints might be regarded as indicative that the Ye family attitude represented the socially desired norm, but for the fact that the T family does not appear to suffer any disadvantages from its behavior.

Even among families whose heads are brothers and first cousins (patrilineal) there is little solidarity. Most of them do not like each other. Only when there is trouble with outsiders do they tend to unite to some degree. But such unity is very temporary.

The typical West Town clan is one in which striking and uniform external features combine with an anomalous internal organization. Nothing which will materially increase the clan's external pomp and clannish appearance is left undone. Yet much which would aid in the clan's solidarity is disregarded.[8]

---

[8] Writers who are in the habit of saying Chinese clans are strong or weak often do so without good foundation. Fei and Chang say, for example: "Clan organization is stronger in Yunnan than in other parts of China. Here the clan possesses common property" (H. T. Fei and T. Y. Chang: *Earthbound China*, Chicago, 1945, p. 11). This statement is erroneous even on the strength of the authors' own evidence. In all three villages few clans are collective owners of land and the amount of land owned by such clans as a whole is small. (In Luts'un, 690 *mow* are privately owned and 237 are owned by groups. Out of the latter, only 82 *mow* are owned by clans (see *ibid.*, pp. 53–55). In Yuts'un, out of a total of 555 *mow* of rice field and 108 *mow* of vegetable garden, only 80 *mow* of rice field and 2 *mow* of vegetable garden are "village lands, the clan lands, and the temple lands" (*ibid.*, pp. 221–226). In a study by Hanseng Chen we find that clans in some areas of Kwangtung Province own from 23 to 40 percent of all cultivated land. In some Kwangtung areas clans own 75 percent of such land (*Peasant and Landlord in China*, New York, 1936, pp. 31–35). Nor were Fei and Chang aware of the fact that clans in other areas, such as West Town, as a whole own, if anything, even less than those in the Yunnan villages which they investigated. Furthermore, is ownership of some common property by any clan good evidence for strength in clan organization? The large amounts of land owned collectively by some Kwangtung clans are often so appropriated by a few powerful and self-fattening families in the clans that they add causes for much intra-clan hatred (*ibid.*).

CHAPTER VI

How Ancestors Live

ELSEWHERE in China old age means enjoyment of authority and if the family is well-to-do, freedom from work. The younger members of the family, sons and daughters-in-law, are the objects of authority, and the burden of the work falls upon them.

Aged fathers in West Town, as we have seen, do not necessarily enjoy much authority over their male children once the latter are married and have taken a portion of the family property; nor do elderly women work less hard than their daughters-in-law, whether a family is divided under the same roof or not.

Old men and women in West Town are definitely resigned in their attitude. It is difficult to ascertain exactly at what age this resignation begins. The observable thing is the following contrast: there are a number of young people who are interested in making more money, building up a grand family home, going to distant cities, and actively participating and competing in all communal affairs. Their worldly ambition cannot be mistaken. On the other hand, there are any number of elderly people, men and women, who are interested only in reading scriptures, becoming devotees in temples, ensuring the quality of their coffins and graveyards, and preparing windsheets. Their resignation to avoid active life is fairly obvious.

The tombs in a family graveyard are, if the family can afford it, prepared during the lifetime of the persons to be buried. The coffin of an elderly person will be made and stored in a side room of the clan temple. The site of the tomb in the graveyard will be decided upon by a geomancy seer, and the stone structure of the tomb which contains the coffin will often be built under the supervision of the person himself.

The extensive graveyard of the C clan may be taken as an example. Here the tombs are situated on several widely separated terraces. I visited this graveyard during a *Ching Ming* festival. I chatted with members of one branch of the family: an aged father, three sons, two daughters-in-law, and several children. The old man, who was then still the head of the *pao*, asked me to sit down on the stone bench in front of a small cluster of three tombs. One of the sons was painting the upper part of one of the tombs. The women were busy preparing food. The three tombs were arranged in two rows. The two in the first row were that of the old man who had invited me to sit with him and that of his wife, who had died a couple of years earlier.

Structurally the two tombs were the same. The surprising thing was that the old man's tomb, though empty, was fully inscribed. On his wife's tombstone the inscription stated that here lay "a noble lady, waiting to be conferred the honor of Ju Jen in the imperial dynasty, who enjoyed the advanced age of 78." On the old man's tombstone the inscription said that here lay "a noble man waiting to be conferred the honor of Wen Lin Lang in the imperial dynasty, who enjoyed the advanced age of 85." At the time the man was sixty years of age. When death actually comes to him, the top part of the structure will be lifted, and the coffin will be lowered; then the tomb will be closed again.

The old man talked to me about the various tombs, including his own, with the same sort of pride that a person would display about his family residence. The only sign to show that one tomb was empty and the others not was given by the red couplets posted on them. As noted in Chapter II, red couplets are posted on portals to family homes during ceremonial occasions and the lunar New Year. Since tombs are family homes for the dead, couplets are also posted on the front portion of many of them which are visited by descendants during the *Ching Ming* festival. The tomb of the old man's wife bore couplets like those found on clan temples, while the old man's tomb bore only a large red square paper with the word "blessing," which often decorates the doors to family homes.

In Chapter III we have also seen how hard one aged lady in a well-to-do family worked, not from necessity, but for the express purpose of saving for her funeral and coffin. Not only the parents themselves think along these lines. Many grown-up sons with whom I discussed the matter would not conceal the emphasis of their concern. A young man, who is father of a two-year-old daughter and the oldest son of a seventy-year-old father, made the following statement to me in front of the latter, without much questioning on my part.

> A family such as ours, which is of the fourth class (Ting Teng), will at least have to put on a 70–80 table feast in case of my father's funeral. The minimum cost will be $100,000 (1943), not to say anything about coffin and the tomb. . . . We all have to be prepared for it.
>
> The gifts from sympathizers will be light. . . . In West Town the custom is for such gifts (called *jen ch'ing*) to be small. It really makes matters very difficult. . . . *"Li cheng"* (correct ceremonial and ritual ways) is very important.

This resignation does not stop at preparing an abode for the body. Many would like to make sure that their spirit will not suffer from disabilities. On many birthdays of gods and goddesses, such as those of the Goddess of Mercy, of the Dragon God, and of Mother Wang, women of all ages participate in the ritual offerings. There is always a group of women more zealous than others. These are, as a rule, elderly women who voluntarily form a company of their own, stand or kneel in front of the altars, and chant the scriptures loudly. During such chanting some of them hold a bundle of incense; others beat a small wooden fish; still others merely hold their two palms together in front of them. Such chanting often lasts the better part of the festive day. Other occasions for scripture chanting are the 1st and the 15th days of every Moon. On these days women from the same neighborhood or women who have relatives or friends will go in twos or threes to one or another of the temples to do the same thing.

In the section on *The World of Spirits* an attempt will be made to obtain a picture of the spiritual world and man's relation to it. Suffice it here to observe that the women who are so religious have no explanation except that their acts will increase their merit in the world of spirits. Elderly men do not seem to go in for this form of worship. In addition to participating in ritual festivals, they prefer to go to the temple called Sheng Yu T'ang (a temple organization), where they can smoke a pipe and study the scriptures with each other. Those who are well-to-do give generously for the performing of séances in that temple.

As far as present-day West Towners can remember, there have been two instances in which such a changed orientation in life took a more extreme form. One instance concerned a widow who had no relatives. She had a little money, and she built herself a small temple in the middle of the mountains to the south of West Town. The temple was called Chung Shan Temple (middle mountain) and had installed in it some sort of an image. She did nothing but recite the scriptures many thousands of times a day. The informants were not clear as to how she managed to support herself. She died about seven or eight years ago. West Towners added that other widows had been known to become devotees in the past, but could cite no specific examples.

The other instance concerned a man who was still living at the time of this investigation. He lived in a temple dedicated to a West Towner who, the legend had it, became a god after death many years ago. The temple is located in a village south of West Town, at the foot of the mountains. The male devotee is a vegetarian and reads scriptures throughout each day.

In one of the foregoing paragraphs I observed that the

usual reason given by female devotees is that such acts augment their merit in the world of spirits. The higher hope is really the implicit desire of becoming a god (Fur). Just as at present few ordinary men in the street would openly profess the desire to become a high official of the government, they would not as a rule assert that their religious devotion will lead them to godship. But the kernel of their spiritual aspiration is unmistakable.

There are many tales which allege that men or women have become gods after death. The most popular instance is the case of the nationally known scholar who lived in the Ming Dynasty, H. S. Y., who was a native of West Town. The popular tale goes thus: Soon after Y's death a villager who was cutting some fuel wood in the hills met the scholar on the road. Not knowing about his death, the villager conversed freely with the scholar. The villager was asked to go to the scholar's house and tell the family where a certain pair of his (the scholar's) shoes was. Mystified, the villager went as instructed, and learned about the scholar's death several days before. To everybody's great surprise, the family were just searching for that pair of shoes; they found the shoes where the spirit directed. Everybody agreed that it was a holy apparition (*hsien sheng*). A special temple was built for him, which still stands in the hills today.

This man's title in the other world, the local priests said, is God of Charity (Pu Chi Chen Chun), and he is an important official in the world of spirits. He figures largely in the rituals of communication with the dead.

Another case was a man named Yang, who was the recorder in many séances and was very devoted to spiritual life as a person. After death he was given the title of God of Record (Chi Lu Chen Chun). The portraits of both of these gods appear as lithographs in a Rooting Misery Scripture (*Pa Koo Chen Ching*).

In addition to the above there are at least three instances of local men who were alleged to have become *cheng huang* (patron gods, each of which is in charge of a district). In one case the man was asked to take the post by one of the spiritual world judges and graciously declined the offer.

Only one case was known in which a woman had become a goddess. The woman died in 1940, when she was about 60 years of age. She lived in a village near the West Town side of the lake and was very pious during her lifetime. Her husband had died many years earlier. She had three married daughters and one unmarried son, who was a peddler. On a certain occasion after her death, the son consulted a witch woman. The witch woman told him that the family from then on should burn yellow paper money to the deceased mother, not white paper money. She told him that the old mother had become a goddess. The yellow paper money is reserved for gods. White paper money is reserved for spirits of dead humans only. Many people believed this story.

THE WORLD OF SPIRITS

In order to understand the place of the dead it will be necessary to form some idea of the world of spirits. For this purpose I interviewed eight local priests, two of them leading ones, and analyzed five complete sets of religious documents from the local temples. Four of these documents are scriptures, and the fifth is entitled *A Precious Bell for Awakening the Ignorant*. The scriptures were verbatim reports dictated by various gods and taken down in elaborate rituals in one or another of the temples, in the presence of large crowds of believers. One of the scriptures was taken in 1932, in Chungking, and has enjoyed wide circulation in Yunnan. The second and third were both taken in 1938 in the temple called Sheng Yu T'ang in West Town. The origin of the fourth scripture was unknown, but "had been given by gods many years ago." *A Precious Bell for Awakening the Ignorant* was produced in 1927 in a temple called Tze Yun Shan, West Town. The last volume is not verbatim dictation from the gods. It contains: (1) a systematic description of the mediums in their journeys through the spiritual world day by day, for a period of two weeks, and what they saw; (2) a number of cases of reward and punishment given the good and evil people respectively; (3) a number of items of advice given by various gods, mainly judges in the Lower World of Spirits.

The manner in which the mediums worked and the mechanisms of communication with the spirits will be described later. I shall proceed to relate the general structure of the world of spirits as given by local priests, in the scriptures, and in *A Precious Bell for Awakening the Ignorant.*

The world of spirits is as follows: A boundary line marks out the World of Man from the World of Spirits. At this boundary line is the distinction between what man understands as life and death. Immediately beyond this line there are two main roads: one broad highway leads to heaven or the higher world of spirits, and a narrower passage leads to the lower world of spirits.

Soon after a spirit enters the narrower passage he comes to a "Three Branched Cross Road," where there are shops, hotels, and restaurants. It is similar to any street scene in the world of man. Some distance beyond this is the Gate of Ghosts. This gate is really a castle in itself, like the main gates of any city wall. It has a registration office for the newly dead and other roaming spirits and a reception room for honored guests. This gate is protected by ghost guards.

Inside this gate are many *cheng huangs,* or magistrates. Their duty consists of recording the good or bad behavior of individuals in the respective districts they govern. They have to submit their records to the judges, who are their immediate superiors. Sometimes they themselves have to punish the bad men and women. They know about a death or a birth in their locality as soon as it occurs. The families concerned have to report such events at their temples.

Above the *cheng huangs* are the ten judges, each with a specific title, assistant judges, and recorders. Eight of the judges possess prisons or hells and implements of torture for the evil and one or more guest houses for the deserving. Each judge resides in a palace surrounded by a wall. The entrances in this wall are covered by ghost guards. The judge does not know who wants to see him or what is going on outside. He receives orders from above and has to be informed of visitors by his staff and guards.

The ten judges are under the control of the Supreme Ruler of the Lower World, variously known as Yu Ming Chiao Chu or Ti Chang Wang. This ruler receives instructions from superior authorities and relays them to the judges. The palaces of the ten judges are arranged in a sort of circle, the palace of this Ruler being in the center. But the area occupied by these palaces is very extensive. Several priests, as well as *A Bell for . . . the Ignorant,* indicated that it coincides with all China, the palace of the first judge being located somewhere in Changan, Shansi; that of the second judge, in Wu Chang, Hupei; and so forth. The priests' geography was not very good, for they did not realize that Changan is not in Shansi, but in Shensi.

The eight judges who have prisons or hells and implements of torture for evil persons are the second to ninth judges, inclusive. Each of these has one large prison or hell. Within each large hell there are sixteen small ones. In these prisons or hells spirits of bad men and women will be confined permanently or be waiting for hearing, torture, or transfer to another judge.

There is special mention of two platforms, one called "mirror of evil deeds platform," the other called "looking over home village platform." The former is in the palace of the first judge, and the latter, that of the fifth judge. The former is a sort of crime detector. Very often spirits of evil persons deny before the judges the evils they committed when they lived in the world of men. Such spirits will be forced to mount this platform and stand before the mirror. The mirror will reveal in detail how such persons committed their various sins and crimes.

The "looking over home village platform" is one from which the spirit may have a last glimpse of his or her own home, neighborhood, and the inhabitants thereof. This picture usually makes the spirit very homesick and dejected. As a rule only spirits of sinful persons are made to mount this platform.

Beyond this Lower World of Spirits there appear to be at least two other realms of the spirits: the "Higher World of Spirits" and the "Western World of Happiness," also referred to as "Supreme Heaven" and "Western Heaven," respectively. Supreme Heaven is headed by the Jade Emperor, from whom all final authority emanates. Under him are various ministers, the most important of whom seem to be Kuan Sheng Ti Chun (the God of War who was a hero in the Three Kingdoms) and Chang Huan Hou Ta Ti (the former's sworn brother, who lived in the same period). Somewhere under the Jade Emperor were the heads of the three religions: Confucius, Buddha, and Lao Tze, founder of Taoism. The heads of the three religions are always mentioned together, and the emphasis is on their being of the same origin. These three heads of religions are not active. The most active ones are the aforementioned two ministers and a host of other lower officials or gods. No one knows how many gods there are under the regime of the Jade Emperor. In one scripture I counted 608, including the names of Jesus Christ and Mohammed, who are called sages and are subordinate to the Jade Emperor. Then the account proceeds as follows:

> In addition to the above, the following gods are hereby invoked: Gods of ten directions; all fairies and sages; all fairy warriors and soldiers; ten extreme god kings; gods of sun, moon, and nine principal stars; three officers and four sages; the stars of five directions; gods guarding four heavenly gates; thirty-six thunder gods guarding the entire heaven; twenty-eight principal stars of the Zodiac; gods for subjugating evil ghosts; god king of flying heaven; great long life Buddha; gods of Tien Kan and Ti Tze; great Sages of Tigrams and Nine Stars; secondary officials of five directions; secondary officials of ten directions; gate gods and kitchen gods; godly generals in charge of year, month, day, and hour; gods and spirits in charge of four seas, nine rivers, five mountains, four corners; of hills, woods, all rivers and lakes, wells and springs, ditches and

creeks, and twelve river sources; all gods; *cheng huangs* and their inferiors; local patron gods; minor local officials (Tu Ti); gods of roads and bridges; of trees and lumber; spiritual officers and soldiers under the command of priests; all spirits in charge of protecting the taboos, commands, scriptures, and the right way of religion.

The titles of most of the gods given separately are fancy indeed. All of them are titles of exaltation. Some examples are: "Emperor of Thirty-two Heavens"; "Great Heavenly Supreme Jade Emperor, the Most Exalted Highest Emperor God"; "West, Boundless, Most Reverent, Heavenly Flowery, Religious Chief, Awakening Emperor, Ancient Buddha, Heavenly Emperor the Supreme God." The titles of the local patron god and his wife in one temple run thus: "Ruling by Divine Decree, Great Sage, from the West, Scripture Protecting, Guarding all Five Mountains, Constructing the Nation, Emperor of Many Gods," and "Protecting Women, in Her Own Right, Understanding Virtues, Sage Mother Goddess" (for the patron god's wife).

Besides the Higher World of Spirits there is the Western World of Happiness. As may have been noticed, some of the gods and goddesses listed above have titles which suggest that they came from this realm. But the exact relation between this and the Higher World of Spirits was not clear to my informant, nor is it clearly indicated in the sacred books. The supreme deity in this Western World is Buddha, often referred to as "Fo Chu," or "Ancestors of All Buddhas." In some scriptures this place is, however, taken by a goddess: The Golden Mother of Western Heavenly Lake, and her full title is "The Ancestor Who Has Produced Heaven and Earth, the Master Who Has Produced Sages and Buddhas, the Mother Who Divides Darkness from Light, the Supreme Deity Who Separates Heaven, Earth and Men."

In the last-mentioned scriptures this goddess has under her command "gods and fairies from ten continents and three islands, sages who became gods after death, heads of religions, ten judges from the Lower World of Spirits and the supreme ruler of that world, dragon gods from five lakes and four seas." In fact, they are all the gods found in the Higher World of Spirits with the exception of the Supreme Ruler himself.

There appears, however, to be some difference between the Western World and the Higher World. The latter shows more signs of being an administrative machinery, the former is more like paradise pure and simple. When the ruler of the Western Heaven takes action, he or she takes the line, not that he is punishing, but that he is relieving the profane world of misdoers, devils, and suffering.

The gods in these two realms, like those in the Lower World of Spirits, do not automatically know of happenings in the profane world and have to learn about them through emissaries and lower functionaries whose duty it is to record and report such happenings to the responsible authorities as they occur. The lower functionaries are called Day Inspecting Gods (who roam about the world of man during the day) and Night Inspecting Gods (who do so at night). They have long legs like stilts and walk by long strides. They report their findings to Heralding Gods of the Higher World of Spirits who in turn report them to the Supreme Ruler.

I have also interviewed a large number of ordinary men and women in an attempt to find out exactly what ideas they have about these worlds. The results are uneven, and the picture obtainable is somewhat hazy. Certain elements and figures universally admitted are as follows:

1. The Lower World of Spirits with the ten judges, The Higher World of Spirits, the Supreme Ruler, and a host of lower functionaries.

2. The *cheng huangs* or counterparts of magistrates in the profane world.

3. The functions of the judges are as above described and the fact that they have hells and tortures, and the functions of the *cheng huangs*.

4. Ideas of the Higher World of Spirits and Western World of Happiness are vague. The one definite thing about these two realms concerns the two supreme rulers. Most

informants assign them to the Higher World and the Western World, respectively, as described by priests and the sacred books. Others put the Golden Goddess under the Supreme Jade Emperor in the Higher World.

5. Buddha as an all powerful, but good-willed, deity resides in the Western World of Happiness. His relation with the Golden Goddess is not clear.

6. The most clearly recognized spirit is the fifth judge, who is universally regarded as being more severe than any other judge.

7. Kuan Kung, the God of War, is the most outstanding of all gods. He is most active in all séances and the most respected, revered, and feared. As noted in the previous description, he was an historical character, and his sworn brother, General Chang Fei, was regarded as holding equal rank with him. According to the informants Kuan is far above Chang.

8. Some of the other gods frequently mentioned are: heads of three religions (Confucius, Lao Tze, and Buddha), Liu Chen Chun (a Taoist god), Kuan Junior (adopted son of Kuan Kung, God of War), Goddess of Mercy (who is thought of as residing in a realm somewhere in the south), Dragon God and Goddess, local patron gods (*pen chur*)—some equate these gods with *cheng huangs*—Wen God (God of Epidemics), and God of Wealth.

Pieced together, the world of spirits is remarkably like the world of the living. The Supreme Ruler of heaven is head of all. He is similar to the emperor or the head of the secular government. His relation with the other gods, high or low, is like that of the head of the secular government with his bureaucrats. This spiritual hierarchy has power of punishment or reward over the living, not only after but also before their death.

There seems to be some difference between the opinion of men and that of women concerning the spiritual worlds. Men tended to be more exact in their statements, and expressed more definite ideas about the structure of these worlds as well as higher deities who figured in them. Women tended to be somewhat vague and in general gave the names of deities who were related to specific functions or ailments. Some of the latter were the fifth judge, goddess of fertility, goddess of mercy, goddess of eyes, goddess of measles, god of epidemic, god of small pox, or local patron gods. These differences can at least be partially explained by the fact that men have more opportunities of looking into the scriptures and conversing with priests than have women, for literate and illiterate males show similar differences to a much smaller extent.[1] But both men and women were aware of the existence of the spiritual worlds and the spirits, even though they could not name all the details and deities. There does not appear to be any appreciable difference in beliefs between the wealthy and the poor.

Most West Towners admitted that it is impossible for the ordinary person to know all about the worlds of spirits and that it is better to consult the priests. One man, somewhat literate, expressed his opinion to me thus:

Each believer (*hsin sse*) only cares about the deities of his or her own faith. . . . He or she cares about the birthdays of these deities only. . . . For example, some care only about the Supreme Ruler of the Lower World of Spirits (Ti Chang Wang), some care only about patron gods, and disregard others. Just as believers in Christ care only about the birthday of Jesus Christ.

Another man said:

We have numerous gods of Buddhism. Every month we have at least ten or fifteen birthdays of gods and other ritual occasions. Even natives of the locality cannot count them.

Nevertheless, bit by bit most adults could give an astonishing number of names and titles of gods and goddesses and describe their life in the spiritual world. They were incoherent and inconsistent at many points, but their belief in the spiritual world as a whole cannot be doubted.

[1] West Towners who are on the college level begin to show ignorance of these spiritual worlds in significant ways. However, in external behavior they still rigidly conform to the social norm.

MAN'S RELATION WITH SPIRITUAL WORLDS

Each person has a body and a *huei,* or spirit. When a person has died an ordinary death from old age or sickness, he becomes a *huei* and goes to the spirit world. If a person has died in expiation of some crime, such as banditry, his spirit will become a *gur,* or ghost. The body of a person who has died an ordinary death is usually buried properly. The body of a person who has been executed is usually left exposed; such exposure as a rule produces a *gur,* or ghost.

Huei is not harmful or malicious to human beings, but *gur* is. *Gur* can be uplifted (transformed) through prayers and scripture reading by hired priests. It then becomes a *huei* and therefore harmless. Only *huei* can reincarnate. The spirit of a person who has been killed by bandits or by accident does not, as a matter of course, turn into *gur.* But if the spirit of a dead person is dissatisfied, it will become *gur* and create trouble.

"Gur" is applied to males only. The female equivalent is *yao.* Several West Town informants agreed that some years ago in several instances a *yao* had appeared, but I was able to obtain the exact location and details of only one apparition, which, the informants added, occurred when West Town had comparatively few inhabitants. The latter statement cannot, however, be reconciled with the facts. West Town has been fairly thickly populated for several centuries, and in order to be so well remembered the incident could not have occurred so long a time ago. As the story was told by the informants, the *yao* (a lot of them) were seen sitting on a stone veranda in the lane just outside a house of C. Quick ritual propitiation prevented disaster from befalling that household or other households. They could not remember any cases in the history of West Town in which execution of women were involved, but they said that when rebels overran West Town about ninety years earlier, a lot of women were molested and killed.

Wai are the images in temples. They are, so to speak, the bodies of gods. Their spirits, corresponding to *huei* of human beings, are *sheng,* or gods.

The duration and the degree of prosperity or misery of a person's life depend chiefly upon two things: the pre-ordained fate and the person's behavior in life. The first refers to the duration of life prescribed for the person when he or she was born; the second refers to whether the person has been a good or a bad person. "Good" and "bad" are defined by tradition and will be made clear shortly. These records are kept by *cheng huangs* and the assistants of the Ten Judges according to reports given them by various gods including: Kitchen God, Day In-specting and Night Inspecting Gods. The *cheng huangs* normally dispatch emissaries to call for or to arrest the spirits of human beings whose time is up either because it was preordained or because it was precipitated by his or her bad behavior. Good behavior will prolong the preor-dained duration of life; bad behavior will shorten it or cause it to be miserable or disease-bound.

When the *huai* of a person leaves his or her body, it has entered the World of Spirits. As soon as it passes the boundary line, it will see two roads; the broad and nice one leads to the Higher World, or the Western World, and the other, not so broad and pleasant, leads to the Lower World. If the deceased was widely known for his or her good deeds in life, the spirit will be received with pomp and led to the broad road. If the spirit is of someone who was not so well known, it will be sent through the Gate of Ghosts be-fore the first judge. The spirits of people notorious for their bad behavior and whose lives were shortened as a result by special decree, will be put in chains.

However, before reaching the first judge all spirits must cross a river by a *nai ho* bridge. This bridge seems to be a precarious structure. The spirit that crosses it is in danger of falling from it and being swallowed by the monsters underneath.

By each judge in succession, the spirits who have committed the worst behavior in life will be submitted to many forms of torture, such as being cut to pieces, ground to cream in a mill, roasted, disemboweled, etc. The severity of the torture depends upon the extent to which they had misbehaved in life. At the court of the tenth judge they may be allowed to reincarnate. Many of the worst ones may be kept in hells permanently and never get such a chance at all. Those who reincarnate may be allowed to become only a lower animal. The somewhat better behaved ones will be made into human beings, but kept in poverty and misery.

The spirits who did not misbehave in human form will be sorted out, on the basis of the records of the ten judges. Most of them are quickly dispatched to the tenth judge and then born into families with means. Those who are more deserving will be entertained for a longer or shorter time in special guest palaces in the headquarters of one of the judges. A few of these will be offered official positions in the spiritual hierarchy. The usual position offered is *cheng huang*, the spiritual figure corresponding to the magistrate. A very few will become permanent higher gods and go to reside in the Higher World or the Western World. Should such a figure reincarnate, it will become at least a high official in the government.

The punishment suffered by a spirit in the Lower World may be mitigated or increased, respectively, by the good deeds or misdoings of its descendants. Prayer services at which hired priests officiate are part of the good deeds. Its destination in the next reincarnation may also be improved or prejudiced, respectively, in the same way.

As has been made clear in the foregoing paragraphs, the fundamental differentiation among spirits is one between "good" and "bad." The following is an analysis of the qualities and behavior, which make individuals and their spirits "good" or "bad," given by six priests, fifteen informants selected at random, and the local sacred books. It is evident that some items given in Columns (I) and (II) overlap each other. The division was made by the informants and the sacred books. In general, Column (I) contains more of the abstract qualities, while Column (II) provides the actual forms of behavior exemplifying the abstract qualities.

All items marked with one asterisk are explicitly stated to be applicable to women only. The last two items of Positive Virtues, namely, Upholding five human relations and eight virtues (for male), and Upholding three subordinations and four virtues (for female) are usually referred to without details. However, all sources elaborate a number of items separately which are part of their contents.

Good and Bad Characteristics

Column I	Column II
A. *Positive Virtues*	B. *Good Behavior*
Filial piety and fraternal harmony	Filial attention to parents and harmony with brothers
* Sexual fidelity (especially referring to widows who refuse to marry again)	Kind to old people and helpful to community
Industriousness and frugality	Honor to teachers and piety to gods
Honesty in business dealings	*Respect toward husbands and parents-in-law
Harmony with neighbors and other members of the community	* Harmony with sisters-in-law
Harmony with members of the same clan	The building of public bridges and roads
Upholding five human relations (heaven, earth, ruler, parents, and teachers) and eight virtues (filial piety, harmony among brothers, loyalty, faithfulness, ceremonial appropriateness, justice, purity, and sense of shame)	The establishment of schools
	Reading scriptures, explaining scriptures and sacred books to the ignorant, disseminating virtuous tales to the public, joining religious organizations (churches), and inviting professional priests to officiate at prayer meetings
* Upholding three subordinations (subordination to father when a maiden, to hus-	Observing sexual taboo days

Column I

Column II

band after marriage, and to
son after husband has died)
and four virtues (fidelity,
speech, work, and appear-
ance)

C. *Negative Qualities*

* Licentiousness

Indulgence in liquor, in licentious practices, in excess
wealth, and in anger and
violence

* Causing disharmony in the
household and the neigh-
borhood

Excessive pride to the extent
of despising others

Purposely ignoring the study
of classics

Blasphemy against the gods
and heaven

D. *Evil Behavior*

Jealousy and fights between
religious creeds

Coeducation

* Divorce

* Free choice in marriage
against a mother's wishes

* Seduction of sweethearts and
adultery

Law breaking

Murder, incendiarism, and
other forms of unruly be-
havior impinging on inno-
cent people

Revolt

Adopting communism

Running a brothel for profit

Running gambling dens

Extravagance

* Impurity of heart while
reading scriptures

Lack of "mouth virtue"
(namely, malicious gossip
about other people's weak
spots) and refusing to help
those urgently in need or
to annoy people or to fail
to give them a hand in an
emergency

Eating and drinking glutton-
ously, and sleeping with
women while in monkhood

From *A Precious Bell for Awakening the Ignorant* we may obtain some further insight. The source of this volume as well as its influence will be dealt with shortly. This volume gives illustrations drawn from "actual cases" to show the types of behavior which would result in severe punishment or high reward after death. For women the worst sins appear to be adultery and causing disharmony in the household. Conversely, the spirit of a woman who refused to remarry after the death of her husband in spite of extreme hardship caused by poverty is reported to have been generously rewarded. The most interesting illustration given is the following.

> The spirit of a woman named Ting from a community north of West Town was seen by the medium to be suffering from various forms of torture in the Under World. In the hope of alleviating somewhat the severity of her torture, she confessed that she committed adultery behind her husband's back and caused her husband to quarrel with his uncle and aunt-in-law (his father's brother and father's brother's wife). She also confessed that her adultery caused him to be without an heir. Later on, she continued, her husband was so annoyed by her behavior that he went to his younger brother for help. His younger brother was commander of a regiment in Kunming. The two brothers arranged a secret plot. A sedan chair was dispatched to her door, with an invitation for her to go away for a visit. She entered it, but instead of being carried to any house, she was soon in the middle of a wild field. An armed soldier appeared and shot her. As soon as she passed away, her spirit was chained and taken to one of the judges. The spirit has been suffering from various forms of torture ever since.

This case shows clearly that for the punishment of an unfaithful woman physical violence amounting to murder, which is explicitly stated as being an evil behavior, is legitimate. It also shows the lack of distinction between spiritual and worldly punishments.

For men the sins illustrated appear to be licentious practices, gambling, opium smoking, liquor drinking, cheating in trade, and failure to be filial to parents. The first appears to be chiefly directed against monks, while the latter two are applicable to all. Conversely the two "actual" cases given at length in the book show that those who are dutiful to parents in spite of poverty, do not cheat in business, and are satisfied with a simple life will be highly rewarded.

The first of these cases concerns the spirit of a man Yang, who lived in West Town some years ago. He describes his life as follows:

> He was born into a poor family and married a very virtuous wife. He began his career by learning to trade under one of his uncles. Unfortunately they suffered from heavy losses and had to return home from the place where he and his uncle had carried on their business. After his return his father passed away. The family was in constant danger of starvation. He and his wife then supported the family by weaving, trading yarn on the local market, and dyeing cloth. His mother often scolded him, and he never disputed her. He never thought of gaining some profit by illegal means. He knew how to play the flute, so he joined the local temple (church) as a member, regularly participating in prayer meetings and séances. During his spare time he worked as a day laborer. However hard up the family was, he tried his best to please his aged mother. He and his wife got on well together. They never blamed each other for any thing. When his mother was ill, he spent all his time trying to take care of her. The old lady died after three days of illness. He begged friends and relatives to take pity on him so that he could bury her properly. After his mother's death he was more resigned from worldly ambitions. He never admired wealth or despised poor people. He never blamed heaven or earth or ancestors for his humble lot in life. Whenever there were any prayer meetings or other good deeds to be carried out, he always volunteered to help. When he had no money, he helped by physical strength. He realized that his fate was preordained, and he was content with his lot. Then he died of illness. He did not think that any good would come to a poor man in the World of Spirits, but as soon as he entered it, he was received with a big sedan chair of green flannel, as would become an official of some rank. He has been *cheng huang* in a county called Hsiu Sui ever since. He asked the medium who took this note to go back and tell his three sons to become pious members of the temple organization.

The other case concerned a man whose worldly lot was equally unattractive, but who was also made *cheng huang* after death.

> He was born in a Yen family of West Town and was married into a Kao family as a married-in son-in-law. After entry into the latter family he began work as a student. He mastered the classics, but failed in all examinations. So he bought a title of the Fifth Degree and was entitled to wear Blue Feather (Manchu emblem of the rank). But he realized that he could not go further. Later he decided to become a silversmith. He owned a shop. Other silversmith shops used highly adulterated silver instead of pure silver. He refused to imitate them and gave customers only pure silver when he marked his goods as pure. He never cheated in any way. He died at the age of sixty-eight, which was about thirty years before the time of the interview by the medium. He was allowed to stay at the guest palace in the headquarters of the fifth judge for nearly thirty years. Lately his sons and grandsons have been pious and active members of the organized temple and increased his otherworldly merits. This fact was noted by inspecting gods and reported to the Supreme Ruler of the Higher World of Spirits. He was appointed *cheng huang* in Ming Shan County a year earlier and has been on his official post for a year. He asked the medium, who happened to be his grandson, to go back and work for the gods with greater zeal than before.

The sex taboo days[2] are generally birthdays or days when a number of gods and goddesses appears. Two such lists, one posted in the temple organization Sheng Yu T'ang and another given in a volume of Taoist literature entitled *Tun Hwa Kuei Yuan* (Sermons on Origins), which several priests recommended to me, were obtained. The lists are in substantial agreement, and both agree with

[2] The term "taboo" is here used in a broader sense than that of Polynesia. The days listed are sexually taboo because of the following reasons: These days are either birthdays of gods or days on which gods are more active. Sexual intercourse, as well as everything that is connected with it, is unclean. By entering into sexual relations on such days the individuals would offend the gods in the same way as individuals who might enter into sexual relations with one another in a temple would offend them.

SEX TABOO DAYS

Month	A. *List in Chapter 1* Dates	B. *List in Cheng Yu Tang*[a] Dates	C. *List from* SERMONS ON ORIGINS Dates
1	1		1
	9	9	9
	15	15	15
2	3	3	3
	5	15	15
	19	19	19
3	3	3	3
	15	15	
	28	28	28
4	8	8	8
		14	14
5	5	5	5
6	24	24	24
7	7	7	7
	15	15	
8	3	3	3
	15	15	15
	27	27	27
9	9		9
	19	19	
10	15	15	15
11	19	19	
12	8		8
	23	23	23
	30		30
	24 days	21 days	21 days

[a] There is good reason to believe that some of the dates are occasionally added freely by the priests. In this list there are two birthdays for Moon God, and the priests in charge could not give any plausible reason for it. It is certain, however, that the main body of the dates in different lists is the same.

the list of popular festival days given in Chapter I of the present work.

I discussed the lists with various men other than priests and failed to get a uniform picture of the extent of their observance. However, the following points stood out clearly: (*a*) Most informants agreed that sexual taboo should be observed on *all* festival and religious days listed *anywhere;* (*b*) most informants were not aware of specific kinds of punishment which would result if the taboo were violated, but maintained that violation would be "bad" and "dangerous"; (*c*) most informants confessed to having failed to observe or to have forgotten about one or another of the dates at one time or another; (*d*) all informants agreed that during any epidemic and when prayer meetings were in session, only fools indulged in sex activities.

No direct information about women's observance of such days is available. However, it is obvious that, in this connection, men and women cannot differ too much. It is also known that all women wash themselves from hair to toe before going to temples for ritual observances.

To sum up, the worlds of spirits are places where human beings go after death. In broad outline they are organized similarly to the world of the living, with a head of the government and a bureaucracy, power to punish and reward, and encouragement for individual achievements. But these spiritual worlds are more than a mere counterpart to the world of the living. The former are really a necessary supplement to the latter. This is especially made clear by the fact that the achievements or sins for which the individual is rewarded or punished in the spirit world correspond closely to virtues or evils upheld or condemned in the world of the living. Moreover, the rewards or punishments originating from the spirits may come to the individual either before or after his death. This is evident not only from the cases enumerated in *A Precious Bell for Awakening the Ignorant* and from the testimony of informants but also from most popular literature. In the volume entitled *Sermons on Origins,* which gives a list of sex taboo days, all specified punishments refer directly to the living: (1) reduction of longevity; (2) sudden death; (3) poverty; (4) still birth or birth of monster in the family; (5) malignant diseases; (6) loss of voice. Also, West Towners often interpret any disaster that befalls the individual in terms of spiritual punishment or causation. When a disaster affects more than a few individuals, such as the cholera epidemic of 1942 or the earthquake to the south in 1926, the whole community is held morally responsible. Prayer meetings are chiefly intended to purify the people from their sins.

In general, the priests' picture of man's relation with the worlds of spirits is the clearest, but not necessarily the most consistent. The priests are also conscious of the fact that not all West Towners believe in or are familiar with all the details. In one scripture a god ordered that "with upper grade people . . . [the priests] should persuade by means of the dangers in their own lives; with middle and lower grade people . . . [the priests] should persuade with the rewards and punishments due to meritorious or evil behavior, respectively." But it is obvious to any observer that not a single West Towner can be found to discredit the beliefs as a whole.

DEATH AND FUNERALS

Death is the event which marks the passage of an individual from the world of man to the world of spirit. All rites in West Town funerals aim at one of four things: (1) expediting the spirit's safe entry into that world; (2) its comfort in that world; (3) expressing sorrowful feelings on the part of the living and their reluctance to let the dead go; and (4) making sure that the death has not created conditions for future disaster through circumstances which are beyond his or her control.

The elaboration of a funeral is in direct proportion to the economic condition of the family and the social station of the dead. It also varies according to age. Dead children are not entitled to any funeral at all. An unmarried adolescent boy or girl may be given a small funeral. Even if the family is very well-to-do and makes the funeral resemble that of a young married person, his or her body may not be buried in the family graveyard and has to be taken to any public graveyard on level ground near the site of the Dog Market. The body of a woman who died during labor is impure and is disposed of in the same way.

When a member has died, the first thing for the family to do is to find out whether death occurred on a "double death" date. There are eight months in which such dates occur, and they are expressed in a rhyme which may be translated as follows:

> *Keng* and *chia* in First and Seventh,
> *Yi* and *hsin* in Second and Eighth,
> As to the Third, Sixth, Ninth and Twelfth Moons,
> *Wu* and *chi* are "double death" days.

In the lunar calendar, a copy of which every family possesses, each day is represented by two words which are one of the combinations of two sets of symbols, the *t'ien kan*, or zodiac symbols, and the *ti chih*, or earth symbols. Any day on which one of the six words (*keng, chia, yi, hsin, wu,* and *chi*) occurs is a "double death" date. As there are only ten earth symbols used cyclically, there are bound to be about sixteen or seventeen "double death" dates in every month.

If death has occurred on such a date, a second death in the family will follow unless the following ritual is performed: A cock is hung with a piece of string by one leg in front of the corpse on the ground. The bird soon dies. A small human effigy, either cut out of paper or made of wheat flour, is put in a tiny coffin made of reed or bamboo leaves. On the day of burial the dead cock is placed on the head of the coffin, and the tiny coffin is carried in a basket by one of the helpers in the funeral procession. When the procession arrives at a cross road on the main highway west of the town, the dead cock is hung by the legs on the lower branch of a tree, and the tiny coffin is buried near it. The death of the cock and the burial of the second coffin will have counteracted the omen of a second death.

If the deceased is a married-in son-in-law or a married woman, his or her parents' family must be informed immediately. The latter will send one or more members to see the body and determine whether his or her death was natural on the one hand, or due to maltreatment or murder, on the other. On no account may the body be sealed in the coffin before the arrival of this party. If any suspicion is aroused, a great row, followed by a lawsuit, is the usual result.

A red date and a white date, the latter tied with colored thread, are put in the mouth of the corpse. An ordinary hat will be put on the head of a male, and a piece of black cloth will be placed on that of a female. Then the whole body is covered with red cloth after having been dressed in the best clothes, which have been prepared for the purpose. Under and covering the corpse are "blessing quilts," made of cotton and red cloth. After the corpse is lowered into the coffin, the latter will be filled with wicks or more cotton quilts to keep the corpse from shifting when the coffin is being carried in the funeral procession. A small jar covered by red cloth and containing two small fish and some water will be buried in the pit underneath the coffin. These measures are to ensure the prosperity of the family. The hour when the coffin lid will be nailed on the coffin, the hour when the coffin will be removed from the house, and the day when the coffin will be lowered into the pit for burial must be decided by diviners or by referring to the Lunar Almanac. This is to ensure that the God of Earth (T'u Ti) will not be offended, and therefore that the dead may not be uncomfortable in the tomb.

Poor families usually have the coffin removed from the house within three days after the death. In that case, the date (not the hour) is merely a matter of convenience. If the funeral takes place on the third day after the death, then the date and the hour will have to be decided by divination. Rich families will remove younger dead from the house within three days, but may retain the coffin of older dead for one or two months. The older and the more important the dead in the kinship hierarchy to the living, the longer the coffin should be kept. A son should keep his parent's coffin in the house longest. But if his grandparents are living at the time, the interval may be shortened.

The length of time the coffin is kept at home indicates the strength of the esteem or the affection of the living for the dead. In life, West Towners, like all Chinese, beg a welcome visitor to stay as long as possible; if no such gesture is made, it is a sign that the visitor is unwelcome. If a well-to-do man fails to retain the coffin of his parent or his grandparent, he will be criticized as having desired the death.

Certain years and certain months of each year are more propitious for certain burial locations with reference to the family dwelling. There are eight directions: south, north, west, east, southeast, southwest, northeast, and northwest, and a diviner must decide which direction is auspicious. If the family graveyard is located on a slope southwest of the house and if the diviner says that this location is not good for the family in that particular year, the coffin will be taken out of the house and deposited elsewhere temporarily. The coffin will not be buried in a pit, but will be laid on the surface of the ground and then covered with slabs or pebbles until the year and month propitious for the southwest location. If a family should fail to follow this rule, the good effects of the family graveyard may be totally annulled. In Chapter II we have seen that "the prosperity of the descendants depends upon the places where their ancestors rest in peace."

The first evening after death has occurred, the dead person's clothes, bedding, and some other articles of daily use will be taken out and burned at the spots represented by *A* or *B* on the map of West Town. Many informants said that this was to ensure that the dead may readily have access to them. One informant specified that some of the articles burned would be those which the dead person liked best, such as a musical instrument. Others said, however, that the burned articles were "dirty" clothes and things, implying that they carried with them the contamination of death. While no definite conclusions can be drawn on this point, we must note the overwhelming evidence for the belief that in the spirit world the dead have needs, wishes, aspirations, and feelings, as they do in the world of living.

As soon as death has occurred, an elderly woman of the household will take some incense and food and report to the local patron god or *cheng huang* at the nearest temple. This is to ensure the good will of the first major god which the spirit of the dead will encounter. Quantities of paper money, but not paper horses, carriages, or houses, as in other parts of China, are burned for the spirit of the dead in anticipation of its expenses in the other world. Paper horses, carriages, and houses are burned only in order to send away undesirable ghosts in connection with sickness. Most West Towners are not very explicit about what will happen to their dead, but all banners of condolence from relatives and friends convey the sentiment that the dead is on his or her way to Western Heaven. In fact, however, most informants agree that the majority of the spirits of the dead will have to go through some unpleasant things in the lower world of spirits.

Three days after death the spirit will have reached the precarious *Nai Ho Bridge*. To ensure the spirit's safe passage it is customary to invite priests to recite the scriptures on the third night after death.

If the family can afford it, another scripture reading by priests takes place on the thirty-fifth day after death. At about this time the spirit, most informants agree, has reached the headquarters of the fifth judge, who is popularly known as being more severe than the others. The function of the priests on this occasion is to make an appeal for the clemency of the fifth judge, so that the dead will not be treated too severely.

On the second or the third New Year's day after the death, the mourning period has been completed. On this occasion another scripture reading takes place. There are no specific comments about this procedure, except that it is the custom and will be of some benefit to the dead. Below are a few of the more salient features of West Town funerals.

Mourning. Death calls forth extreme sorrow. To express this sorrow publicly is the duty of the young to the old and of the younger generation to the older. The closer the kinship relationship, the greater is the expression of this sorrow, which is expressed in mourning dress, wailing, and a total disregard for personal comfort and appearance. Mourning dress is made of coarse white cloth. The children of the deceased must wear the coarsest type and wear it longest. They wear the full mourning garments until after the funeral. After that event they wear a partial mourning of white, but may not wear silk or gay colored clothes until the entire mourning period is over. For the death of the father this period is two years, while for that of the mother it is three years. This distinction, West Towners emphasized, was because the mother's burden had been greater with regard to the care of the children and that, therefore, the children owe her a greater "debt."

As relationship becomes less close, the coarseness of the white cloth, the amount of the cloth, and the duration of its wearing are proportionately reduced. Sons and daughters are under the most strict obligations. Using the parent-child relationship as the criterion, the closeness of the relationship is reduced in two directions: lineally and laterally. The mourning obligations of grandchildren are less than those of sons and daughters; those of great-grandchildren are less than those of grandchildren. Great-great-grandchildren have no mourning duties. Laterally the obligations of brothers' children are less than those of sons and daughters; those of first cousins' children (on the patrilineal side) are less than those of brothers' children. Mourning obligations come to an end with those who are the descendants of a common great-great-grandfather.

On the matrilineal side mourning obligations are limited to the wife's parents, mother's parents, and mother's brothers and sisters only. All obligations for those of the same generation are reciprocal, except between husband and wife. A woman wears mourning for her husband similar to that for her parents-in-law, but a man wears a much lighter kind of mourning for his wife.

For forty-nine days after a parent's death sons may not shave their beard or hair or take a bath, and during the succeeding two or three years sons and daughters may not marry. Formerly it was regarded as very immoral for the wife or the concubine of a man to become pregnant during the period of mourning. This rule is, however, not generally observed today in West Town. During the funeral procession each of the sons of the deceased must look as though he is so grieved that he is unable to stand upright and has to be supported by a cane and two helpers.

Both men and women wail at funerals, but only women (usually the wife and the daughters-in-law of the deceased) do it continuously and loudly throughout the days when the coffin is in the house and during the funeral procession. It is the duty of the nearer relatives to wail more than the others.

The Coffin. Usually an aged person has a coffin made and stored in the clan temple long before death. The quality of the coffin is of as much importance as is the quality of a suit of clothes or a house. If the deceased or about to be deceased is a married woman, her parents' family may object if the quality of her coffin is in their estimation not fine enough. The same objection may come from a man's family if he is a married-in son-in-law.

Two spirit banners lead the bier in any funeral procession. One of them is of red paper and bears words to the following effect: "Spiritual banner of the dead by the name of ——, of the Clan ——, who is being received by the boundless Western Heaven of Eternal Happiness." The other is of white paper and bears words to the following effect: "The Travelling Banner of —— of the —— Clan, who died after enjoying the age of —— [the age is usually inflated], who lived in the Republic of China and was recognized by the whole community as being honest and helpful." Whether the family is rich or poor, some firecrackers are fired off and paper cut in the shape of coins is thrown about on the street during the funeral procession. During the funeral of the old man Ye firecrackers were fired continuously during the procession from the house to the western limit of the community, a distance of about one mile. These firecrackers are to scare away homeless ghosts, and the paper coins are to pay them off, as one would cast coins to beggars, so that the spirit of the dead will have no trouble in going on its way.

Condolence and Guests. All relatives, clan members, and friends have the mutual duty of condoling each other upon the occasion of any death in the family. Guests arrive with gifts of rice, money, paper money, and condolence banners. Such banners are usually of inexpensive silk of blue, black, or white. On them are inscribed sentiments of praise for the dead and the implicit or explicit statement that he or she has gone or returned to the Western Heaven of the Heaven of Eternal Happiness. All guests will participate in one feast or more. These feasts are as elaborate as the family of the deceased can provide. The number and the social origin of condolence banners and guests are important to the living and to the dead, of course, as matters of pride. The higher the social position of the condolers, the greater will be the prestige of the recipient family. In one West Town funeral, at least, condolence banners from General Chiang Kai-Shek and from the Minister of the Interior were displayed very prominently in the funeral procession.

Many mourners who attend the funeral in person are also helpers. The closer friends practically take charge of the whole ceremony. The impression given by all informants shows that death is the time of reckoning. If the dead and his or her family have been unkind, people will not attend the funeral. It becomes, therefore, a matter of plain logic that the number of mourners and their banners indicate the status of the dead and of his or her family in the community's esteem. The funeral performed by the richest family of the town in 1941 was participated in by about ten thousand people from many localities. All of them ate heartily for one, two, or more days at the family's expense. The funeral procession was about a quarter of a mile long. The helpers in the event numbered a little less than one hundred, organized in a hierarchical team, like that found in a public prayer meeting, with directors and managing directors at the top and receptionists, treasurers, errand runners, and others in the lower positions.

Obituary Notices.   Relatives and friends who live in the town will be informed and invited personally by sons or nephews of the deceased. They and all others who live far away will receive an obituary notice. As in all other parts of China, the notices from rich families are elaborate affairs. The notice is usually printed from type or lithograph and contains: date and hour of the person's birth, date and hour of death, age at death, date or dates of public mourning ceremonies, date of the funeral procession, date or dates of the feasts, and a list of the names of the dead person's sons, grandsons, brothers, patrilineal nephews, patrilineal grandnephews, great-grandchildren, and so forth. Then comes a long biography of the dead person. In some cases this is a separate volume. It cites in glowing terms the dead person's early wisdom, scholarly achievements, the wisdom and achievements of his or her parents, the various posts of distinction which he held, the various good deeds which he performed for the public and the nation, his or her various imperial honors, his or her outstanding qualities in terms of filial piety, the harmony among brothers and cousins, his freedom from corruption as an official, etc. etc. Often some alleged or real filial feat according to the classical pattern is included. The favorite feat is for a man, or a woman, when desperately trying to find a cure for his dangerously ill father or mother (or her father-in-law or mother-in-law), to cut off a piece of his flesh and boil it in the pot with other medicines.

The narrations are, as a rule, exaggerated strictly in accordance with the behavior pattern idealized in the classical-literary world. A greater age at death is usually assumed. It is a bad sign for a person to die young and is popularly believed to indicate that the deceased or his predecessors have committed some immoral deed. It would not be far from true to say that the length of life indicated on spirit banners, obituary notices, and tombstones is usually five, six, or more years longer than is justified by the actual facts.

A proper funeral is important both for the living and for the dead. It is to fulfill obligations of the living toward the dead, to ensure the safety and prosperity of the family, to renew a good relationship with relatives and friends, and to express social prestige in one of the most tangible ways. It assures the dead a safe passage from the world of man, provides comfort in the worlds of spirits, and also renews a good relationship with relatives and friends.

West Towners are not very articulate, but the general importance attached to the funeral may be seen from the following comments given me by a shoemaker during one of the funeral processions.

> It is really pitiable if one dies away from home. A man has to have friends and relatives . . . they will mourn you. A man who died without a proper funeral and mourners is like a dead dog. . . .

He went on to give an example of what he meant.

> Take the Chekiang school teacher, for example. He had only a wife and a baby son when he was drowned in the lake. He would really have died a miserable death if his students and the local gentry had not rallied round to give him a grand funeral. . . . That is what I mean by a not-pitiable death.

The teacher he referred to had taught in the local middle

school and had come to the interior as a refugee. He was drowned in the lake near by while swimming for pleasure. His funeral was a pompous affair, paid for by the school and the local gentry, and the procession was participated in by a large number of students and other West Towners.

A spiritual tablet is made for the deceased immediately after death. This tablet is placed in front of the coffin, where it remains during the entire proceeding, and in the funeral procession is carried in a special sedan chair. After the coffin is disposed of, this tablet is placed on the family altar. No worship ceremony before the ancestral altar takes place during death. Just before the coffin is taken out of the house some food is offered at the ancestral altar, but no incense or paper money is burned. Male children who die before the age of twelve will have no tablet in the altar. Those who died unmarried but older than twelve will have a bare tablet. The tablets of married persons are each enclosed in a case made in the form of a shrine, with doors to be opened during periods of worship.

DEATH AWAY FROM HOME

If a person has died away from home, no effort is spared to transport the corpse to the ancestral graveyard. If this cannot be done, a ritual performance calling for the person's spirit takes place at the home as soon as news of the death is received there. This begins in the evening and lasts most of the night. Two or more priests are hired for the performance. Two rows of burning incense sticks are inserted in the ground along each side of the lane between the gateway of the family home and the main street. An armchair is placed facing an offering table in the courtyard just inside the gateway. On this chair are placed one suit of clothes and a wash basin containing water, a comb, and a towel. On the offering table are a number of articles. First, a spirit banner of white paper, similar in design to the ones used in funerals, but with words showing that it is intended for "calling home" (*chao yin*) (not sending away) the spirit of the dead. Next comes a tablet made of yellow paper and with an attached stick inserted in a container of rice. On this tablet are inscribed words to the following effect: "This is the sacred seat of the spirit of Father (or Mother) — of — clan, who is hereby reverentially called with incense and flowers, foods, and uplifting scriptures." Then comes a semicircle of several lotus-flower lamps. Each lamp is a rice bowl containing oil and wick, with pink paper cut in the shape of lotus petals pasted around the edge of the bowl. Each lamp is lighted and looks like a lotus flower. Then there is a semicircle of food offerings: *gana,* tea leaves, salt, fragrant wood, and other things. At the end of the table opposite that of the paper tablet stand two lighted candles.

Connected with the offering table is another table for the priests. There are at least two priests, often five or more. They sit on benches on both sides of the table. The chief priest leads the one or two fully accredited priests in reading the scriptures and prayers for the dead. The apprentice priests for the most part beat drums and cymbals according to a specified rhythm. Often they join in the refrains with the rest of the company. The other priests blow bugles and flutes. Apart from the scriptures used, the external appearance of this performance is the same as that of any other prayer meeting.

The end of the second table farthest away from the chair is near the door of the house. Prostrate on the ground between that end of the table and the house door are the sons, the wife, and the grandchildren of the deceased. They wail continuously at first, but after a time intermittently, because of exhaustion.

About midnight a quantity of paper money, together with the lotus lamps and the spiritual banner, are taken out beyond the gateway and burned. At the same time a bridge-crossing ceremony for the spirit of the dead is performed inside the courtyard. Some informants called this bridge "heavenly bridge." Others insisted that it was *"Nai Ho*

Bridge." In connection with the Lower World of Spirits the first obstacle encountered by the spirit of any dead person is *"Nai Ho Bridge."* The representation of this bridge is made by piling several benches on the ground in the shape of a traditional Chinese bridge. The benches are fastened together and covered with white cloth. While still reciting scriptures, the chief priest, followed by other priests, takes up the spirit tablet of the dead and slowly carries it across the "bridge." Then it is carried into the house, where the sons of the dead are prostrated before the family altar. The several priests chant for some time before this altar, and afterward the spirit tablet is burned in front of it. A proper wooden tablet for the dead is then produced and placed on the altar.

The incense sticks bordering the lane outside the family home are to guide the spirit of the dead in finding its own house. The chair is for it to sit in, and the clothes, as well as the basin, are for its use.

If the body of the dead is taken home later, a proper funeral will take place. If not, then the calling-home rite takes the place of the funeral. There is an apparent contradiction, which bothers no West Towners: the spirit of the dead is called home, but may not be sent away to Western Heaven as in an ordinary funeral.

CHAPTER VII

Communion with Ancestors

ONE OF the outstanding features in West Towners' treatment of the dead is the fact that, far from being afraid of the dead and being anxious to remove the body from the house, they keep it or express an intense desire to keep it as long as possible. It is easy to see how this works in a culture which affirms the principle that because every individual owes his being and everything he has to his parents, he must repay his indebtedness by means of filial piety. Death, far from having severed the relationship of the dead to the living, has merely promoted the relationship to a plane technically different from, but theoretically similar to, that which existed before the event.

The relationship of the living to the dead is maintained, chiefly through ritual, for three general purposes. Some rites are designed to gain knowledge about the dead: their whereabouts, how they are getting along, and when they will be reincarnated. Some rites are intended to provide comfort for the dead: the offerings of food, clothing, and money. Still other rites are performed to invoke the dead to discharge those duties which were practiced in life: giving sanction on marriage and family division and acting as a disciplinarian for the younger generations.

In this section we shall deal principally with the first group of rites—séances which may be described as "communication with the dead." Séances are usually performed within the two- or three-year mourning period, as a rule in Sheng Yu T'ang, the temple organization of the community, on the "birthday" of *Mother Wang,* supreme goddess of the Western Heaven of Happiness. The birthday occurs on the 18th of the Seventh Moon, but the rites usually last for five days, until after the twenty-second of the month.

According to its priests, the name of the *t'ang* (organization), *"Sheng Yu,"* means decree by a divinity or sage. It originated with the God *Kuan Kung,* who is also popularly designated as *Kuan Sheng,* or *Kuan* the Sage.

The interior of the temple is furnished with various religious objects. Against the wall and seated on high platforms are three life-sized images in three shrines: *Kuan Yin,* or Goddess of Mercy, in the center, *Wen Ch'ang,* or God of Literature, to the left, and *Ti Mu,* or Goddess of Earth, to the right. In front of each image is an offering table with ceremonial paraphernalia. In addition to the latter is a row of deities, represented partly by tablets and partly by portraits.

In front of the Goddess of Mercy is the colored portrait of *Kuan Kung,* the god who decreed the establishment of the organization. Flanking the portrait on both sides are eight tablets, each of which bears the fanciful title of a god. Before the God of Literature are three tablets representing, respectively, the Kitchen God (at the left), heaven, earth, emperor, parents, and teachers (in the center), and the chief spiritual officer guarding the organization (at the right). A portrait of Dr. Sun Yat-sen, founder of the Chinese Republic, is in front of the Goddess of Earth. Hanging on the wall are three photographs: that of the last dead chief priest of the organization is beside the God of Literature, that of a group of members just below the first photograph, and that of a dead member (a lady) is next to the Goddess of Earth. A portrait of Confucius is on the side wall at the right. In front of this is the table on which gods or spirits of the dead give their messages.

On the veranda outside the main temple is a large tablet with an offering table in front of it, dedicated to all spirits of those "brave men and women who died in the war against Japan."

The temple was originally built to house and for the worship of the God of Literature and the Goddesses of Mercy and of Earth. About twenty-five years ago, when the organization was ritually "ordered" by the god *Kuan Kung*, the building was borrowed and another row of gods was added. While the activities of the organization are chiefly connected with the second row of gods, the three original images are never completely neglected in the offerings.

The portrait of Dr. Sun Yat-sen and the tablet dedicated to "brave men and women who died in the war against Japan" were added, according to most informants, about two years after the beginning of the late Sino-Japanese War. Some informants maintained that these were for the purpose of protecting the establishment from local hostility. Some West Towners were opposed to the organization on the grounds that it was immoral, charging that men and women believers met much too freely in the temple and that it was a haven for sexually dissatisfied individuals. Others were against it because they discredited its professed functions completely. Still others were jealous of its prosperity. Some even sought to have the whole thing disbanded. But the priests were wise, some informants told me; they installed the portrait of Dr. Sun Yat-sen and the tablet for the war dead, and thereby silenced all opposition.

If some West Towners were opposed to this particular organization, the majority of them have always taken the priests' functions and similar organizations for granted. In one form or another the priests and the *t'ang* have, as far as all informants could remember, always existed in the community. Before Sino-Japanese hostilities began, this particular society was said to enjoy much greater patronage. Whether this statement merely shows a longing for "the good old days," I have not been able to verify. The fact is that as late as the middle of 1943 the society had an active membership of more than two thousand individuals; more than half were women. Since there are no membership dues and no definite ceremony of initiation, the active members are those who from time to time donate money or occasionally take advantage of the services of the organization for a fee.

Regularly in charge of the organization are three or four professional priests, including the chief priest (*cheng tu*) and the chief assistant priest (*fu tu*). During the festive celebration of the "birthday" of *Mother Wang,* when séances for communication with the dead are held, additional helpers are enlisted from among the active members. The number of helpers usually amounts to thirty or more, distributed in the following way.

HELPERS AT SÉANCES

Duty	*Number of persons*
Chief priesthood	1 (regular chief priest)
Assistant chief priesthood	1 (regular assistant chief priest)
Taking care of incense	6 or 7 (they also serve tea to other officers)
General management	1 (senior member)
Taking charge of and manipulating the spiritual recorder	3 (one or two of them are priests)
Providing music	15 (or more)
Purchasing	2
Recording spiritual messages	2 or 3
Reporting spiritual messages	3

These officers are named by the chief god, invoked through the spiritual recorder. The recorder consists of three parts: a tray filled with fine sand, a stylus of willow wood, which has a holder and a point affixed perpendicularly, and a smoother. The smoother is used to give the sand in the tray a level surface. The stylus is held by two officers sitting opposite each other, with its point touching the surface of the sand. After the proper rituals of invocation have been performed by the priests the stylus moves as though "automatically." The spirit or god invoked uses it to convey a message. The stylus writes one word at a time. The reporter pronounces it, and the recording officers write it down in a book. All spiritual messages are obtained in this way.

The "birthday" of *Mother Wang* occurs on the 18th of

the Seventh Moon. But those who want to find out about the deceased members of their family begin to register in the hall on the 15th of the month. Each registrant does so by giving the name, birthday, and hour, as well as the day and hour of death of the person about whom the information is desired. Each registrant paid, in 1943, a fee of twenty national dollars. In 1943 the total number of registrants was about 120, of whom about 70 percent were women. A survey of the requests shows that the contact desired was usually with a member of the individual's family: father, mother, brother, sister, wife, or husband. Grandparents and others rarely appeared on the list.

The ritual of invocation begins on the "birthday," and briefly is as follows: All persons present in the temple, other than officers who have duties to discharge, kneel on the floor. Early-comers kneel on the veranda in front of the main hall; others kneel in the courtyard in order of their arrival. They will kneel until after the arrival of the God for the Day's Work. The chief priest, helped by his assistants, officiates before the center shrine of the hall and pronounces the formal opening of the séance by chants, amulets, and incense. He then ceremonially invites the spiritual heads to the séance (in 1943 the spiritual head invited was the Central Emperor, one of the most powerful local patron gods, and the assistant spiritual head was Exalted General *Chao*). The chief priest then kowtows before the center shrine—at first three times, then six times, and then nine times. When he begins to prostrate himself, it is a sign of the arrival of the two principal spiritual heads of the séance. Music, by the orchestra of string and wind instruments, also begins when the chief priest first prostrates himself. The music continues intermittently throughout the séance under the direction of the priests.

The chief priest then pronounces the Ten Commandments of the séance. The Ten Commandments are:

1. Thou shalt not forget about filial piety and harmony among brothers;

2. Thou shalt not violate the law of the nation and offend and cheat the ruler;

3. Thou shalt not forget about the dignity of teachers or show signs of ingratitude;

4. Thou shalt not disrupt relations within the lineage and clan;

5. Thou shalt not fight or seek revenge so as to disturb the village and the neighborhood;

6. Thou shalt not refuse to come to the rescue of those who are urgently in need;

7. Thou shalt not cheat and be unaware of the necessity of accumulating spiritual goods;

8. Thou shalt not take advantage of special positions and privileges and cause inconvenience to others;

9. Thou shalt not expose other people's secrets;

10. Thou shalt not disobey any Commandments.[1]

After the Ten Commandments are pronounced, offerings of wine and ritual homage are given every god in the hall. On this occasion, in addition to the usual gods inhabiting the temple, numerous banners bearing the titles and names of hundreds of other gods, similar to those found in any prayer meeting during a cholera epidemic, are hung on the beams, walls, and other structures in the hall. The ritual homage covers them all.

Then the chief priest presents a petition to the Supreme Ruler of Higher Heaven. He does so by kneeling before the

---

[1] These commandments were supposed to have been imposed by Kuan Kung, the god who "founded" the present organization. In all prayer meetings for emergency purposes the priests announce some commandments, but there are not necessarily ten. The "ten" commandments in the present connection probably came about by way of missionary influence. The priests in charge insisted, of course, that they were entirely from their own gods. On the other hand, priests in the community were very conscious of the presence of missionary and church workers. Some of the latter tried to persuade the priests out of their jobs. A few took a more belligerent attitude. The priests answered by incorporating Jesus Christ into their indigenous beliefs. Christ was installed as one of the ministers of the Supreme Ruler in the Higher World of Spirits. Some of the priests had a cursory knowledge of the New Testament.

central shrine, holding with both hands a document written on yellow paper, and reading it aloud. The petition reads approximately as follows: "On such and such a date, the people of West Town, of the district —, represented by priest —, have such and such needs and request hereby the Supreme Ruler of Higher Heaven to dispatch some gods to this séance." This petition is often lengthy; its reading may take fifteen minutes or more. After the petition is read the chief priest and his assistants sing a benediction, while the orchestra plays. The benediction is a seven character poem, as follows:

> Earnest and honest wishes of the populace are behind the petition,
> They will make the — [one word title of the god] Sage take pity and give attention,
> This morning all four corners of the earth are illuminated by godly light,
> Ten thousand sins are cleared away, and ten thousand blessings are the destination.

The document is then burned with more offerings of incense.

The God for the Day's Work will then arrive. While the priests are singing out the benediction, the two officers in charge of the stylus have already held it in position on the surface of the sand. As soon as the benediction is over, the stylus begins to move. The first words usually identify the god, who announces his arrival first by a whole stanza of seven-character verse, and then gives his title and name. After this, all kneelers stand up.

Each registrant in turn gets his message. The procedure is as follows. After burning a bag of paper ingots with the name and the dates of birth and of death of the deceased, the registrant kneels on the spiritual recorder platform. The priest writes an amulet on each of the registrant's palms, after which the person holds the palms together for a while. Then he or she sits in the chair on the platform. With eyes closed, the registrant touches the stylus. The stylus moves. Music now is played till the end of the séance.

The idea is that the God of the Day will find the spirit of the dead. The god either makes the spirit tell the interested relatives some vital facts about his or her present condition or gives the information himself by words written on the surface of the sand.

The message is invariably in the form of a seven-character poem, occasionally with an additional line of information. Eight examples are given below:

(1) This was from a young man who died at about 27 years of age. His wife requested the information.

It was the natural result of my last life that I died so early;
It is a pity that two birds in the same bush have to be separated by one departing before the other;
However, decrees have been issued for my reincarnation;
It is hoped that my behavior will vindicate me during my next life.

(2) This was from a woman who died when she was about 70 years of age. Her son, about 40 years old, requested the information.

It is a happy thing that I died a natural death;
It is a result of good accumulated in my last life;
Happily my case has been noticed, and I have asked for immediate reincarnation;
Already I have the document and am only waiting for my turn to say farewell to the Tenth Judge.

(3) This was about a man whose age at his death was not indicated. His sister requested the information. His spirit was not present in the séance. The query was answered by the god.

This man is specially favored by superior deities;
He suffered from no restrictions or punishments at all;
Scripture reading since death has raised him to guest house;
He is waiting for opportunities to enter the worlds above.

(4) This was about a man who died when about 25 years of age. His younger sister requested the information.

He bore stains of evil deeds committed in his last reincarnation;

On top of that, he persisted in doing what he should not
   have done;
Previous sins will be forgiven if and when good deeds are
   accumulated;
Never should the thought of reincarnation and of being
   good be lightly taken.

(5) This was about a woman whose age at death was not
indicated. Her son requested the information.

This is a woman who lived up to her womanly virtues;
She entered the world of spirits, but never suffered tortures;
Happily she passed a festival when all spirits were in-
   spected;
She was given special honor and is now Heaven due.
[After the above verses, the stylus continued to move and
   scribbled the following:]
She has already gone to the West.

(6) This was about a young woman whose age at death
was not indicated. Her younger brother made the request
for information.

She failed to live up to her womanly virtues in her last
   life,
But she mitigated her circumstances by earnestness and en-
   durance high;
She was called back to the Lower World of Spirits as pre-
   ordained,
But she has accumulated good and expiated her sins, and
   soon will see light.

(7) This was about a woman who died when middle
aged. Her husband requested the information.

She failed to abide by commandments for women in two
   lives,
After last death Mirror of Evil Deeds has revealed her
   vices,
However, a recent decree of general clemency has reduced
   her punishment by half,
But her detainment in hell will continue for a long time.

(8) This was about a man who died when about 22 years
of age, in Paoshan (about 200 miles south of West Town).
He had been a soldier. His younger brother requested the
information.

Accumulated debt of evil follows him all the time;
After death his punishment became revengers' delight;
Scripture reading has already improved his circumstances;
His suffering in this life has also helped.

All of the messages are recorded in a book kept in the temple. Each registrant takes away a copy of his or her own message. Toward the end of the séance, when all individual messages have been received, the god in charge will give a "grand message," intended for everyone in the community, telling them how they should conduct themselves in the coming year.

Upon request, séances of a similar nature, but on a much smaller scale, may take place on other dates, usually the first and the fifteenth of each month, in the same temple.

It may be asked who the patrons of these séances are and how seriously they take the messages. No analysis of the social station of all participants is available, but there are a number of illustrative facts. As mentioned before, more than half the participants are women. General observation seems to indicate that without doubt women, on the whole, take it much more seriously than men. Most women are illiterate, but all messages are carefully explained to them by the record keepers. I watched some such scenes and saw women drinking in every word. In not a few instances tears flowed from their eyes. The atmosphere of the entire séance is in sharp contrast to that of any temple fair; in the latter there are serious scripture readings and prayers, but there is also a feeling of gay festivity. During a séance there is no gaiety; there is only seriousness. As soon as the women get home they produce the message and have the literate members of their family verify what they have been told in the temple.

It is most interesting that faith in these séances is sustained in the face of damaging evidence. A woman of about thirty years was one of the registrants in Sheng Yu T'ang in 1943. Her husband had died the year before at the age of 35. Before his death he was a peddler of miscellaneous merchandise. The message which she received in that séance indicated that her husband had already been elevated by scripture reading and reincarnated. Later on, this woman went to a place about ten miles north of West Town and participated in another séance for the same purpose. She got the message that her husband had to wait for another three years before obtaining his chances of reincarnation.

This woman was illiterate, and the messages were explained to her. When she was asked about the evident conflict of the two messages, she simply dismissed the question by saying: "The ritual methods of the two places were different, that's all."

The position of male participants is equally interesting. A few men admitted that they participated because they believed in the séances. Several of them admitted that "although these things may be branded as superstitions, they are often very *ling*" (efficacious, true as popularly represented, etc.). Most West Towners are familiar with the popular slogan *"Mi hsin, mi hsin, pu te pu hsin"* (which means that although they are superstitions, one cannot help but believe in them). This is probably an answer to charges of the school people. Outstanding cases can be given in support of these views.

The sons of a rich Yi family, for example, communicated with their old father shortly after the latter's death in 1942. The message said that the old man's spirit would be raised to heaven if the sons would be more generous in giving alms, especially in order to provide the poor dead with coffins. The sons followed the instructions closely for some time.

A very large number of men explained that their participation was due to the requests of their women folk. High on the list of contributors in 1943 was, for example, the man L. K. Y., who was the vice-commander of a regiment under the Ministry of War and a student returned from Japan. All informants insisted, however, that he contributed money merely because his mother had told him to do so before her death. Another young man named

W. F. C., who was one of my informants and has had business experience in Burma, admitted to me that he was once a musician in the orchestra, but nothing else. A few days later, I mentioned his name to one of the two younger priests in charge. The young priest at once said that "Mr. W. F. C. used to be one of the officers in charge of the spiritual recorder." When I told W. F. C. about this, he strongly denied it. Probably his denial was caused by some suspicion on his part that, although I was interested in knowing about the séances and other local religious practices, I really disapproved of them at heart. Some days later, when we knew each other better, W. F. C. admitted to me that he did act as an officer in charge of the spiritual recorder. He at once added, "I went because my stepmother wanted me to go."

A number of facts show, however, that there is no real lack of interest on the part of the male. An examination of the contributors for the 1943 séance shows that men's names made up four fifths of the total. The list of contributors for the 1929 séance which produced *A Bell for Awakening the Ignorant* confirmed the proportion. In both cases, too, the larger single donations were given by male contributors; the gifts of female contributors were much smaller. It may be argued that men's names dominate the lists because men control the purse strings. But it is to be remembered that the majority of West Town women work for profit and have some income of their own. The only partially plausible answer is that in a patrilineally constructed society many things are done in the name of the family head, who, as has been shown in Chapter V, is as a rule, a male. This ostensibly explains the fact that donations openly given by women are smaller, because they may originate from broken, and therefore poor, families.

The above answers are rather specious, because if the males really lacked interest in the séances or were otherwise opposed to them, they would certainly not have been active participants, or they might even have found means of preventing their wives and mothers from participating. The least they could have done was perhaps to keep their names from being posted publicly as active supporters of such practices. Since no male opposition could be substantiated in any form, and since a fair number of them do take active part in the séances, the natural conclusion would seem to be that, though men are not as ardent believers in the séances as are women, they are by no means as wholly uninterested in them as some assert that they are.

PILGRIMAGE TO GRAVEYARDS

We come next to one of the usages which concerns the provision of comfort for the dead. A family makes at least one ceremonial visit each year to its graveyard or graveyards. This takes place about the festival of Ch'ing Ming, in the Third Moon. The festival occurs on the 5th of April every year according to the solar calendar, but its occurrence varies between the 10th and the 20th in the Third Moon according to the lunar calendar. The visit is not necessarily made on the day of the festival. It may be made on any day within the Third Moon. Practically all West Town graveyards are situated on the side of Ts'ang Mountains facing the lake. On any bright and clear day within this period a long and almost continuous procession of men, women, and children, with or without baskets, pack horses, and riding horses, and carriers with pots and pans, and so forth, may be seen streaming in the general direction of the mountains. They leave the town in the morning and return toward evening.

If a family has two or more graveyards situated in different areas, it will take two or more days to make the separate visits.

The visitations are made to provide the dead with food, money and clothes as well as to have a reunion with them. The latter is especially comparable to a social call among the living, in which it is the custom for junior members of the family and clan to ask about the health of senior ones, or otherwise pay their obeisance.

This usage will, I believe, be best illustrated by the description of a typical journey to a graveyard, in which I participated in 1942. The family concerned was headed by the merchant Y.C.Y. The whole family went on the pilgrimage—Y.C.Y., his wife, his concubine, his two sons (12 and 14 years of age), his two daughters (11 and 15 years of age), and his four nieces (brother's daughters, 7, 16, 17, and 19 years of age). The mother of the nieces had died some years earlier. Their father lived with a concubine in Kunming and disregarded the children. Two female affinal relatives (both about twenty-five years of age) also accompanied us, and two remote male clan members who happened to be living with the family at the time. Three male affinal relatives went along as hired helpers for the day. They and a pack mule carried the foodstuff, pots and pans, blankets, kindling, and articles necessary for ritual offering. Everybody walked.

The family possessed two graveyards at the time. The one visited was the newer of the two. It was situated just below one of the minor peaks in the mountains. The distance from West Town to the foot of the mountains is about 12 *li* (about 4 miles); from the foot of the mountains to the graveyard there was a stiff climb of 5 *li*. Parts of the slopes were very slippery with dead leaves, loose earth, and pebbles. All the women except the two daughters and the four nieces had bound feet. One of the two female relatives was at least six months pregnant. We walked in three groups: the family head, two male clan members, and myself formed one, the three helpers and the mule formed a second, while the ladies formed the last group. It was amazing that although we kept ourselves slightly ahead of the female group all the way and although I was completely exhausted when we reached our destination, without exception the ladies appeared more energetic than ever.

Upon arrival at the graveyard the family head took out the blankets and spread them in an open space. He, the male clan members, and I sat down on the blankets, while the three helpers and the ladies started to work. The ladies first carefully put the flowers, which they had gathered on the way up, in front of the two main tombs. Each tombstone was covered with a large straw hat, which most of the unmarried girls wore for the occasion. Almost simultaneously the helpers kindled a fire, while the ladies prepared for the cooking. The helpers did the rough work, such as carrying water from a spring and gathering large pieces of firewood. The ladies first made some tea, which the two boys served to the men on the blankets. They then proceeded to shell the peas, cut up the meat, and wash the vegetables.

The graveyard was not a big one, but it conformed in every respect to the best of West Town standards. It had three terraces, hacked from the slope of the mountain. On both sides of each terrace were two pine trees, and on both sides of the lowest terrace were two engraved stone pillars marking the front entrance to the graveyard. Below the plot was a heavily wooded slope. Flanking this particular height were two larger mountain ridges, which nearly joined each other, but just failing to do so, left a narrow gap between them. Viewed from the family graveyard, these ridges were like outer walls with the gap serving as a gateway. Through that gateway a person standing in front of any tomb could see part of the lake.

While the ladies cooked and the helpers hacked wood, our group, sufficiently rested, began to visit some other graveyards scattered at various points on the same mountain. At all of them were signs of activity and cooking. Some families had just arrived; others were beginning to eat. We visited one graveyard which occupied several hundred mu^2 of space and in which several hundred individuals were grouped near the tombs of their own lineages. We visited a humble graveyard in which the tombs were mere heaps of earth, by which only a few living members

---

[2] One acre equals 6.6 *mu*.

of the family were gathered. We discussed the merits and demerits of the various graveyards. When we came upon a group which was just sitting down for the grand meal of the day, we were offered some wine and food.

Upon our return to the Y. graveyard, the meal was ready to be served. All the dishes prepared, together with warm wine, were neatly arranged before the two main tombs, which were those of the family head's parents. The family head then took some burning incense and wine and made a ceremonial offering, first before one tomb, then before the other. He kowtowed nine times before each. As he did so, paper money was burned. The other male members of the gathering followed suit, one by one. As a guest, I made my incense offering according to the custom, but when I offered to kowtow, the family head prevented me from doing so, saying that I did not have to be so polite. When the men had finished, the ladies went through the same procedure. When each person had had a turn, some dishes were taken to the tomb on the lower terrace, which was that of the younger brother of the wife of the family head. There a simpler ritual offering was made, only by the family head, his wife, and all the women.

In the meantime, the young female relative who was pregnant left the group and went to visit a small graveyard about fifty yards away. There were two tombs, both very humbly constructed. One was that of her mother, and the other was that of an aunt. This young relative made some incense offering, sat leaning against the front part of her mother's tomb, and wept deeply for a long while. Later, other female members of the party with great difficulty persuaded her to desist and to leave the tomb.

With all offerings completed, everyone sat down to the hearty meal. The men sat in one group, the women in another. There was ample wine, meat, deliciously cooked vegetables, and a portable fire pot similar to those used in North China during the winter months. This outdoor meal was thoroughly enjoyed by everyone in the party.

After the meal came tea and pipes. When the two groups

felt that time enough had elapsed, the women and the helpers began to clear away the food and wash the dishes. At
about three o'clock in the afternoon the party started on a
leisurely return to West Town. En route to the graveyard,
as well as on the way back, we met hundreds of other
travelers on the same mission.

Such a visit is chiefly intended for members of the same
lineage, particularly for those who are closely related. The
usual objects of such visits are tombs of parents, husbands
or wives, or grandparents. In the big graveyard mentioned
above, which occupied several hundred *mu* of space, the
tombs of some earlier ancestors received visits and offerings
from members of many lineages descended from them, but
meals were, without exception, partaken of in groups of
five, ten or more, each clustering near the tombs of those
to whom the partakers of the food were immediately related. The same is true of the wailing, which is accorded
only to near relatives who have recently died.

Y.C.Y. told me that two similar visits might be made
during any one year, one about the 15th of the First Moon,
and another about the 15th of the Tenth Moon. This statement was subsequently confirmed by other informants. Actually a much smaller number of families practiced the
optional ceremonials, and they were never attended by the
whole family like the one just described. Y's wife told me
that as far as her family was concerned, only her husband
and a few men made the other visits, partly for the purpose
of taking care of the graveyards. She said that the distance
was too great for her.

ANCESTOR FESTIVALS

Each household has a family shrine. The shrine is situated in the central portion of the second floor of the west
wing of the home. It is installed on the ground floor only
when the house is a one-story structure. Occasionally the

shrine is for ancestors only, but more often it houses a number of popular gods.

Ancestors are represented in such a shrine either on a large scroll or on separate tablets. The scroll is a large sheet of mounted paper containing names, sex, and titles of the ancestors who are (theoretically) within *wu fu,* or five degrees of mourning. As mentioned in Chapter II, this rule is not always observed. On the scroll of a poor and illiterate Ch family only a small number of the ancestors were represented, because "the old scroll was destroyed by fire and these are the only ones we can remember." On the scroll of a Y family many ancestors beyond the five degrees were represented, because they "have not had another scroll made yet." The tablets are made of wood, but if there is no time to have one made, a paper one will be substituted.

The popular gods in all family shrines are three: *Kuan Kung* (the warrior from Three Kingdoms), Confucius, and one or more Buddhas. A fourth popular figure is the Goddess of Mercy or Fertility. As a rule these gods are represented by images. In addition, there are often other spiritual figures in family shrines which the family members cannot identify. In at least one shrine there was a large tablet for Confucius as well as his supposed image. Before the shrine is an offering table, on which there are two incense burners, one for ancestors and one for the gods, two candlesticks, and a flower vase or two. At the foot of the table are two round straw cushions for the kneeling worshiper.

Incense is offered in each burner daily, usually by a woman of the house. This act is performed every morning just before breakfast. There is no offering of food except on occasions of marriage, birth, division of the family, and during the ancestor festival.

The festival occurs around the 15th of the Seventh Moon, but in effect it begins on the 1st of the month and ends on the 16th. On the 1st of the month the portion of the house containing the shrine is cleared of non-essential articles and cleaned. Offerings of the following items are made:

fruit, preserves, candies, two or more bowls containing growing rice sprouts, one or more dishes containing fragrant wood, some lotus or other flowers in the vase, and a number of dishes or bowls of cooked food. Red candles are inserted in the candlesticks. A new cloth, as well as a front cover, is placed on the offering table. If the tablets are encased, their covers are removed. The offerings and arrangements may be made by both men and women. The offerings may be replaced with fresh ones from time to time throughout the fifteen days.

If the family can afford it, as many West Town families can, one or more priests are invited to read scriptures and perform certain rituals before the shrine during this period. Such priests may be hired for one day or for several days, depending on how much the family is willing to spend. The greater the number of priests and the longer they are utilized, the more beneficial it will be for the dead and for the living. If only one priest is hired, he sits on a stool at the right of the offering table. His equipment consists of a wooden "fish," a pair of cymbals, many volumes of scriptures, the family's complete genealogical record, as well as the names and birthdays of all its living members. These data are written on a long folder of yellow paper. The priest recites the scriptures and performs all the pertinent rites continuously for the entire period of his employment, stopping only for meals and opium, but uninterrupted by the family's work on the shrine.

The function of the priest in connection with the dead ancestors was clear to all informants: to report the names of the dead to superior deities and to uplift them by scripture reading so that they will be able to proceed to the Western Heaven of Happiness as soon as possible. The reason for a complete list of the names of the family's living members is not clear to all. Some insist that it is to bless the living; others say that it will make the dead happier by showing them what worthy descendants they have.

In the middle of 1943 the daily wage for each priest performing this function consisted of: $40 to $50; half *sheng*[3] of rice or beans; meals; opium to smoke during work. During the same period of 1943 laborers in the field received an average daily wage of $25 without food.

Some time during the first thirteen days of the month a married daughter makes a visit to her parents' home. She takes with her the following gifts: a number of loaves of sweetened bread; two or three pounds of pork; pears or other fruit; and a number of bags filled with ingots made of paper for members of the parents' family who have died within the last twelve months. She will be entertained at a specially prepared meal upon her arrival. She presents these gifts to her parents, pays proper ritual homage before the family shrine, and is supposed to remain for three days. In practice, however, most married daughters have to leave sooner because of the pressure of work in their husbands' households. After a woman has died, her daughter-in-law makes this visit on her behalf. When the latter has also died, then the granddaughter-in-law will make the visit. Informants agreed that this ceremonial relationship was always kept up for several generations. Every married woman must return to the home of her husband before the 14th of the Seventh Moon for the big ceremony.

If a member of the family has died within a year of the Seventh Moon, the family will make a special offering and ritual homage to the recently deceased. This occasion always includes the burning of a quantity of ingots made of paper and sealed in bags, each inscribed with the names of the recipients and their immediate descendants. This ritual is generally designated as *shu* (burn) *hsing* (new) *pao* (bags).

If there has been no death within the last twelve months, the family worship takes place on the afternoon of the 14th. The service is performed in one of two ways, depending upon family habits. Members of the several branches of the household can perform the worship together, with joint offerings of food, wine, and incense, or

---

[3] In West Town sheng equals 15 pounds.

they can perform it separately, with individual offerings. The dishes offered on this occasion are all elaborately prepared and contain chicken, pork, fish, and vegetables. Each dish is topped with flower designs. If the household worships as one unit, all dishes, together with at least six bowls of rice, six cups of wine, and six pairs of chopsticks are laid on the offering table in advance. Members of the household then kowtow one after the other before the altar. Generally men kowtow first, followed by women and children. But this rule is not rigidly kept. Sometimes children perform the act of homage before adults. On occasion there is considerable confusion as to who has and who has not yet kowtowed. Adults tell children and each other to *dou dou bao* (kowtow); they also ask each other, *"Dou he le ma?"* (Have you kowtowed?)

If the several branches of the household perform the ceremony separately, each branch will use its own offering trays. One tray contains six or eight bowls of chicken, meat, fish, etc., and a second tray contains two bowls of rice, two pairs of chopsticks, and two cups of wine. These trays are presented at the shrine by one or two male members of the branch, followed immediately by the other members. They kowtow before the altar, the elder before the younger, and men before women. The usual number of kowtows appears to be four, but often individual members perform this obeisance five, nine, or even more times. Various branches of the household may come into the shrine room with their trays at approximately the same time, or representatives of one branch may arrive before those of another have completed the ritual. Indeed, the whole second floor of the wing may be crowded and noisy.

The atmosphere among the worshipers on this occasion appears to be greatly influenced by whether or not the male members of the family or household are scholarly. If some of them are, the atmosphere is more serious than otherwise. In all cases the West Town worshipers seem to be much less serious than the families in North China which I observed before 1937 on such occasions. As far as West

Town is concerned, the atmosphere is much less restrained on such occasions than in any prayer meeting during an epidemic. Adults joke with each other and make mistakes. Children feel playful, chatter, and have a happy time. In only a few instances do the family heads wear their best attire.

When the offerings and homage at the family altar terminates, the same dishes are taken by a male member of the household (or branch of the household) to the clan temple. There the food is briefly offered at the main altar, and the male who delivers it kowtows a number of times. After this, the offering food is taken back to the house, and all members of the household come together to feast on it. If it is not enough for everyone, more food will be added until all are satisfied. Male and female members of the household eat at the same table.

During the day incense sticks are inserted at numerous places in the family home: on the lintels of all portals, special parts of the walls, and in many sections of the courtyard. During the ceremony at the family altar practically equal amounts of homage are given to ancestors and to the gods beside them. In some families the offering dishes are placed between the two groups. In others, identical offerings are placed before each group. In some families, all kowtows are intended to be shared by both; in others, all members prostrate themselves twice, once before each group.

After the meal the *shu pao* (burning the bags) ceremony begins. Each bag contains a quantity of silver ingots and bears the names of a male ancestor and his wife, of the descendants who are providing the bag for them, and the date on which this is burned, together with a brief plea entreating the ancestors to accept it.

In general it is the custom to provide one bag for every direct male ancestor of the lineage (whether he is in the family shrine or not) and his wife or wives. By the word "direct" I refer to those deceased members, however remote, who are lineal ancestors of the person who is providing the bags. In other words, they are father, father's father, father's father's father, etc., not father's brother, father's father's brother, etc. Most families keep a list or a separate book containing the names of those ancestors who figure largely on this occasion. If first and second cousins live in the same household, each will thus provide for his own parents and grandparents until they come to a common ancestor. For the recently deceased, the number of bags per ancestor is at least doubled and may be much larger and more elaborately decorated. Each bag is burned with some coats and trousers cut out of paper.

In very rich families, music may accompany the ritual homage before the family altar as well as the *shu pao* ceremony, but this is unusual. A big container with some ashes and a bit of fire is placed in the middle of the courtyard just outside the west wing of the house. A young member of the household then kneels on a straw cushion beside the container, facing the west wing. The rest of the household may be sitting or standing around him. All the bags are heaped beside the kneeler. He first picks up the bag for the most ancient lineal ancestor, reads slowly everything that is written on it, and then puts it on the fire. As he does so, another member will throw on the same fire one or two suits of the paper coats and trousers. This procedure is repeated with all the bags, and in many cases it may take one or two hours to complete the ceremony. After all bags are burned, the ashes are poured into a stream which finally carries them into the lake.

Shortly after the household ceremony and sometimes while it is still going on, the worship in the clan temples begins. Families who have no clan temples omit this ceremony; those who have them never fail to perform it. Although this is more formal than the worship at the family altar, the degree of formality varies from clan to clan. I watched such ceremonies in five temples in the years 1942 and 1943 and have had several informants describe for me the ceremonies in four others. The most elaborate and formal ceremony appears to have taken place in Yi temple.

In 1943 the clan was represented by one or two male members from each household, totaling about 140 individuals. Two men were elected in advance each year from among the senior and more active members of the clan to act as treasurers as well as general managers of the ceremony. With the help of junior members of the clan they had the temple cleaned before the occasion, the altars decorated, and the kitchens made ready for use. A team of volunteer cooks who prepared a number of special offering dishes was chosen from among the clan members. In the temple a pair of big candles was lighted on the table before the center altar. The tables before the side altars held incense burners, but no candlesticks. Large numbers of lighted incense sticks were inserted in each burner.

As soon as the hired bugler and drummer arrived, the ceremony was begun. All male individuals present, including those who had cooking and other duties to perform, stood in six or seven rows of about twenty each facing the main altar in the hall. Without regard for wealth, power, or learning, the rows were arranged in order of seniority with regard to generation and age. The older men of the senior generation came first, followed by the younger ones of the same generation, and then the older men of the succeeding generation. One member stood aside and acted as master of ceremonies. After giving an order for the rows to be formed and another order for them to kneel down, the master of ceremonies knelt down too and proceeded to read aloud from a document written on yellow paper. This was a general report about the clan and its prosperity. It was called Piao and contained the names of all living male descendants of the clan. The names were included by order of seniority in generation and age, as in the formation of the rows. After the reading, the document was burned. While it was being burned, the master of ceremonies gave orders for the kneeling congregation to kowtow: once, twice, thrice, and a fourth time. He then shouted "Stand up," and pronounced the completion of the ceremony.

Musicians played during the ceremony, except for the

period when the general report was being read aloud. As soon as the ceremony was completed, five bags of paper ingots were burned to the ancestors. One large bag with some special decoration was marked for the "very first ancestor" (the ancestor of origin). The other four were marked for "all ancestors of all generations." All five bags were provided by "all descendants of the Y clan." After this event the company sat down at various tables to eat a hearty meal. The seating was also more or less in accordance with seniority of generation and age.

In sharp contrast to the lack of formality at household altars, generally the temple ceremony calls for the wearing of one's best clothes. Most of the elders wore the ceremonial short coat on top of their gowns. The atmosphere during the entire proceeding was very solemn. There was no joking, laughter, or unnecessary noise or movement.

On the same day, however, the ceremony in the T clan temple was much less formal and orderly. T family, it is to be remembered, is one of the wealthiest families in the community, and the difference cannot, therefore, be explained on an economic basis. The ceremony in this temple was also accompanied by music. A "report" was read and burned. Then members of the clan knelt and kowtowed, two at a time, before the central altar. It was not specified who should make up the pairs, nor did the worshipers perform in order of seniority of age or generation. What relaxed the atmosphere more than anything else was the fact that on each side of the veranda just outside the main hall two tables of majong were going full swing. Both tables were crowded and noisy. The gamblers, among whom were some of the most important members of the clan, did not take their turn in performing the ritual worship until they had finished settling the final score of their game. It should be mentioned that the manner of worship in the T clan temple was not typical.

Observation and information concerning the ancestor festivals in other ancestral temples showed that none of them were similar in atmosphere to that of the T clan.

The ceremony at lesser ancestral temples, such as those of Ch clan and a Y clan, was performed without the accompaniment of music, but with much solemnity. A likely explanation for the aberration at T clan temple is that those present at this temple were largely young men. The more venerable members of the clan were absent at the time.

The cooks for these events may be hired professionals rather than volunteers from among members as in the cases described. If volunteers are depended upon, women usually come and help generously. In a Ch clan temple women members came into the main hall and conversed with other members of the clan. They also distributed bits of the food from the offering to members who were sitting on two benches on the platform outside the main hall. They did not, however, partake of the feast.

Generally the expenses incurred during the temple service are met in three ways: (1) "share money"—equal amounts paid by different households of the clan, (2) income from clan property (if there is any), and (3) surplus cash left over from a previous temple service (if any). Such a surplus is usually lent to one or more clan members at interest. Both the capital and the interest will be paid back to cover the expenses of the next temple service. If there is a deficit, it is invariably covered by some wealthy member of the clan. In one case the amount of "share money" was not even fixed in advance. At the end of the rituals, members of the clan who were present discussed it in the most friendly manner. Most members, in view of the expenses, wanted to pay $30 each for the occasion. But the man in charge of the service for that year demurred. He emphasized that each member household should pay $10.00 or at most $15.00 and that he would make up the rest. He was the wealthiest man in the clan. Finally, most members left $20 with the temporary treasurer.

In larger clans a balance sheet showing income and outgo is posted on the wall of the temple shortly afterwards. The smaller clans tend to be informal and save themselves the trouble.

COMMUNAL WORSHIP

Between the first and the fifteenth of the Seventh Moon, although homage is rendered ancestors at all family altars, a number of communal services also take place. These meetings are based on areas within the community and may be on an extensive or a limited scale. In 1943 there were at least six such meetings, organized and performed by hired priests. The most elaborate one was held at the most important temple of the community, Chiu Tan Shen. It lasted four days, from the sixth to the ninth of the month. To this meeting 98 shops or firms and 140 household units contributed, including all the prominent citizens of the community.

The meetings have two main purposes: on one hand, they will save all spirits who are ancestors of the town's inhabitants, so that they may be freed from the consequences of any possible sin committed before death; on the other hand, the meetings uplift and give comfort to all spirits who have no living descendants and may be roaming about the town, causing the spirits to leave the vicinity and thus not be potential sources of trouble for the living.

A few days before the 1943 communal service, a board of managers was organized by elders who volunteered. They, in turn, appointed an impressive array of other officials, similar to those in charge of any cholera meeting.[4] Before the event, this body mounted large posters everywhere, bearing the following inscriptions: GREAT CHUNG YUAN PRAYER MEETING: PRAY AND ABSTAIN WITH ALL EARNESTNESS, DIRT AND UNCLEANLINESS ARE FORBIDDEN (in large characters). The family members of the recently deceased and those who wished to have him uplifted were advised to apply with full particulars at the temple on the seventh of the month. The procedure of registration was

[4] F. L. K. Hsu, *Magic and Science in Western Yunnan*, p. 11.

similar to that of communication with the dead. Any household which had made a donation, however small, was entitled to register, and the ancestors so registered might include not only the recently deceased but also those of a number of generations earlier.

Descendants whose ancestors were thus registered had no further responsibilities; the priests did everything on their behalf. The whole ritual, though arduous and continuous for four days and four nights, was comparatively simple in terms of its component elements. The first day was mainly occupied by invoking the gods and presenting to them a petition for leniency. On the same day a special trip of invitation was made by all the priests and their assistants. They went in procession to a temple on the hill west of the town. A huge bell was temporarily moved to the temple in town where the prayer meeting took place. A similar trip was made to the temple of one of the local patron gods. The second and the third days consisted of extensive chanting of the scriptures by the priests. Quantities of offerings in food and paper money were also made. Papers on which the names of various deceased family members were written were first put on the altar and then burned. The last day was occupied by a "sending-home visit." The same priests visited a temple on the hill and that of a local patron god. During these visits the priests would pay homage to any temple or images of gods met on the way. The entire proceeding was accompanied by drums and stringed and wind instruments.

The gods worshiped during such a communal service included most of those listed in Chapter VI. The idea behind it was that the more gods supplicated, the better the chances of those who were to be uplifted. Figuring largely among the gods invoked was, of course, the Supreme Ruler of the Lower World of Spirits. It is to be recalled that that world is the destiny of the majority of the dead, who may be honored, sent on to the Western Heaven, given official posts, tortured, imprisoned in hells, or refused another chance of reincarnation, according to their merits. The large numbers of ancestral names registered on this occasion indicates the important place that the practice holds in the minds of the local populace.

The Third Moon pilgrimage and the Seventh Moon festivity are duties that all descendants must execute for their ancestors. The descendants must provide comfort for the dead: giving them food, clothing, and money, paying their respects, and spending a period of time with them. It is, however, dangerous to display food and comfort before the hungry and the needy without giving them part of the food and comfort. To do so is to arouse those spirits who may roam about penniless, having no place to rest their tired feet. These unknown and dissatisfied spirits may create difficulties in two ways: they may either cause the living to get sick and destroy their houses by fire, or they may give trouble to the more fortunately situated spirits. These are, so to speak, the potential thieves and bandits in the world of spirits.

The two most important ways of dealing with these vagabond spirits are: the *sa pai jer* ritual and the institution of public story-telling during the entire 7th Moon of every year.

Sa pai jer literally means "spreading of porridge." The ritual is performed as part of the communal worship of ancestors or for overcoming an epidemic, and is part of the ritual at the clan temples. In all three instances the procedure is identical. The difference lies in the fact that it originates in particular clan temples in the third case, while in the other two cases, it begins in the temple where the prayer meeting has taken place. In all cases it is performed primarily by young people of the community. On the evening of the 15th of the 7th Moon every clan which has a temple observes this ritual.

Toward the evening which marked the conclusion of the prayer meeting in 1943, a huge quantity of porridge was cooked in several boilers in the courtyard of the temple. A group of male volunteers gathered. Two of them carried one of the boilers on a pole; a third man had a long wooden spoon, a fourth a basketful of paper money and paper coats and trousers, a basketful of incense sticks was brought by a fifth person, and two others held torches. Lastly, several men carried and played a gong, a drum, and a pair of cymbals.

Starting at the gate of the temple, the man with the spoon spread some porridge on the ground. Following him, another man laid some paper money and a suit of paper clothes (consisting of one coat and one pair of trousers) near the porridge. Another man placed some lighted incense sticks on the clothes while the latter were being burned by the torches. When this was done, one of them shouted: "One string of money, one coat, one pair of trousers, and one spoon of porridge. Nobody is allowed to retain more." This procedure was completely repeated at six or seven-foot intervals covering the entire distance from the gate of the temple to the big tree which marks the community's boundary on the west side and at which all formal funeral processions stop. The distance is about three quarters of a mile and the ceremony takes about two hours. The porridge, the clothes, the incense sticks, and the money are provisions for vagabond spirits, and the idea is to insure that they leave town after this event.

The most interesting practice observed in this ritual, however, reveals an important West Town attitude toward spirits. So far we have evidence of two classes of spirits in addition to higher gods: ancestors and relatives on the one hand, and vagabond and unrelated spirits on the other. The disposition of the first group of spirits is friendly without question; that of the second group is ambiguous, for the unrelated spirits are at best indifferent and may be very dangerous if offended or too hard pressed by want. But to West Towners there is evidently a third group of spirits—those of the Mohammedan dead. The Chinese Mohammedans, it should be recalled, do not worship ancestors and have great cultural differences from the rest of the Chinese. The most striking contrast is their attitude toward pork.

In many instances, at the end of the foregoing order of "One string of money, one coat, one pair of trousers, and one spoon of porridge, nobody is allowed to retain more" the shouter added:

> Hu huei tze tou bai zou,
> Na t'ao-ge-na dai zou niu
>
> If despicable Mohammedans come,
> Give them a segment of pig's intestine.

Since the Mohammedans do not eat pork, the mention of pig's intestine is calculated to drive their spirits away from the provisions. But inasmuch as all West Towners are aware of the fact that Mohammedans are sensitive about pork, so they must also know that these words will certainly not please their spirits. Yet few West Towners appear to worry about this point. As a matter of fact, in practically all performances of *sa pai jer,* both in 1942 and in 1943, this additional sentiment was proclaimed freely. The shouters only refrained from adding it when the party came to a point along the route within hearing of the Mohammedan village. Informants told me that in the past years some bloody fights had occurred between West Towners and inhabitants of the Mohammedan village as a result of those words.

The animosity between the two communities is beyond the scope of the present volume. One conclusion that may be drawn from the above evidence is that only vagabond spirits of the dead who are of the same *in-group* as the living may be harmful to the latter if unsatisfied and offended. West Towners are evidently not afraid of offending Mohammedan spirits of the dead.[5]

Public storytelling takes place on any day or days during

---

[5] I am not certain that West Towners consider inhabitants of the neighboring Mohammedan village as of a different racial group in the same sense as they would Europeans. It is definite that the Mohammedans are not regarded by West Towners as members of the same community.

It is interesting to note that preliterate peoples are not, as a rule, afraid of enemy magic. Also, taboos do not operate on children or others who are entirely innocent of them.

the entire Seventh Moon. Usually one or several well-to-do families hire a storyteller. The latter will relate their tales for one to three days in or outside the courtyard of one of the patrons. Every performance is open to all—men, women, and children. In any normal year five or six men will be contracted for storytelling during this month. The storytellers are usually from some distant village, although some West Towners are expert storytellers and often take part on an amateur basis.

In 1943 I watched several such performances. One of them was held in the courtyard of a Ch family. The storyteller and his musician assistant sat on a temporary platform, and the audience sat on benches and stools. The story was very long. It was partly sung in rhymed verses and partly spoken in prose. The singing part was accompanied by the plucking of a three-stringed musical instrument. The sessions, lasting more than three hours, took place during the day as well as at night. In the evening, the gathering was illuminated with petromex lamps.

Other performances had similar arrangements. The largest gathering listened to a storyteller in the Market Square (Ssu Fang Kai). He and his musician were paid by donations from the entire community. They gave six performances, lasting three days and three nights in all.

Some of the stories told were popular everywhere in China, and others were peculiar to West Yunnan. One of the widely known tales was that of Liang Shan Pai and Chu Ying T'ai. It is a love story bearing a strong likeness to *Romeo and Juliet* and depicts two young lovers who died by mistake, but evidently became united for eternity. One of the local stories described the misery of a young man who squandered the inheritance bequeathed him by his parents. He was obliged to make a long trip to locate his patrilineal first cousin who had passed the imperial examinations with the highest honors. Later the young man reformed and also prospered.

These performances obviously provided ample amusement for all West Towners, but their major function was to soothe the vagabond spirits and make them harmless. There was some difference of opinion among the informants as to how this aim was to be accomplished. Some informants thought that a number of stories were about the reincarnation of spirits and that the tales had the effect of uplifting the unfortunate ones. The majority felt that the stories were mainly based upon themes of loyalty to the ruler, filial piety, fidelity of women, and righteousness. The tales would pacify the malcontents so that they would feel happier and leave without getting into any mischief.[6] One informant put it thus: "Some people have died a natural (good) death; others a bad death. Some feel that they should not have died and have their minds bent on revenge. These stories will make their spirits see the light or perhaps persuade them to go away more readily."

[6] A small number of West Towners insisted that these stories were for the purpose of amusement only.

CHAPTER VIII

Introduction to the Ancestral Ways

EDUCATION, formal or informal, is the means by which all groups maintain their social continuity. Education may be focused on the future—on experimentation and the development of the young as young—or it may be concerned with the past—with shaping the young according to the image of the old.

Many shades exist between the extremes, but education in West Town is almost exclusively the inculcation of the ancestral tradition. The past is the model of the present, and both are charters of the future. We have seen how the bond between old and young is not broken by death. Instead, this bond is perpetuated by the ritual of communication with and worship of the dead. Moreover, ancestors are not only worshiped, but also held to be the sources and bases of the socialization of younger generations. At any given period of time the family, in the minds of West Towners, is but a continuation of past generations and a preparation for the coming descendants to live in accordance with the wishes of the ancestors. One cannot talk about ancestors without in some way relating them to grandsons and great grandsons, nor can one talk about future members of the clan without constantly keeping in mind their source or origin.

BIRTH AND CARE OF INFANTS

A pregnant woman has to observe various restrictions and taboos, some of which are intended to influence the foetus. A pregnant woman must not get angry or quarrel with anyone. If she does so, her child will have a bad temper. She should not work on jobs which require the lifting of heavy weights or reach for things high above her head. She must not go to temples to look at certain images, particularly those of the cow-faced and horse-faced gods. She must not look at an eclipsed sun or moon, but neither must she sleep during any eclipse. Violation of this taboo means that her baby will be born with a harelip.

If a woman remains happy and not quarrelsome during her months of pregnancy, her baby will be good-natured and clever.

Often a pregnant mother consults a diviner before giving her unborn baby a name. This will be the baby's "small name," which is used at home. This procedure will insure the coming baby against illness and evil spirits.

The birth of the baby is assisted by a local midwife, who knows nothing about sterilizing. There are a number of such midwives in the community. The modern hospital, though within reach of every family of moderate means, is not resorted to by all of them. There is a strong prejudice against sending women folk to a public institution, especially on such a critical occasion as child birth.

A difficult labor is caused by ghosts who are ill-disposed toward past or present members of the family. In such a case, a witch (man or woman), who is supposed to have spiritual eyes, is invited to the house to examine the nature of the ghosts. Ghosts which give West Towners trouble nowadays come mainly from one of five spots in the community (indicated on the map in Chapter I). About twenty years ago a group of strongly organized bandits came south from Teng Chuan district and entrenched themselves in West Town. They had a good time until they were rounded up by a strong government force. Most of them were executed at these five spots. Ever since, their ghosts have lingered near the places of execution. For the past twenty years the witch man or woman has usually given one of the spots as the source of trouble for all cases under consideration. The witch often deduces that the woman passed one of these places while pregnant and somehow offended one of the ghosts of the dead bandits. The injured ghost followed her home and at the time of the birth of her child wanted to oust the rightful soul and thus be born as her son. The struggle caused difficult labor.

When such is the diagnosis, the mother-in-law of the pregnant woman and some other relatives will go to the designated place and perform a rite of propitiation. The ritual consists of prayers and offerings. The elderly women take five pairs of straw sandals, one or more bunches of incense, some paper money, paper clothes, and three or more items of food. At the designated spot they arrange the five pairs of sandals in a circle. Inside the circle they burn the paper money and clothes, together with the incense. Outside the circle they place the items of food. After kowtowing and praying (requesting the ghost's departure in persuasive tones, etc.), the assembled women partake of the food, throwing some of it on the flames, which are beginning to burn the sandals. If there are passers-by who care to take some of the food, they are welcome. The women say that when passers-by partake of the food, the spirits will be even more pleased.

A few days after the child is born a ceremony called "Celebrating the *sao chu*" takes place. *Sao chu* means "three days" (after the birth of the child), but the celebration may take place much later. Wealthier families, for whom this is a big event, require many days for preparation. The celebration usually takes place only for firstborn children. The birth of other children, though in some cases hailed with ceremony, is marked by much less elaborate events. These take place without regard to the sex of the newly born, though that for a male child may be more impressive.

The celebration of birth has its ritual and social aspects. Of a ritual nature are the following: offerings to ancestors, to the kitchen god, to all gods in the family shrine, and (most important) to the local patron god. These offerings are made partly to express gratitude and partly to report the arrival of the new member. The first two offerings are simple, like those made on the first and fifteenth of every moon, except that there are more items of food on the offering table.

The offering to the patron god is more elaborate. It is usually made by the baby's grandmother. In her absence, some other female relative will make it. She assembles a number of items of food and incense, and, usually accompanied by some children of the household, male or female, goes to the temple. The food offering usually consists of *gana* (a kind of fried rice cake, very thin and dyed in various colors, which is always an item in any ritual offering), one wheat cake, a salted pig's head, one chicken egg, one goose egg, a kitchen knife, wine, and some tea leaves. They enter the temple, put most of the food in front of the main shrine, and then prostrate themselves to pay homage to all gods and goddesses of the temple.

The old lady will begin at the main shrine, go next to the two shrines on each side of it, and lastly go to the minor altars in the same temple, including the dragons on each of the two pillars. She will kowtow about fifty times before each of the gods in the first three shrines and about eight or nine times before each of the other gods and the dragons. Before she leaves the main shrine, she puts part of the offering on a tray and places it in front of each of the shrines which she successively visits, burning a small quantity of paper money at each shrine. She kowtows while the paper burns.

The social side of the occasion may be celebrated as is a wedding, but on a smaller scale. Practically all the guests are women, however, and most of them are fairly close relatives. The family of the new mother figures conspicuously. All guests carry with them gifts: some red eggs, some reddened walnuts, baby's garments, or some ornaments for the baby, such as a silver locket. The guests are feasted to the best ability of the family (in some cases

150–200 guests are served) and each receives one red egg on departure to take home for its blessing.

A month after the birth, a pair of new shoes is made for the baby. The next important occasion is the one hundredth day after birth. In some families this is a more elaborate occasion than the one on the third day, but in general the same kind of social and ritual requirements are fulfilled.

On the first birthday a boiled egg is given the child to eat. Offerings are made at the family shrine, and better food than usual is served to all in the household.

A woman in confinement cannot pass through the main portal to the family home, because her "unclean" body will give offense to the gods guarding it. If she is obliged to go out by the house door, she must wear a hat.

During the period of confinement, which usually lasts about a month, the mother is usually assisted by her mother-in-law or some other relative. Rarely does her own mother come to her for this purpose. After the first month, the baby is cared for by its mother, unless she is too busy, in which case her mother-in-law or someone else in the household may attend to the infant's needs.

All infants are fed at the mother's breast as a matter of course. If the unfortunate mother has no milk, porridge or cow's milk will be administered freely. The local people feel that an infant whose mother has no milk has rather poor chances of survival. The breast is given the infant as soon as he cries and is taken away when the little one has gone to sleep, even in the middle of a feeding.

Handling the diaper is exclusively a woman's concern, largely the mother's. At each change of diaper, the lower part of the infant's body may be rinsed with water. Apart from this, there is no idea of a regular bath. Diapers are changed as soon as the mother can manage it. If the mother is hard pressed by work, the infant may stay wet for a couple of hours. But from the time the infant is two or three months old, it is seldom left alone. If the mother is not with it, some other member of the household, a girl or older woman, and occasionally a man, will be there to hold it, give it food, fondle it, or make it smile. When the mother goes to the market, the infant is often tied securely to her, its stomach against her back. In this manner it may be carried for considerable distances. When the infant is a male, he may be carried in this way until he is two or three years of age. Females are as a rule carried for shorter periods.

Every infant illness, as is difficult labor, is attributed to evil spirits who may be unfavorably disposed toward past or present members of the family. Some medical advice is sought, but invariably the first step after the discovery of a child's illness is to propitiate the spirits or to consult a seer or a witch. The most common symptom of ailing infants is insomnia. It is interpreted to mean that the child has lost its soul. The standard cure for the trouble is as follows: The child's mother, grandmother, or father's sister takes a bowl filled with raw rice, in the center of which an egg has been stood on end. The bowl is taken to a street corner outside the family portal. Here two incense sticks are inserted in the ground, some paper money is burned, and the rice and egg ritually offered. After kowtowing, the child's name is called continuously, while the elderly woman walks home with the rice and egg.

In the case of a more serious illness, a seer or a witch is consulted. The witch will indicate one of the previously mentioned execution spots as the source of trouble. A propitiation ritual, such as that which takes place in the case of difficult labor, is performed without delay.

Every cure known and believed in by the people will be resorted to in order to restore a child's health. Of course, the effort expended for a male child is considerably more than that for a female.[1]

After the death of a child less than one year of age no ceremony takes place. The little body is simply taken out of

---

[1] For a wider discussion of the attitude and treatment of illnesses in this community the reader is referred to F. L. K. Hsu, *Magic and Science in Western Yunnan,* Institute of Pacific Relations, 1943.

the house, rolled in a straw mat, and buried in some unused ground outside the town. Wild dogs will search it out and eat it. Rich families have been known to use coffins for their children who died less than one year after birth. There is no rigid rule on this matter, however, and it seems to be decided by the financial ability of the family.

If more than one child dies in close succession, a different mode of disposal of the body is used. This is especially true after two or three children in one family have died within the span of a few years. Then the face of the second child who dies will be slapped by shoes, and its body will be thrown into the lake instead of being buried in the ground. The belief behind these actions is that such repeated deaths are caused by *Tou Sa Guer,* or Life Stealing Ghosts. These ghosts come and go, exacting services and goods by being born as children into innocent families. If thrown into the water, the ghosts will not be able to reincarnate again. The people believe that the soul of a person will reincarnate four months after death, but that a person who died by drowning cannot reincarnate unless he gets a victim to substitute for him.

Instead of the shoe slapping, a little soot from the under surface of a boiler may be smeared on the face of the dead baby. The resultant mark is supposed to discourage the same ghost from coming into the family again, because it could then be recognized.

Instead of throwing the bodies into water, some families hang them on trees, because of the current belief that any soul whose body does not touch earth has lost its power of reincarnation.

These measures are resorted to regardless of whether the dead children are male or female.

EDUCATIONAL OBJECTIVES

The aims of education in West Town are primarily intended to mold members of the younger generation after the pattern of their parents, grandparents, and remoter ancestors. There is no idea of helping children to develop as children, each with his or her individual personality. Attention is directed only to preparing children to assume their traditionally prescribed roles in adult life as soon as possible.

Educational objectives may be classified into three main groups: training for livelihood, for social adequacy, and for ritual appropriateness. Before proceeding, we must clarify two social categories, the rich and the poor.

It is difficult to decide, as noted before, the exact line of demarcation between rich and poor. But at any given point of time the extremes are not hard to observe. In West Town there are those who live in huge and elaborate family homes, have much money and many shops, have possessed actual or pretended official connections in the past or now possess them, will put on extravagant celebrations for funerals, weddings, or other occasions, and will have their names high on the list of contributors to any communal cause. On the other hand, some live in humbler one-story dwellings, can barely manage to make ends meet, do not show any sign of bureaucratic aspirations, and are small spenders on all occasions. Between these two groups of extremes there is a middle ground, consisting of many grades. Within this last group are borderline cases which are difficult to separate. For convenience, hereafter one extreme will be designated as the "rich," and the other as the "poor." The number of people who may be classified as rich is, even in West Town, in the minority; but the number of those who may come under the other category is much larger, even approximating a majority.

Aspects of livelihood activities have been examined in Chapter III. We have seen that in this respect there is fundamentally little difference between the sexes. What we did not touch upon is the fact that insofar as livelihood activities are concerned there appears to be a wide gulf between the rich and the poor. The rich rarely work in the fields. Members of the literati or their sons always have higher aspirations. Trading is engaged in by a very large number of West Towners. Both rich and poor find their way to the markets not only as buyers but also as sellers. But while in families of moderate means both men and women enter the market places, in families of wealth and social distinction only women do so. The wife of B. B., for example, whose brother is the principal of the local middle school and whose family is one of the wealthiest, is often seen in the market carrying a basketful of rice and waiting for a customer. The young concubine of the old man of the same family may be similarly engaged. Girl students of the local middle school have been seen in the market selling cloth. No males from families of corresponding status have been observed so occupied.

In shops and large firms the same division of training is observed. The sons of the owners of small shops will learn their trade from the bottom up. They must work as hard as their parents do if they want to exist. For the sons of very wealthy families, on the other hand, the story is totally different. First, it would be considered a social indignity to their parents if they should work even in their own firms, let alone as apprentices in other establishments. It is more usual for the boys to go to school in a half-hearted manner or otherwise idle away their time. If the young people are interested in business, more likely than not they will attempt to make "killings" by starting their own "half-baked" enterprises with resources supplied by their rich fathers.

In education for social adequacy there are four component elements; the first is filial piety, which is the foundation stone of West Town social organization. It would be no exaggeration to say that it is the measuring stick of all behavior and of the worth of the individual. It provides the most important reason, consciously upheld, for the cult of ancestors. Filial piety as understood by Confucianists, as well as by West Towners, means that children (especially sons) must please, follow, and support their parents while the latter are alive; they must mourn and ritually serve them after their death. In addition, it is incumbent upon any man to continue his male line. We have seen how, in its functioning, filial piety is far from being a one-sided matter.

The second element in social adequacy may be described as estrangement between the sexes. This is necessary primarily because, as has been shown, the development of a close relationship between the sexes is considered detrimental to the supremacy of filial pity. Estrangement works out differently for the two sexes. In the first place, women must not be attractive to men and must not display their personal charms. Those who do so are regarded as licentious. In the second place, sex is considered unclean, and women carry the burden of this uncleanliness. That is why there are various taboos on mothers who have just given birth and on women during menstruation. Thirdly, women are inferior to men and must assume a strictly subordinate role. Parents show greater preference for and indulgence to boys. Older brothers can punish their younger sisters, but older sisters may not punish their younger brothers. It follows, therefore, that on the men's part there is generally a disrespectful avoidance of women. If a man, for example, encounters an angry woman who is not related to him and avoids her wrath by a quick exodus from her presence, it is not because he lacks courage, but rather that getting involved in a quarrel with an unrelated woman is an ill omen.

The pattern has probably never been put clearly by any West Towner, but the norm would seem to be this: Men must never fight women other than their wives and sisters; if they do, it will be a bad omen for them and they will have degraded themselves. Women have to respect their husbands, fathers, older brothers, and other related senior males; if they do not, they will find themselves becoming social outcasts.

The third element of social adequacy is the emphasis on

loyalty to the household, clan, affinal relations, and the community. But there is considerable ambiguity about each category. We have seen that the really basic point of cohesion is the individual family and that it requires the clever device of division under the same roof to hold the joint household together. Therefore, the degree of loyalty tends to diminish as we come to the larger and more inclusive groupings. These circles of loyalty tend, also, to become more or less temporary, for such loyalty is only reiterated when there is a conflict of interests between two groups. If two members of the same household quarrel, loyalty to the household is usually set aside. On the other hand, if two persons of different clans quarrel and a third party from one of the two clans happens to be a disinterested bystander, it may actually result in friction between the two members of the same clan—because by being disinterested the bystander showed no loyalty to his clan.

It is to be recalled that the wealthiest and the most powerful family of the T clan has often been criticized for not giving the best opportunities to its own clan members.

Interest in these several wider circles of loyalty is influenced by another factor, the social status of the individuals involved. That is, those whom we have classified as "rich" tend to be much more interested in these wider groupings than those whom we have classified as "poor." This fact is closely connected with the fourth element in social adequacy, competition.

At first sight it is hard to appreciate the importance of the sense of competition in a social organization based upon filial piety and ancestral authority. But there is really no incompatibility. The sense of competition may be expressed along conventional lines or it may be expressed in the opposite direction. In West Town, the former is the case.

Within the bounds of convention there is, however, a wide range of choice both as to methods and objects. Here we come upon the most important distinctions between the rich and the poor. The sons of the poor will try their best to get ahead by hard work in order to reach some degree of social and economic comfort. The sons of the rich, on the other hand, will receive every encouragement to out-rank others by exaggerating their paternal and ancestral prestige and power.

To reach their respective objectives, the poor resort to economy and industry, while the rich resort to extrava-gance and ostentation in graveyards, family homes, and ceremonials. The greater their excesses in these and other respects, the greater will be their prestige and power.

This sense of competition among the rich also involves giving alms to the poor and contributing to communal rain pleadings or cholera prayer meetings. These are all tra-ditionally "good deeds." New items of competition have occasionally been added in recent years. The hospital and the several schools in the community were built with dona-tions from a few top-ranking families. That these are not contributions to causes inherent in the function of the in-stitutions thus built may be seen from the fact that the same families are also generous supporters and active par-ticipants in cholera prayers and rain-pleading parties. Again, when the T people talked about building a middle school in the locality, the Ye people and the Y people wanted to be on the list of contributors. The T family decided that the institution had to be recognizably T or nothing. The final decision was that the T family should provide all the build-ings, and the Ye all the furnishings. For several years the T family could not supply adequate sums of money for all the planned buildings. They decided to build them part by part, as most West Towners build their family homes. The head of the T family was born in the "Tiger" year (one of the horoscopic signs in a twelve-year cycle), so on the front of the main building of the school is painted a tiger in bright colors.

Thus, we have a situation in which both the poor and the rich exhibit a strong drive for competition, but the methods and the objects of their competition are different. For the poor, the method is hard work and frugality, and the object is some degree of social and economic security. For the rich the method is exhibition of arrogance and excess in wasteful consumption, and the object is parental and ancestral glory.

This competition does not aim to annihilate equals or superiors, but each individual and his group attempts to reach a more favorable position on a traditionally defined hierarchical social framework.

However, it is not to be supposed that the object of social adequacy of the category of families which has been designated as "poor" will permanently remain as I have described it. In fact, even while the people have to be frugal and industrious to make ends meet, they tend to regard frugality and industriousness as but necessary evils of the poor. As soon as circumstances permit, that is, as soon as the fortune of the family has risen, they or their sons tend to follow the other line of competition, the line of families which has been designated as "rich."

Apart from two points of difference, social adequacy for the female is substantially the same as that for the male: the women are subordinated to the authority of the male, and because of the principle of sex segregation goals of competition for women are largely confined to household or minor business affairs. The result is that they are, so to speak, social inferiors to the male, and they exert much less influence over their husbands and male children than the males do over them.

The third and last category of educational aims deals with spirits. The spiritual world is a supplement of the social world. Ritual appropriateness is therefore a supplement of social adequacy. As had been made clear, from the point of view of man's relation with them, spirits are divided into four broad classes: (1) ancestral spirits; (2) spirits of persons not related by kinship or marriage; (3) spirit officials; (4) spirits of a different culture. To living descendants their own ancestral spirits are always benevolent, never malicious, and never offended by the descendants. The attitude of the descendants toward their ancestors is strictly defined in terms of filial duties and, therefore, of more social than ritual importance.

The disposition of the spirits in categories (2) and (3) is varied. They are of all levels. The spirit officials, who rule over a multitude of spirits including ancestors and descendantless spirit vagrants, are arranged in a hierarchy, like that of the official hierarchy in the world of the living. These spirits may be kindly, helpful, benign, malicious, or severe.

The spirits of another cultural or racial group are merely irrelevant entities. They are neither feared nor welcomed. They do not influence the West Towner's relation with the other world at all.

As a result, West Towners attend to mainly the second and third categories of spirits. The essential principle of action is never to antagonize any malicious spirits, lest they do you harm, never to alienate the kindly ones, lest they refuse to come to your aid when you are particularly in need. To play safe, it is necessary to please or at least to avoid offending all these spirits, a complicated problem, for which there is no single solution. Taboos must be observed; if they are broken, some spirits will be offended. Sinful behavior must be eliminated; if it is committed, the kitchen god or other spiritual inspectors will have it reported. Ritual offerings to the proper deities must be made at the prescribed time; if they are overlooked, the expectant deities will be annoyed. But suppose one has broken some taboos. Suppose one has committed sinful behavior. Or suppose one has neglected important ritual offerings. It still does not mean the doom of the culprit, because special propitiatory rites may be performed to pacify the angry gods.

In this connection the basic psychological process involved in achieving ritual adequacy can be demonstrated.

The special propitiatory rites are either efforts to win lost favors by more extensive ceremonies and richer offerings to the same gods or gestures of submission to still higher authority, by invoking deities more exalted than the ones offended. The more serious the crisis, the clearer becomes the evidence. The best example of such propitiation rites occurred during a cholera epidemic in the early part of 1942, when a heavy toll of life was taken. The epidemic was caused by the wrath of certain deities as a result of Man's sinful behavior. In order to ward off calamity it was necessary to perform more and greater rites and to make more and richer offerings. It was equally necessary to invoke more and higher gods. The chief priest of the largest prayer meeting held in the community gave me the following statement.

> In order to avert the disaster, it is necessary to invoke the mercy of superior deities who will require the Wen God to retract the Wen spirits which he let loose earlier. It is necessary to invoke as many superior deities as possible. . . . More deities are invoked each day of the prayer meeting, so that a one-day affair may invoke a much smaller number of deities than a two-day one. The latter, again, is less effective than a three-day affair. Usually three days and four nights are an adequate duration, but for real perfection seven or eight more days are desirable.[2]

During the crisis sixteen prayer meetings were held in different sections of the community. To organize a meeting like that of other suppliants was not enough. A section that was financially able would try to perform a bigger and more elaborate ceremony than any other group. The competitive efforts were not intended to destroy the opportunities of other sections, but merely to achieve a more favorable relation with the deities concerned.

The aims of education discussed in the foregoing pages may be seen in tabulated form as follows:

[2] F. L. K. Hsu, *Magic and Science in Western Yunnan*, p. 15.

EDUCATIONAL OBJECTIVES IN WEST TOWN

	Livelihood	Social adequacy	Ritual adequacy
Male	Work in fields Trading Work in shops and firms Scholarship	Filial piety Sex estrange- ment Interest in household, clan, etc. Competition in livelihood activities or power, pres- tige, and honors	Pleasure to all spirits that are powerful. At least no offence to any of them Submission to all higher spirits and their author- ity. (They will reward you for good behavior and punish you for bad be- havior.)
Female	Home work Work in fields Trading Work in small shops	Filial piety Sex estrange- ment Interest limited to household Subordination to male Competition in trading and life at home	Individual com- petition for good favors of the higher spirits. (More ritual restrictions on the fe- male, because of her men- struation and association with preg- nancy and birth.)
Rich (male)	Executives in firms Work as boss	Filial piety Sex estrange- ment	

	Livelihood	*Social adequacy*	*Ritual adequacy*
Rich (male)	Scholarship and officialdom Being idle at home	Interest in wider groups more intense Competition in power, prestige, ancestral glory, and in being able to do no work	
Poor (male)	Work in fields Trading Work in shops and firms Work as executives in firms when opportunity becomes available	Filial piety Sex estrangement Interest in wider groups very limited Competition in work for livelihood	

METHODS OF EDUCATION

Direct Participation. The reasons for the different objectives in competition between the rich and the poor are the close father-son tie and the big family ideal, which express themselves most clearly in the methods of education.[3] The most important method of training the young in West Town is direct participation. There is practically no verbalization of the ancestral ways. Children learn by examples.

[3] In writing this section the author has particularly been benefited by a study of O. H. Mowrer and Clyde Kluckhohn: "Dynamic Theory of Personality," in J. McV. Hunt, ed., *Personality and the Behavior Disorders,* 1944, I, 69–131.

As long as they are within the prescribed limits, they are let alone. When and if they blunder, they are told off rather bluntly. There is little effort expended on reasoning with children as to *why* they cannot do certain things. Nor is there an abrupt point at which children are said to be initiated and to have reached adulthood. They are gradually introduced into the life and work of the family and the community.

In general, as we have seen, babies come into contact with a number of individuals besides their mothers. If their mothers are busy, their older sisters, aunts, or grandmothers will administer to their needs. If there is a rule, it is the rule of convenience. We may say that from the point of view of the growing child there is a tendency for these women to merge; that is, in the eyes of the growing child, one woman is likely to be as good as another. On the other hand, in terms of frequency of contact the mother undoubtedly stands out above everybody else both before and long after weaning.

The time of weaning varies. A child is always weaned as soon as the next one is born, but lacking a younger sibling, a child may be fed at its mother's breast for two, three, or even four years. This fact obviously has an important bearing on the child-adult relationship. In a society which emphasizes direct participation, the older a child is when weaned, the older it will be when initiated into the adult world. Elsewhere in China it has been demonstrated that the size of a family seems to correspond with the size of its farm; holders of large farms appear to have large families.[4] From this it may be inferred that children in

[4] C. M. Ch'iao, "A Study of 143 Rural Families in Ch'ing Yuan, Shansi Province" [in Chinese], in *China's Population Problem*, Shanghai (1931), pp. 267–273; C. M. Ch'iao, Warren Thompson, and D. T. Chen, *An Experiment in the Registration of Vital Statistics in China*, Oxford, Ohio, 1938, p. 15; H. F. Feng: *Outline of Rural Sociology*, Shanghai [in Chinese], 1931, pp. 128–132; and Ta Chen, *Population in Modern China*, Chicago, 1946, pp. 30–31, 94. In the last mentioned study two facts are shown: rural population as a whole has higher birth rates than urban population, but among urban population, wealthier classes (those under modern influence excepted) appear to have more than poor ones.

wealthier homes tend to be weaned, and therefore pushed into the adult world, sooner than those under poorer conditions. Unfortunately, we do not have the necessary data on this subject for the community under our consideration.

After weaning, the mother remains the most intimately in contact with children of both sexes for a number of years to come. She is responsible for their clothing, laundry, regular feeding, safety, and discipline. The other women, with the exception of the grandmother (that is, her mother-in-law), will do favors for her children, and they, including the grandmother, will often call her when and if her children are crying in her absence.

Some toilet training occurs when a child is one year of age or older. The child, regardless of sex, is periodically held with its back against the mother's abdomen and both of its legs lifted to induce urination or defecation. But no punishment of any sort has been observed to be inflicted on children in this respect until the youngsters were three or four. There is little or no systematic training or enforcement of diet habits. Children eat with adults as soon as they can; they eat at any other time when and if they can get hold of some food.

In many respects the two sexes are trained for different roles and to assume different attitudes toward life and each other. The point to be emphasized here is that children of both sexes enter the adult world much sooner than do American children. Their childish activities are tolerated, but never encouraged. There is no idea of helping children to play as children. European and American children may worry their parents by behaving like adults; in fact, such parents may consult an analyst or a psychiatrist. West Town children, on the other hand, delight their parents for the same reason. In fact, parents are definitely proud of children whose behavior is mature.

Three elements can be distinguished in participation—observation, imitation, and conscious instruction. In West Town life the first two are most apparent; the third is less frequently encountered.

Most boys and girls are early acquainted with periodic markets. Those whose parents own shops, are soon familiar with shops. If the family home is back of the shop, any member of the family may help with business transactions. If the shop is located in separate premises, young members of the family visit it frequently. For somewhat larger shops the apprenticeship system is used. In such cases only boys are engaged.

The apprentice system is similar to that which is found in other parts of China. It requires the initiate to be apprenticed for about three years or a little more. During this period the boy receives at best a very meager allowance and must work from morning until night at any job ordered by the owner or the master of the shop, who lives in the shop. If the apprentice is the son of the owner, he will be given opportunities to master the job quickly; otherwise a large part of his time will be occupied by the duties of a personal servant to the master. Under such circumstances, the extent of his learning depends upon his own initiative and upon his powers of observation and imitation. When the apprentice begins to handle some of the trade jobs, he will from time to time receive some deliberate instruction from some of the accomplished workers or the master, but rarely is the instruction systematic. Certainly there is nothing comparable to classroom work, nor is there any theoretical elaboration. It is, in other words, a kind of home training transplanted into the shop.

The informal nature of the training is most clearly demonstrated in connection with ritual matters. Boys and girls learn ways to please spirits early in life; they also learn how to avoid offending them. An average boy or girl of thirteen or fourteen must have witnessed a few hundred ritual celebrations or ceremonies, and have participated in a somewhat smaller number. The celebrations of births, deaths, marriages, 15th of the 7th Moon, New Year, birthdays of gods, prayer meetings, and other festivals are the big occasions. All families make offerings to their family shrines on the 1st and the 15th of every moon, and most families do so daily in the morning and in the evening.

The following is an account from my notebook showing how children learn to deal with spirits.

Today I saw old Mrs. Yen with two grandsons and three granddaughters in the Pen Chu Temple. Offerings are made to every "god" (that is, every image) in the whole temple, both inside and outside the main hall. Even the dragons winding around the two main pillars of the main entrance receive a share of the "food and money."

The old lady first burns paper money in front of the three main shrines. There are four gods occupying these shrines. As the paper burns, she kneels down to kowtow fifty times to each of the four gods. The center shrine is occupied by Pen Chu, the local patron god. The shrine to its left is occupied by Niang Niang, or Goddess of Mercy. The two gods occupying the other shrine are not identified. The old lady does not know what they are.

When these gestures of homage are over, she takes some of the food offered at the main shrines and puts it in a tray. She takes this tray and offers it in front of all the images in the temple, one by one. In front of each image the procedure is as follows. She offers the tray by lifting it up with both of her hands to a position above her head. She lays it on the table. She burns some paper money. She kneels down to kowtow eight or more times.

She prays to only the first four gods as she kneels down to kowtow.

Her oldest granddaughter present is twelve. She follows her grandmother. As the old lady finishes kowtowing to one god, she kneels down and kowtows eight times. Following her grandmother, she does the same to all the other images.

The other two girls, four and five years of age respectively, are also learning to kowtow as does their grandmother, but do not do it very well yet. From their appearance it is evident that they are serious about it.

The two boys, who are about the age of the latter two girls, are more playful than serious. They kneel down in front of the images in the wrong order, face them aimlessly, and nod their heads any number of times. Sometimes they look as though they were shaking their heads.

The floor of the temple is brick paved, but dirty. That fact, however, worries no one. Every person kneels down freely, with two hands on the floor.

On this occasion the old lady went to the temple to report to the local patron god on the third day after the birth of a grandson and to express gratitude therefor. Many old ladies visit the temples for various other reasons. In fact, such offerings are common sights in any temple at all times of the year.

But girls soon learn how they differ from their brothers. West Town adults never appear naked in public. They also try their best to hide their unclothed bodies from their children. However, inasmuch as children of seven or eight or older sleep in the same room and often in the same bed with their parents, it is obvious that they are not completely in ignorance of certain physical facts. I know of a number of cases in which a boy of nine or ten has slept in the same bed with his grandmother.

I cannot make a definite statement regarding the age at which male children are no longer allowed to occupy the same bed with their mothers or grandmothers, but I do know of one twenty-year-old son who lived in the same room with his widowed mother, and of a girl of seventeen who lived in the same room with her widowed grandfather. The girl was suitably married just before I left the community, and neither case was considered extraordinary. However, individuals are not allowed to display curiosity about the naked features of the opposite sex. Generally at the age of about four or five the differences in the roles of the two sexes begin to manifest themselves.

As has been pointed out, the nature of education is such that much is taught by way of direct participation. Therefore, the first stages and much of the later stages of the socializing processes are never verbalized. In general, boys follow the examples of their fathers, and girls, their mothers.

Girls begin the process of participation earlier than do boys. For example, at six or seven a girl can already care for her younger brothers and sisters, clean grains, and wash small pieces of clothing at a stream. Shortly afterward she will begin to help with the harvesting and the cooking. When boys are twelve or thirteen they still roam about the town doing whatever they like, while girls of comparable age have already taken over a considerable portion of their mother's burden.

Again, there are wide ritual differences. Boys, for example, are never barred from any occasion of ritual importance; girls, on the other hand, are excluded from most prayer meetings. Boys have very few taboos to observe; girls suffer from a good many ritual disabilities. A girl's clothes, because of their association with her body, cannot be displayed or sunned anywhere in the courtyard as are other clothes. Her menstrual blood, ritually speaking, is the worst kind of impurity. It offends and alienates all spirits. Therefore, during menstruation she must avoid any ritual activity. After the birth of a child she must observe numerous taboos which virtually immobilize her.[5]

The social and ritual differences between the training of the male and that of the female are important, but they are pale in comparison with another group of differences— those between the rich and the poor. These differences do not come about because the culture prescribes them, but because of the existence of the father-son tie and the big-family ideal. For the same reason, the differences between the rich and the poor apply for the most part only to males.

Under the guidance of these two principles the adult male and his sons are inalterably bound together. All parents see some part of themselves in their children. But West Town fathers tend to be more anxious than others to see their sons measure up to their envisioned heights almost from birth. For no part of the adult world, except that of sex,

[5] Of course, the taboos concerning women in confinement have the effect of insuring her recovery, because they probably save her from heavy work, but that is not the way they are phrased or understood by the West Town people. The taboos on a woman in confinement are genetically part of all taboos on women in West Town, and have as their purpose to keep the impurity of the woman's person from coming into contact with spirits which might be alienated or offended.

is closed to the growing child, and no part of the child's world is exclusively his own. No West Town parents are known to have given their children a weekly or monthly allowance with which the youngsters have to make their own ends meet. Every child has as much money as he can get from his parents. Thus, children (especially sons) of the rich tend early in life to indulge in excessive spending. Their parents make little effort to restrain them. In fact, that they are able to squander so freely testifies to the pride and prestige of their parents. Children of the poor, on the other hand, tend, early in life, to realize the disastrous results of any waste. Their parents can give them no pocket money at all.

What is true with regard to money is even more true with regard to other habits of consumption. Rich children tend to indulge in excessive eating; poor children constantly have to tighten their belts.

In this way, the sons of the poor are as poor as their fathers, and the sons of the rich are as rich as their fathers. Normally, therefore, children of the poor learn early to be frugal and industrious; while those of the wealthy are encouraged to be extravagant and carefree. On the poor sons is impressed the importance of earning a living, of making ends meet, and of saving for a rainy day. Subsistence comes to them the hard way. On the rich sons is impressed the pleasure and the dignity of being served and provided for and the importance of being children of the highly placed. It is unnecessary for rich sons to consider whether the cost of their extravagances and vain displays are within or beyond their means. Like their fathers, they do not worry about want. Having power, money will come to them as a matter of course.

In the same way, the sons of the poor or the rich share, respectively, the humility or power of their elders. This, again, means that in the normal course of events children of lowly birth begin life by being humble and careful, while those of the highly placed begin life with the firm belief that they have most of the world in their grasp.

Reward and Punishment. West Town rewards appear in three forms: praise for achievements, wealth, and happy ancestors and prosperous descendants.

Praise may come from parents, family members, or others. It may be given to children as well as to adults. Whether for children or adults, it is given for proficiency in trade, skill in manipulating delicate social situations, extraordinary filial acts to parents, ritual decorum, generosity toward the clan and the community, and individual achievements in scholarship and officialdom. In other words, children are praised for behaving like adults, and adults are praised for success.

Praise may be given verbally, by one person to another, or it may be given by spirits (through mediums) during one of the séances. In the latter case, the person praised is usually dead and is serving as an official somewhere in the spiritual world.

Wealth is sometimes an object of praise, but the sentiment felt toward wealth demands something stronger than praise. Wealth is undoubtedly the immediate incentive to work for the majority of the community. The person who has successfully acquired wealth is often regarded as having done so as a result of his or her ancestors' good deeds and moral character. Conversely, a penniless man is often regarded as having lowered his status by evils committed by him or his forbears.

Happy ancestors imply prosperous descendants, and when descendants are prosperous, ancestors will be happy. Each individual is part of the infinite continuum of the lineage. There is little that West Towners will not do to make their ancestors happy. Those who are successful feel that they have come up to the expectations of the past members of the clan and that they are setting a glorious example for their descendants. Those who are not doing so well hope that sooner or later they will come up to such expectations and set a better example for their descendants.

Women do not come under this system of reward to any great extent. They are often praised socially or by spirits for being dutiful. They also enjoy the feeling that they have happy ancestors and will have prosperous descendants. But no woman is in control of large wealth, in spite of trading, and all women are regarded as being supplementary to their husbands and sons in the family continuum.

Undoubtedly related to their insignificance in the system of earthly reward is the fact that women appear to strive much more for some compensation in the world of spirits than do their husbands, brothers, and sons. This remains true in spite of the fact that only men have been known to become spirit officials with definite ranks after death. At all times the number of women devotees in temples and at home is much larger than that of men.

In contrast to their small connection with the reward system, women figure largely in the punishment system. They are objects of punishment as much as men, if not more so. The simplest form of punishment is scolding or nagging by the parents. The father has the final authority at all times, but the mother deals with children of both sexes before they are ten or a little older. Up till then the father comes into the picture infrequently. When the youngsters are more than ten the father will discipline the male children and the mother the female children. Older brothers can also discipline their younger brothers and, in the absence of the father, occasionally their younger sisters.

According to principles inherent in the kinship structure, authority is also vested in the hands of those who are situated on the same generation level as, or on a higher generation level than, that of the father. The reality is quite different. No father will consciously admit that uncles are without authority over nephews and nieces, for such extended authority is the generally recognized right thing; yet, if the principle is faithfully carried out by some unsuspecting uncle, the parents of the punished children may be so hurt that they will at least silently resent it and are likely to show actual hostility toward the uncle. At least once I came across a situation in which a daughter-in-law developed a serious quarrel with her father-in-law because the latter had punished his grandson. Public opinion did not support the young woman, but the matter became so unpleasant for the old man that he would probably think twice before taking any such measure again.

It is not that the pattern of authority and submission does not extend to uncles and nephews, but merely that the father-son tie is so much stronger than anything else. The identification between father and son is so predominant that other principles are often overshadowed.

As a result, as long as a man or a woman is alive, whether he or she is at home or not when a child needs disciplining, the tendency is to regard no other member of the kinship group as the possessor of any final authority over his or her children. His brothers may take the responsibility of disciplining the youngsters only at the risk of unpleasantness between the older people. The result is that only parents have both theoretical and real authority over their children. The others do not count and tend, therefore, to avoid such responsibility unless the actual parents have passed away.

Punishment takes a number of forms. Beating is frequently resorted to, but severe beating has never been observed in West Town. In fact, if the stricken children cry out as though they are being murdered and yell that they will "never do it again," as they usually do in such cases, the angry parents usually stop punishing them. In contrast to the males in many parts of China, male West Towners apparently show no great determination to punish their children. They are no more severe than their wives.

Another form of punishment is disinheritance, which in West Town language is, as elsewhere in China, to "chase him (or her) out." This form of punishment is theoretically resorted to when the young person involved is regarded as hopeless. A girl who has lost her honor will deserve such a fate.

Actually, no such punishment has been observed or recorded in West Town. To my knowledge two girls who were apprehended for sexual offense were merely beaten by one of their parents (father or mother) and then secretly married into families well below their own families in standing and situated in some distant community. Of course, the girls so married may suffer a great deal, for in such a marriage the two affinal families rarely maintain social relations. A girl who cannot look for any backing from her parents is at the complete mercy of her husband's family. There is no evidence in West Town that a boy has ever been disinherited.

Finally, it must be pointed out that parental discipline in West Town is more severe on girls than on boys. Fathers do not have very much to do with their daughters, but mothers, who have complete control of their children before ten, are more severe with their daughters than with their sons. Compared with some parts of China, however, West Town shows mild parental discipline, and is not very consistent—that is, for the same offense a child may get punished at one time, but not at another—depending upon chance or the mood of the parent concerned. Interference by grandparents and other members of the household within the pattern of family division under the one roof tends to increase this inconsistency of discipline tremendously. Elsewhere in China, when the family is divided, the component units are scattered at once, so that incidence of such interference is reduced.

In discussing communal punishment, it must be said at the outset that communal punishment is never inflicted by the whole community or applied automatically. It is always initiated and carried out by some group of individuals who, in some way, are interested in the offense. Sometimes the active party is a group of clan members who feel disgraced. Sometimes it is a group of unrelated West Towners who dislike the inroads of new ways of behavior between the sexes. Sometimes it is merely a group of individuals instigated or even hired by the offended party. Clan, as such, is definitely not an outstanding factor in communal punishment.

Communal action is usually directed at things concerning morality, more particularly those with reference to filial piety, loyalty to kinship, affinal groups, and the community, and control of sex. All adults with whom I discussed the subject said that any extremely unfilial son might be severely beaten by his clan members or even by others. No such action has ever been taken. To merit that punishment a son would have to commit an act such as beating his parents, but no son has ever done such a thing. Short of the extreme, all grades of unfilialness, such as disobedience, quarrelsomeness, unsatisfactory support, always exist, and they excite gossip, ridicule, and a mild ostracism within the community.

"Immoral" sex behavior is attacked by gossip, ridicule, and ostracism, but it may lead to more violent forms of punishment. By "immoral" sex behavior is meant, of course, any behavior which fails to agree with the customary ideas on the subject. Any man and woman who make public signs of affection may be the objects of public punishment. One instance well remembered by the people of West Town was that of the young man and his bride who had a bucketful of human excreta thrown over their heads because they were walking hand in hand on the street.[6]

If beating or other violence is involved in a communal action, the punishment is usually much more severe than that inflicted by parents. Such communal action occurs only when the culprits have no parents, or when the latter are weak and socially insignificant. The case of the college student who fell in love with a local girl will serve as one illustration.[7] While the two were walking in the open country an armed band waylaid them and threatened their lives. The lovers were then marched to the magistrate's court at Tali. Later they were transferred to the district court in the same town, where they were released. In this case the offenders got away lightly, because the boy was an "outsider" and had the backing of his college. Further-

[6] For details see Chapter I.
[7] For details see Chapter IV.

more, the girl's widowed mother had given complete agreement to the courtship.

Where there is no such backing, the punishment of an offender, especially a woman, may be very harsh. Just before my first visit to the community, the following incident occurred. A woman who was not satisfied with her husband eloped with her lover. Both had been residents of another district, but settled in West Town after the elopement. Her husband and his family sent emissaries to many localities, and one of them finally spotted the woman in one of the West Town markets. He left and gathered a small force. Returning, they seized the woman and beat her nearly to death. Her lover fled. The reaction of West Towners to this event was typical. They told the gang that they might beat her to death, but that they must do it outside the confines of the community. The underlying significance of this ultimatum was that: (1) such a woman deserved death, but that (2) they did not want to have her death contaminate the town.

Disloyalty to kinship groups and the community is hard to define in general terms. We have seen in a previous connection that loyalty to these groups was ambiguous and transitory. There are, however, specific instances of such disloyalty. One example is for a man to refuse help when he is obviously capable of doing so; another example is an act of bad faith. The former results in general, but mild, criticism; but the latter causes severe ostracism.

For example, the two largest firms in the community both employ a large number of clan members, relatives, and other West Towners. That this is socially desirable is shown by the fact that the family which owns T concern (one of the two largest) has been criticized for failure to give the majority of opportunities to clan members, relatives, and other West Towners. A more interesting fact is that the activities of neither of these firms have been hampered by corruption, embezzlement, or inefficiency through the employment of related individuals or other members of the same community.

This is in sharp contrast to the conditions of officialdom, in which all varieties of evils have resulted from nepotism.

The contrast is to be explained partly by the conditions of work, but especially by the communal sanction against acts of bad faith within the community. First, let us consider the conditions of work. After completing their apprenticeship, all initiates become working members of the firm. Whether they are relatives of the owners or not, they are treated alike and are given rewards according to the quality of their work. Each receives a fixed wage. In addition, at the end of the business year each will receive a large or a small bonus, again strictly determined by the quality of his work. The simple principle of justice, of reward for the deserving and punishment for the unfit, which is so sadly disregarded in Chinese government and on various levels of the bureaucracy, is enforced as a matter of course in private establishments.

The owners of shops, large or small, cannot, of course, afford to let favors disrupt the success of the firms. Nor can the workers, on their part, afford to let their employers down by corruption or embezzlement, because of the pressure of public opinion in the community. Practically all workers in the shops operating in West Town are natives of the community or of near-by areas. The branch shops situated elsewhere employ a number of natives of the areas where they are located, but key positions invariably are held by West Towners.

Now the existence of the evil of corruption in Chinese government is not influenced by possibility of the culprit's detection. There were numerous cases of corruption among officials in which the facts were perfectly clear. To be sure, there has been a growing distaste among some sections of educated Chinese toward such corruption. Some newspapers and magazines have repeatedly attacked it in general terms. But in private circles a man who can embezzle from public funds and get away with the crime is far from being ostracized. In fact, such a person, especially if he is generous with those who know his dealings or are related to him, is, to them at least, an object of admiration and re-spect. The illiterate public is too ignorant to know that the corruption exists and tends to look upon such a man either with indifference or with awe. The result is that by his own circle of acquaintances, relatives, clan members, and fel-low natives of the same district he is shielded against all public denouncements.

Unlike the complicated and remote public affairs, which are always baffling to the ordinary small-town citizen, the affairs of firms owned and managed by members of the community become known easily and quickly, especially if they involve some grievance of one party or another. Any-one who corrupts the shop of a relative, a clan member, or a fellow member of the same community would never be able to raise his head in West Town, even if he ever dared to return home. The sentiment for home and the home town is too strong to allow a West Towner to lead the life of a stranger permanently. For such a person the power of local mores and customs is much more notice-able than broader ideals such as pride in the national achievement or social and economic improvement of the country as a whole. Under such circumstances few indi-viduals, if any, dare to run the gauntlet of ostracism by members of the local community. The very loyalty to kin-ship and local ties is thus a protection against the evils which might otherwise have been produced by such loyalties.

In this connection it is important to draw a distinction between employees of a firm who are lineal descendants of the owners, and those who are not so related. If the latter group of employees committed acts of dishonesty, the social pressure outlined above would be applied; but if the former group committed exactly the same misbehavior, the local people would consider it as merely a father-son affair.

The last type of punishment to be discussed is the su-pernatural: the fear of evil ghosts and judgment in the world of the dead. It is difficult to separate the two sets of fears, but the overwhelming concern is with what may happen during one's present life, with the living parents and their descendants, rather than with the spirit, or *huei*, once it has left the body after death. When some West Towners say that good deeds will be rewarded with good and that evil behavior will be punished with dire consequences, they refer usually to life in the world of man rather than to that of spirits.

Spiritual rewards may be honorable posts among the spirits, but the rewards immediately desired are, as we have said, praise, wealth, and the prosperity of ancestors and descendants. Punishment by spirits may be torture in hell, but the immediately important results of wrongdoing are sickness, poverty, unnatural death, lack of descendants, fire, theft, and other forms of bad luck.[8]

It must be pointed out, before drawing this section to a close, that ancestors do not come into the punishment picture at all. If a man is punished by spiritual officials, in some sense his ancestors share the punishment as well. In fact, it is up to the latter to get him out of the trouble if at all possible.

Genealogical Records.   The institution of public storytelling during the period of the Ancestor Festival must have its far-reaching influences, but the most explicit and strongest force for shaping the young is to be found in genealogical books. Here again there is a distinction between the rich, on the one hand, and the poor, on the other. It is the rich who compile extensive genealogical books, some of which run into many volumes. The comparatively poor merely have records of a few generations of ancestors. The rich have books which not only are records of ancestors and their positions in the family tree but also con-

[8] One example of such punishment is as follows: if a man and woman, whether married to each other or not, should sleep together in a room which they did not rent, the owner of the room would be indignant, not because of infringement of his property rights, but because the sexual relation in such circumstances would excite evil spirits or make the good ones angry, so that the house might be destroyed by some accident.

tain highly systematized material, often manufactured by the descendants. A T clan record states its aim as follows:

> The functions of a genealogical record in every clan are manifold: on the one hand, it will show all outstanding cases of loyalty, filial piety, freedom from corruption [integrity], and chastity [of widow], which will serve as forces of persuasion or punishment; on the other hand, it will clarify the propinquity or the distance between different lineages, which will enable future descendants to comprehend the importance of repaying what they have taken from those sources and of honoring their remote ancestry, as well as respecting their elders and loving their parents. Moreover, such a record will provide material for future district gazetteers and other volumes.

Different records are arranged in different ways, but most of those I examined include the following items in addition to the plain genealogy: (1) introduction (purpose of the records, various efforts expended on them throughout the past generations, changes concerning the clan temple, the remoteness of the ancestry and its authenticity, etc.); (2) ancestral edicts (various virtues to be observed by all); (3) plans of the clan temple and the ancestral graveyards; (4) outstanding literary gems connected with the clan (including those written by members of the clan, past and present), condolence sentiments presented at the funerals of outstanding members of the clan, imperial edicts, and edicts from other government officials which had special significance for the clan; (5) records of outstanding ancestors and their achievements.

From the point of view of this chapter, the last category is the most important. One record mentions outstanding ancestors under the following categories:

1. Those who attained high examination honors.
2. Those who achieved outstanding merit through excellencies of personality (such as extraordinary harmony with the community, helpfulness to younger members of the community who show signs of promise).
3. Those who demonstrated outstanding loyalty and mar-

tyrdom (such as those who died in battle during some specific dynasty, without mentioning the particular emperor under whom they served, etc.).

4. Those who performed kindly deeds (such as repairing public bridges and roads).

5. Those who have performed outstanding acts of filial piety and fraternity (including one who was killed by bandits while defending his mother and another who patiently served his mother in poverty without a word of complaint against his more prosperous brother).

6. Those who have performed outstanding feats of chastity and filial piety (for women only). This section includes one lady who refused to remarry after the death of her husband, another who worked through great hardships to raise her only son, and a third who chopped off a slice of her flesh as an ingredient for her mother-in-law's medicine.

7. Those who have attained high literary achievements, including that of calligraphy.

8. Those who have been elected to public offices since the Republic.

9. Those who have served as officials (not elected).

10. Those who have served as officials and have made outstanding contributions during their period of appointment (including those who have been praised in newspapers by the local populace which they governed).

11. Those who have achieved military victories for the emperor.

12. Those who served as military officials.

13. Those who have graduated from middle schools or higher institutions of learning (one member of the clan was said to be studying in the United States). Ten such graduates are listed; there are no girls yet.

14. Those who have served as border officials.

15. Those who preferred to stay away from officialdom (in this category are mainly those scholars who were unsuccessful).

16. Those who achieved outstanding spiritual relations or

a special place in the medical field (listing one who was said to be able to call for wind and rain, as well as decipher dreams, another who knew the art of turning ordinary material into gold through a special process given him by a spirit saint, etc.).

In addition to the above, the following story is recorded concerning one ancestor whose achievement is not categorized:

> This ancestor returned a bag of money which he had picked up on the road to its rightful owner and was praised by his contemporaries. He used to trade in . . . district. He owned a horse. He let the horse loose in the hills day and night. When it was time for him to attend one of the periodic markets, the horse would automatically gallop to where the man always mounted. The horse would not leave the spot unless the man came along and rode on its back. The same routine went on for more than ten years without failing even once. When he died, the horse died (cause not specified). The horse died on the day of his funeral. This shows that true faithfulness and kindness can affect and influence animals.

Statements such as these, which might have some truth in them, but are obviously elaborated with legends, permeate all genealogical records. The question may be asked, of course, as to how many members of the clan are actually familiar with the contents of these volumes. Since a large number of the inhabitants are illiterate, how can they read them? An answer to this question is not difficult. First, the general literacy rate is higher in West Town than elsewhere in China. Secondly, of greater importance is the fact that the tales given in genealogical records are usually traditional tales perpetuated orally. They are told in after-meal conversations, in family gatherings, and especially during an Ancestor Festival. In this way even illiterate women know a good deal about them. Moreover, in a number of instances the literate record-makers raked the memories of illiterate elders for information concerning their various ancestors. Lastly, a talk with any adult member of the community, whether he be literate or illiterate, will leave little doubt as to the high degree of familiarity of the individual West Towner with stories elaborated in the genealogical records of his own clan.

A review of the so-called "outstanding achievements" given in the genealogical record and analyzed above shows a very interesting discrepancy between these selected emphases and the general life pattern of the community. On the male virtue side, as embodied in these "achievements," we have filial piety, fraternity among brothers and family members, harmony and kindness toward the community. On the female virtue side, we have filial piety and chastity. For the male, the following items of behavior are considered outstanding: charitable acts, spiritual feats, examination honors, literary production, official posts, and accomplishments as officials, military or civil. For the female, the following items of behavior are considered outstanding achievements: faithfulness to husbands and untiring attention to parents-in-law.

These points conform to the life pattern in general, but differ from it in one specific aspect. The records emphasize the importance of scholarship and official ranks as achievements, but fail completely to mention trading or commerce, which is the backbone of West Town life and for which the individual is rigorously trained.

It may be plausible to explain this omission on the basis of the imperial policy of past centuries—the practice of discouraging commerce and encouraging scholarship and officialdom. On the other hand, the last and enlarged edition of the genealogical record in question was made less than fifteen years ago and well after the fall of the imperial dynasty. It is therefore at least plausible to conclude that such an omission indicates the actual social ideal. Finally, since only the comparatively rich have genealogical books of this nature, it is obvious that they tend to be responsible for differences in training between the rich and the poor. Among the latter the emphasis in training is on the livelihood activities as such; among the former, although commerce may still be important, the emphasis in training is on living up to the high standards of power and prestige.

SCHOOL AND SCHOLARSHIP

So far we have been concerned mainly with informal education. We shall now examine the more formal counterpart.

As mentioned in the introductory chapter, in 1942 the three local schools had a total enrollment of about 1,400. Even granting that 50 percent of these pupils came from areas other than West Town, the enrollment figure, when compared with the total population figure of 8,000, is impressive. For a community to have about 10 percent of its population in school is certainly not typical of most known parts of China. Such a high rate of school attendance seems to speak well, without doubt, for West Towners' high interest in schools and scholarship.

Yet a closer examination brings out other facts. First, school education is taken lightly by most parents. Children are sent to the schools when they are not needed at home. Any sort of family occasion would be sufficient reason to tell the children to ask for leave of absence from their classes. Secondly, sons of rich families, far from being kept in school continuously, tend to remain idle when they feel like it. Thirdly, there is very little regard for higher learning. For a community of West Town's wealth, the number of young men who have been graduated from the middle schools and have gone away to college is negligible. The vast majority of the pupils attend school to learn something about reading and writing so as to enable them to be more successful in business. This attitude of disregard for higher learning was most clearly revealed when inflation forced college professors and graduates who stuck to educational jobs into serious financial predicaments. The attitude of West Towners toward these "poor" scholars was one barely short of open contempt. As long as these scholars received incomes much higher than the ordinary business men, they retained their traditional prestige. As soon as their position was lowered economically, they declined socially. The proverbial high esteem for the scholar and scholarship as such was certainly not evident.

For awhile I worked on the basis of the hypothesis that this lack of concern for scholarship had come about since the fall of the imperial dynasty and the abolition of the examination system. Most older West Towners I talked with emphasized the fact that formerly there were fewer students because the community was poorer, but that then there was more "solid" scholarship. The same informants also said that in the old days any talented student could, through the examinations, rise to fame, power, and wealth. The contradiction between the first and the second statements shows that, even in former times, the so-called interest in scholarship was solely the desire for the social and economic advantages which scholarship brought about. This observation is further buttressed by the fact that in West Town, unlike other parts of China, tutor schools according to the old system disappeared completely as soon as the new schools were established. Judging by the conservatism of West Towners in other spheres of life, the quick disappearance of tutor schools can only be explained by lack of interest in scholarship as such.

However, the new schools, though built with money intended to enhance the donor's family and clan prestige, cannot but introduce notes jarring to tradition. The informants were not outspoken on this point. In fact, they were very reluctant to admit it. The schools, though still teaching filial piety, have introduced coeducation, emphasized patriotism, and deplored evils of the "big family" system. There were some cases in which schoolboys had become too independent. There were even two incidents in which school girls had eloped with their sweethearts. The schools warn against superstition, whereas the community is very much given to cholera and other prayer meetings. The schools teach something about agriculture, banking, history, geography, and trigonometry, but the home, the farm, and the family business have little use for these classroom assignments.

Despite this, the new schools have become the fashion of the day. West Towners are therefore torn between the new current and the old tradition. Consequently, there is a good deal of confusion and ambiguity. Parents send their children to school, but they do not care whether or not the children are interested. Boys are taught about public health and hygiene, but they spit on the floor at home and participate in epidemic prayer meetings as a matter of course.

With regard to externals the new school education and the old tutor school scholarship are sometimes equated. Graduation from the modern school has been treated more or less like the old examination honors. But the similarity does not go very far, and West Towners are not too happy about it.

CHAPTER IX

The Ancestors' Shadow

WE ARE now in a position to summarize the culture which we have described and analyzed in the preceding chapters. The first and foremost element is the father-son identification. This identification is at the root of and based upon two general principles which govern the entire kinship structure: patriliny and generation.

The term identification is applied to the father-son relationship because, far from being one-sided, the responsibility and privileges of the relationship are quite mutual. The father must provide for the sons when they are young, educate them in the ancestral tradition, and get them suitably married. The older man is obliged to do these things not so much because he owes it to the youngsters, but because he is obligated to their common ancestors. The son owes to his father absolute obedience, and he must support his parents, mourn for them,[1] bury them according to social station and financial ability, provide for their needs in the other world, and take all necessary steps toward insuring the male line. The younger man is obliged to do these things not only because of his duty to his parents but also because he is indebted to his and his father's common ancestors.

Thus, from the point of view of the kinship organization as a whole the father-son identification is merely a neces-

---

[1] A son wears mourning for two years for his father, but three years for his mother. This longer mourning for the mother, it is expressly stated, is because of her greater hardship in giving birth to him and bringing him up. But a woman's role is on every occasion regarded as subsidiary to that of her husband and even that of her son.

sary link in the great family continuum, with numerous ancestors at one end and innumerable descendants at the other.

The second element is what I call estrangement between the sexes. On the one hand this pattern prescribes sex inequality, and on the other it necessitates the elimination of all erotic expression. Both measures are means for subordinating the husband-wife relationship and enhancing the father-son relationship. In West Town we see an outright superiority of men over women. Not only are husbands above their wives, but brothers are also superior to their sisters. This inequality is implied in the life of the people and clearly stated and recognized by both sexes without reserve or hesitation. Only when a relationship involves two generations is the principle overshadowed. Inequality means that punishment for sexual offense is much more stringent for women than for men and that the remarrying widow is in a much poorer position than the remarrying widower. In fact, the latter is encouraged to remarry, while the former is told that to do so involves disgrace. The remarried female has, therefore, seriously lowered her social prestige. This being the custom, there cannot be any preference for levirate, which very rarely and informally occurs among the poor in some parts of China.

Elimination of erotic expression affects a wide range of behavior. Men and women may not meet preliminary to marriage, for romantic love has no place in this configuration. Marriage, since it is instituted in order to acquire daughters-in-law for the husband's parents and to continue the father-son line, is parentally arranged according to customary rules, including those governing preferred or disfavored matches. The emphasis on the continuation of the father-son tie means that the behavior and the ideas of new or prospective members of the family must be predictable so as not to sever this tie. Romantic love is, in theory at least, unpredictable, and the emphasis is on individual attachment between the spouses. That is why gestures of intimacy in public, even between man and wife, are socially disapproved.

The third element is the big-family ideal. From the point of view of the smooth functioning of the father-son relationship and its continuation, this ideal is important for obvious reasons. In any given family and in any given generation there is likely to be more than one male born of the same parents. This being the case, it means that the father-son relationship in any given instance probably refers to a father and several sons. It is easy to see how constant disharmony between the latter could interrupt the interplay of authority and duty inherent in the father-son identification. If the sons quarrel so that they disperse, the father-son line might even be in danger of extinction.

To promote this big-family ideal, it is necessary to develop two factors: on the one hand, there must be an esprit de corps, and on the other, unity of purpose. The esprit de corps is brought about by sharing honors and maintaining harmony. That is why there are displayed the ranks, virtues, and other achievements of remotely related individuals of the same clan in family homes, ancestral temples, graveyards, and on all ceremonial occasions. That is why if a fight among the children under the ancestral roof comes to the notice of the adults, according to the social ideal the parents will show greater consideration for children other than their own. The unity of purpose is expressed in a community of interests and of material goods. That is why before the division of the family all incomes and earnings go to a common household pool, and any significant deviation from the rule is a sign that the household can no longer be held together. That is why the ideal family is one in which its property is undivided and its members all live under the same roof for many generations. During the late imperial dynasty, sons who broke away from their parents or divided the common property without the older people's consent could be criminally punished. Needless to say, once the emphasis on the big-family ideal is established for two generations of lineally related individuals, it tends to extend to larger and larger collateral groups.

The fourth element is the pattern of education, which for lack of a better phrase may be described as education for old age. Differences between the psychology and behavior of the younger and those of the older members of the society are recognized. But whether the member in question is five years old or twenty years old, the keynote in his or her training in life is the same. Children are not trained to develop as children, but at every turn they are encouraged to imitate and to participate in the ways of the adults, which are, in turn, ways of the ancestors. The sense of kinship continuity, the big-family ideal, ideals of harmony with members of the clan and community, and the conservatism of the spirits are imparted to the young as early as they can absorb them. There is very little intention on the part of the parents to encourage differences in temperament among their children. On the contrary, the more the youngsters conform to the ancestral tradition, the better. This process makes it clear to the young that it is not very desirable and comfortable to be young, but that it is advantageous and dignified to be old.

This education is built on the supposition that all the living are in the shadow of their ancestors. Death does not sever the relationship of the departed with the living; but merely changes it to a different level. Far from being characterized by fear, the attitude of the living toward departed members of the family or clan is one of continuous remembrance and affection. In fact, the custom requires for a departed relative a considerable heightening of the kinship sentiments along established lines, at least for a short period of time. As might be expected, custom requires the greatest demonstration of these sentiments for parents and the least for wives. The amount of demonstration required lessens in intensity in direct proportion to the closeness of the recognized kinship relationship, both lineally and laterally. The dead need the same things to which they have been accustomed in life, and it is up to those whose duty it has been to support them before their death to continue doing so afterwards.

The attitude of the dead toward the living is completely in line with that of the living toward the dead. There are, in all, four classes of spirits: (1) spirits of members of the same kinship group and of the group of relatives by marriage; (2) spirits of persons not related by kinship or marriage; (3) officials and functionaries in the worlds of spirits; and (4) spirits of dead persons from unknown or unfamiliar racial or cultural groups (such as those of the Mohammedan dead). The fourth group of spirits are regarded as being irrelevant; they simply do not count, and they are neither harmful nor beneficial. The third group of spirits may be benevolent, benign, or malicious. Most of them control or are in some way related to the destiny, good fortune, bad luck, sickness, disaster, or death which may occur in the life of every individual; many of them are known by name and nature. They are part of the spiritual order, just as magistrates, provincial governors, cabinet ministers, emperors, generals, soldiers, and policemen are part of the social order. The individual can secure their favor or refrain from offending them, but cannot completely get away from their rule. The disposition of the second class of spirits is uncertain; those who have living descendants are usually happy and content and, therefore, not dangerous at all. The dangerous ones are those who have died an unnatural death or are no longer worshiped at any family altar or clan temple. They may become so extremely jealous of the happier living members or so destitute that they will be out to harm everybody and everything on which they can lay their hands. These spirits must be propitiated with offerings and incense and kept at a distance. The first class of spirits differs from all others. They are always well disposed and never malicious toward the members of the families to which they are related. In fact, the question does not arise at all. Their good will is so taken for granted that any inquiry on that point appeared to my West Town informants as pointless and ridiculous.

The ancestral spirits will help their own descendants whenever they can. They are the spirits upon which the living may depend without any question and to which the living are related, for better or for worse and without any possibility of change. Their behavior in life, as well as in the world of the dead, exerts influence on the fate of their descendants. In turn, their fate is also influenced by the behavior of their descendants. They are never offended by their descendants, and they never cause disasters to befall the coming generations. In fact, it is their natural duty (for they do not have to be invoked for such purposes) to use every possible means to protect their descendants in case the latter get into trouble with spirits of the second and third classes.

It is clear, then, that the attitude of the living toward the dead and that of the dead toward the living are functionally one. The relation of the living with the dead is essentially modeled upon that of the living with the living. It is, however, more than that. By glorifying the dead it both idealizes and sets the standard and pattern for kinship relationship. This pattern determines, it seems, the worldly attitude of all spirits, and the worldly orientation of the majority of West Towners. The majority of West Towners are interested in accumulating spiritual "goods" by prayers, observance of taboos and offerings, but they do so largely because they desire certain tangibles: to be free from disease and want and to have living heirs, proper burials, adequate graveyards, prosperous descendants for many generations to come, and honored places in their clan temples. These things, it should be noted, are also objectives desired by ancestral spirits, either for themselves or for their progeny.

The world of spirits is approximately a copy of, and strictly a supplement to, the world of the living. West Towners, like all Chinese, deduce the existence of the world of spirits from the existence of the world of the living, but not vice versa, as in Christianity.[2] By the same token, the cult of ancestors derives its existence from that of the family organization. The cult as it is found in West Town is not primarily a matter of belief. A belief is usually accepted by some and denied by others within the same culture. The cult of ancestors, as it is found in West Town, is more nearly a matter of plain everyday behavior. It is not accepted by some and denied by others. It is a fact to which every sane West Towner subscribes as a matter of course and which no sane West Towner ever challenges. No question of belief ever arises. The ancestors of West Town literally live among their descendants, not only biologically, but also socially and psychologically. Therefore, this family religion requires no validation by means of miracles, as was once asserted by Bronislaw Malinowski, for the miracles are inherent in the family continuum, through birth and death, which are an integral part of the configuration. The family is a part of the religion; the religion, a part of the family.

The five elements of the culture outlined thus far have a common denominator: *authority*. Authority is centered in father-son identification, expresses itself freely in relationship between the sexes, big-family ideal, and education, and is backed up by the wishes of dead ancestors.

However, equally important in the culture is the factor of *competition*. Where there is authority there is no equality. But authority in West Town culture only applies to relationships which involve two generation levels, to those which involve both sexes, to those which involve widely different ages, and to those which involve men of different statuses (the rich or higher officials versus the poor, commoners, or lower officials). Manifestly it does not apply to relationships which involve related persons of the same sex and the same generation level (for example, brothers) or to certain others (for example, common citizens of the com-

---

[2] It is, therefore, wide of the mark to say that the Chinese are animistic. See the absurd arguments of J. J. M. De Groot, *The Religion of the Chinese*, Leiden 1910.

munity who have no official titles). Among these groups equality in large measure prevails.

Between those whose relation with one another is marked by the authority-submission pattern there cannot be competition. But between those whose relation with one another is marked by equality, there can and is bound to be competition. In a family organization which prescribes that all sons, regardless of age, have equal claims to the ancestral inheritance, that all sons have opportunities to head independent family units, and that every son may become the favorite son of parents and ancestors because of personal achievements, this drive for competition tends to receive additional encouragement. It is responsible for the struggle for more wealth, for larger family homes, for more "advantageous" graveyards, for bigger clan temples, for costlier ceremonials, and for a host of other measures which are calculated to increase the welfare and prestige of the living and of the dead. It is also responsible for the weak condition of the clan. Theoretically, the stronger the paternal authority, the more remote the ancestors worshiped, and the stronger the family-unity ideal, the more cohesive the clan organization will be. The sense of competition has, however, destroyed any chance for solidarity of the clan. The individual family cohesion is so strong that even the joint household has difficulty in maintaining its existence. The clan, being composed of members who are much larger in number and much more remote in relationship than the joint household, finds the difficulty greater.

SAFETY VALVES

It is generally acknowledged that every culture selects and emphasizes certain psychological drives and potentialities on the part of the individuals living in it and that every culture eliminates or curbs others. Such selections and emphases express themselves in cultural patterns. While a good many observations have been made on the variability of cultural patterns,[3] no conclusion has been reached concerning the total range or nature of the psychological drives and potentialities which cultures select and emphasize or eliminate and curb.[4]

If we possessed conclusive evidence on the range and the nature of all psychological drives and potentialities, some of the anthropological investigator's work would be greatly simplified. He would be able, for instance, to ascertain the probable areas within which a conflict between cultural and psychological forces will occur, by comparing the cultural demands with the psychological needs.

In the absence of conclusive psychological evidence, I have used an alternate, but less exact, method to determine some of these conflicts. First I ascertained the basic orientations of certain cultural patterns. Then I looked for customs and conditions which are contrary to such basic orientations, but nevertheless somehow function smoothly as a part of these cultural patterns. Wherever such customs and conditions operate in this manner, my inference is that they correspond to certain psychological needs which have to be satisfied in a roundabout way. I call these secondary customs and conditions "safety valves," in the sense that they prevent the culture pattern from breaking down due to inner conflicts.

The first of these safety valves is found in the pattern of parental authority. West Town culture admonishes the male, as soon as he is able to understand, to obey his parents, especially his father, to the fullest extent; that it is bad behavior to question his wisdom or decisions; that it is good to do whatever he wants done without the slightest regard for one's own feelings; that it is not desirable to commit oneself to any independent line of action; that it is sinful to do anything which disturbs his father in any

[3] See Ruth Benedict, *Patterns of Culture*, New York, 1934; Margaret Mead, *Sex and Temperament in Three Primitive Societies*, New York, 1935. Ralph Linton, *The Study of Man*, New York, 1936.

[4] See discussion by Otto Klineberg, *Social Psychology*, New York, 1940, pp. 55–165, and Gordon W. Allport, *Personality*, New York, 1937, chap. iv.

way; in other words, that he is to keep himself ready at all times, as long as he lives, to please him, to agree with him, and to be of all possible service to him. What is more, socially the son will never become mature as long as his father lives.

The basic orientation of this pattern is that sons, as long as their parents live, will have little, if any, opportunity for self assertion. Whether we agree with Alfred Adler that self-assertiveness is all important, the observable fact is that instead of following through its basic demands, the pattern of parental authority is coordinated with the custom of division under the same roof, which drastically modifies the authoritative position of the parents. It may be recalled (see Chapter V) that West Towners, while not encouraging division of the family, look upon it as inevitable. Under this custom, as soon as the sons are married, or when one or more children have been born to the younger wives, the household is divided with regard to living quarters, daily meals, and property or the income from the common property, but the household remains united in religious matters and in social relationship with the clan and the outside world.

The most important consequence of such a division is that real power of decision may then pass from the father to the sons. In this respect a great deal of diversity of behavior is observed. In some cases fathers who appear to be more capable than their sons retain the power. The old father of a Tuan family effectively prevented his sons, who are heads of individual families under the same roof, from gambling. In other cases, a father who appears to be inferior in ability will relinquish the power to his sons. He may be consulted on important issues and may maintain his authority on the surface, but his sons have unlimited freedom of action. The Ch family, cited earlier, conformed to this pattern. Between these extremes there are families which show various intermediate adjustments between the old and the young.

In this way, although the prescriptions concerning paternal authority are severe, there is room for the mature individual who does not subscribe to them. Such an individual may find his place without causing a breakdown of the existing system. The custom of division under the same roof, in a cultural pattern which stresses the lifelong authority of the father over the son, thus serves the function of a safety valve. Its existence is indicative of the individual tendency to self-assertion against overexacting parental authority.

The second safety valve is found in the cultural pattern of estrangement between the sexes. The culture says to the male: No upright man shows signs of intimacy in public with any woman, not even his wife; your primary duty in life is toward your parents; if a quarrel occurs between your mother and your wife, there is no alternative for you but to take the side of your mother against your wife; you may have to divorce your wife if your parents cannot be pacified; you must *love* your parents with all your heart and must show them every consideration, but you must be stern with your wife and make her defer to you.

It says to the female: To be attractive to men is unnatural; in fact it is a crime of the worst order, for such attraction is equivalent to sexual offense, and sexual offense would end your life; it is shameful to be sexually attractive, even to your husband; it is good manners to avoid talking to him intimately in public; your main duty is toward your parents-in-law, for if you must choose between serving your husband or your parents-in-law, you must serve the older persons; you are to be obedient to your parents before marriage and to your parents-in-law and husband afterwards.

The basic orientation of this pattern is that, while the gratification of sex in the physiological sense is not barred, all possible awareness of it is to be eliminated, and all secondary expressions, such as tenderness of feeling and mutual possessiveness which are normally associated with sex, are to be banned. While there is no evidence that these secondary expressions of sex are necessary accompaniments to the conjugal relationship, we must also observe that once again the basic orientation of the cultural pattern is not consistently followed through.

First, division under the same roof serves here also as a safety valve, because it tones down the severity of the restraints on husband-wife relationship. Since the several individual families of a household live, feed, and manage their economic affairs separately, they have obviously much greater scope for conjugal intimacy than would otherwise be possible.

Of greater importance in this connection is the economic factor. Generally speaking, the husband-wife relationship in poor families fails to conform to the cultural ideal. In such families there is, to be sure, no public expression of conjugal intimacy as Americans understand the term, but the two spouses are undoubtedly closer to each other than either is to the husband's parents. The reason is simple. To begin with, in a poor household the husband as well as the wife has to work hard. This means that husband and wife often have to work cooperatively on the same project. In a rich household, while the wife has to work as hard as any woman in the community, the husband does not have to work at all.

In the matter of treatment of the wife, the rich and the poor also differ. We do not know what West Town wives think of the idea of their husbands giving them less consideration than they do their mothers, but we have observed a good deal of variation in behavior. Some wives take their socially ordained position without a murmur. Others fight back in a number of ways. One may start an open quarrel with her husband. In such a case, the man could beat her up, but that would by no means settle the argument. She may refuse to cooperate with him, by neglecting his clothing and food, or if she is really angry, she may return to her mother. In extreme cases she may even commit suicide. When we consider that parents usually do not care to give their daughters to the poor and that marriage of a daughter is in any case a serious economic problem for the not well-to-do, we shall realize the efficacy of these female weapons on their husbands and their influence on the socially approved conjugal pattern.

The man in a wealthier household lives under a different set of circumstances. He is not so dependent upon his wife for personal services. He can easily get another wife should the first one choose to run away or commit suicide. Besides, he can also get a concubine.

The result is that while the rich male often adheres to the cultural pattern of sex estrangement, the poor male is often forced by circumstances to behave contrariwise. These facts indicate that, at least among a large part of the population, the pattern of estrangement between the sexes is counterbalanced by the tendency to greater conjugal intimacy.

A third usage which may be regarded as a safety valve is the importance attached to form. The duties of a son to his parents are, if executed fully, very arduous. They mean not only complete obedience to the older man's authority but also deprivation for oneself and for one's wife and children, if necessary, in order to make the parents comfortable. They may mean indefatigable and continuous attention to the parents and complete stoppage of one's work if and when one of the older persons is indisposed. In other words, no conceivable form of sacrifice on the part of the sons for the parents is too great. No wonder not many individuals can measure up to such an exacting standard of conduct. Does it follow, then, that most individuals have a guilty conscience? Not at all. The importance of form works out in two ways. First, most parents are not willing to admit to outsiders that their sons have been undutiful. This is part of the pattern of father-son identification. In fact, they like to be able to boast to the contrary. Secondly, sons may have failed to be dutiful during the lifetime of their parents, but they can free themselves from a guilty conscience and earn themselves a good name in public by providing an elaborate funeral for the deceased parent. Although no one will admit it, pompous funerals and regular services of worship, which are much more tangible to the community at large than happiness or sorrow within the four walls of a family home, are usually the things by which West Towners judge each other. The importance of form thus has made filial obligations much more tolerable than otherwise.

The importance of form also helps to ease a difficulty concerning sex. As mentioned before, after a daughter-in-law has given birth to children, it would be considered shameful for her mother-in-law to become pregnant. Sexual relations in marriage are for the purpose of providing heirs for the family. When that function has been fulfilled, there is no longer any permissible excuse for the continuation of such relations. The situation is adjusted by abortion, which avoids the consequences which the society no longer favors. When the right thing has been attempted by a public gesture, the blame is removed.

IN THE PENUMBRA

We have, so far, discussed the culture as it applies to the life and the behavior of normal members of the community. These normal members are, in the terminology employed in the present volume, well under the ancestors' shadow. There are, on the other hand, some who for biological, social, or accidental reasons are less fortunate and cannot function normally. In West Town this group of individuals may be described as "in the penumbra."[5]

Normally the duty of sons to parents and the responsibilities of parents to sons are adequate to satisfy both the older and the younger persons. But what about the couple

---

[5] The author is indebted to Professor Ralph Linton for suggesting the use of the word penumbra. According to *Webster's Universal Dictionary*, 2 vols. (New York, 1937), "penumbra" is the boundary of shade and light in painting or the partial shadow between the full light and the total shadow caused by an opaque body intercepting the light from a luminous body, as in astronomy.

who are without sons in old age and the boy or girl who is without one or both parents while very young? The observable fate of such individuals is sad. Sympathy for them will be offered by everybody in the community, but little else. The sonless couple will, while they can, do everything possible to increase their fertility. If the family has money, the husband will take a concubine. When every expedient for begetting a son fails, they will, if they have a daughter, secure a married-in son-in-law. The last resort is adoption of a son of the husband's brother or a remoter relative. In the opinion of all informants with whom I have discussed the matter, adopted sons are not comparable with actual sons. They tend to show greater allegiance toward their real parents. They are likely to be undutiful and get beyond control. Sooner or later, the old couple may helplessly watch a growing independence on the part of the young man and his arrogant liberty with the property of his adopted parents. Sons of brothers or cousins know that the barren couple's property will belong to them anyway, whether they take good care of their adopted parents or not. If the unfortunate couple are poor, their position will be much worse. They may find that they cannot even adopt a son.

In this situation a barren woman's life is more precarious than that of her husband. At first she may encourage her husband to take a concubine. After the arrival of the new woman, the wife's place may be better or much worse. If her husband is good, he will treat her with consideration. At worst, the concubine may be selfish and jealous, and the husband may no longer care for his less attractive wife. Under such circumstances the wife will have no allies in the house at all.

Unattractive as this picture of the life of a barren woman may be, it is many times better than that of a woman whose husband dies when she is very young. Only when we consider the life of such a woman can we understand why any wife should encourage her husband to take a concubine. For a widow's honorable salvation lies in her sons or, in the absence of the latter, married-in sons-in-law. In the latter case she is at least lineally related to her daughter. Very poorly situated is the widow who has to resort to adoption of the son of her husband's brother or of some other near patrilineal relative of her husband. The case of z is a good illustration. z was married when she was 23, and her husband left for Japan three months later. He died in Japan one year later. She never even saw his corpse. The family was well-to-do, so she hung on and adopted the second son of her husband's older brother. At the time of the investigation z was about 37, and the boy, a middle school student in Kunming, was nineteen. All was well on paper, but the disheartening thing for z was that she could get neither the sentimental satisfaction nor even any of the formal respect due to a mother. When the boy came home, he would neither address her as he would a mother nor come to live in her wing of the house or eat with her. He simply went to his own mother and ignored z. But z and the boy both realized that however poorly he treated her, there was no other person to inherit her husband's share of the property. The law of the Republic says that a person has complete freedom to choose an inheritor for his property, but the custom says that the property of a sonless person goes to the son of his brother (if adopted) or to all sons of his brothers (if no formal adoption took place), and custom is still the deciding factor in West Town. This is why, I think, although socially it is more honorable for widows to adopt sons and remain faithful to their departed husbands than for them to remarry, a large number of widows do prefer the latter way out, in spite of the fact that the remarriage of widows is treated with much social and ritual censure.

The position of a child who loses a parent or both parents early in life is even less enviabl.e His position will be particularly precarious if the lost parent is his mother, in which case one of two things takes place. Either the father remarries and the child is put under the tutelage of a step-mother, or the father does not marry again and he is left in the hands of a grandmother, unmarried aunt, older sister, or older brother's wife. None of these individuals, except perhaps the grandmother, is likely to pay much attention to the child, and the little one is often left to fend for himself. When the older brother's wife has children of her own there will be discrimination against the motherless child in every respect.

Such a child may experience something much worse if the father remarries. The child under a step-mother is usually an object of popular pity. At best she may be kind to him. More often she will dislike him and mistreat him. After she has given birth to one or two children of her own, the child of the deceased wife will definitely enter the dog house. So obvious is this matter to West Towners that every informant told me that a child in the care of its step-mother would, to say the least, have a difficult time.

Another group of individuals who are in the penumbra consist of girls from poor families whose parents need their price for food, or girls from better class families who have committed sexual misbehavior. The former were sometimes sold as slaves, but usually they become concubines; the latter become wives or concubines. Concubinage is an accepted custom, but nobody wants to be one. So strong is the aversion, that even the poorest person will be angry if it be suggested openly that his or her daughter might be a concubine. All concubines in the community come from some far distant locality. It is generally admitted that the family of a concubine and her husband's family rarely maintain any social relationship at all.

A concubine may suffer in two ways. If her husband is strong and can show his favor to her while the wife is not particularly jealous, the concubine may have a very good time. As pointed out before, she may even relegate the wife to the dog house and become the queen of the family group. But if her husband is not so strong, worse still, if he is henpecked by a jealous and harsh wife, the concubine may live in a man-made hell. She may be treated like a slave, and she will have no parental protection to fall back upon.

The second source of suffering is failure to give birth to a son. If her husband is wealthy, he will get more concubines, and soon the barren one will be completely ignored. Of course, if her marriage took place after her husband already had an heir, the position is somewhat altered, and she may retain his favor much longer. Even so the latter part of the life of a concubine without sons may be very miserable. Concubines, because they are younger, usually outlive their husbands. When the husband is dead, the sons of the wife or of other concubines will not pay much attention to her and her needs. When the lineage already has an heir, a concubine has no right to adopt a child. This means that such a person will merely wither on the vine. She has no certain place on any ancestral altar.

To the best of my knowledge there are no slave girls in West Town, but the life of a few of them in adjacent areas would chill the blood of any unlucky woman. These unfortunate girls are completely at the mercy of their mistresses and their children, who in most instances treat them like animals and beat them for sport. Their only way out is to run away by stealth. But after they succeed in getting away from the house of their bondage, their lives are still no "bed of roses." When they were first sold, they were mere children. Their buyers usually lived in some area far away from their home town. Having completely lost contact with their parents, they might not even know how to find their way home. Being ignorant and illiterate, they as a rule do not go to the police. At any rate, even up to a few years ago the police did not regard slavery of this type as being illegal. Going to the police might result in being returned to their former owners and more ill treatment. The most popular way of escape was to follow some man, met by chance, who had promised marriage. Often they are resold to a new owner or to a brothel elsewhere by their husband-by-promise, who appropriates the sale price.

Another type of individual in the penumbra is the unmarried. Since the role of the individual is to be a link in the great family continuum, a bachelor or a spinster is socially lost. This is particularly true of the old maid, because a woman has no place in life apart from marriage. At the time of investigation there were any number of widows and widowers in West Town, but there were no old maids or bachelors. Bachelors may leave town and make good elsewhere. But once a woman has passed the reproductive age, she has lost her chance of marriage forever. The best solution for such a person is to reside in a temple or become a female diviner or priestess at home. She will pass her days in reciting scriptures and performing ritual homage to various spirits. Because of her virginity, such a devotee may become a powerful healer and a good candidate for immortality.

It is interesting that in spite of such spiritual advantages no female in the community has been known to choose this particular way of life. It gives strong additional evidence to the fact that in spite of the abundant rituals and séances and the great importance attached to life after death, the basic orientation of West Towners is worldly rather than other-worldly. Their supposition is that a right place in the spiritual world follows automatically a right place in the social world.

This analysis of individuals in the penumbra has, I think, thrown some additional light on the nature of West Town culture. There is, as was pointed out before, good evidence for the existence of a strong desire for competition and success among males and, in a limited way, among females. We can see that no success will ever be complete unless the individual has first attained his or her right place in the family organization. In fact, the individual who has not attained such a place is disqualified before the race has even started. On the other hand, the life of an individual who has not made good in the American sense of the word can, if he has parents and sons, be well satisfied. An individual who has a rightful place in the kinship structure and lives among the members of the structure who owe him, or to whom he owes, duties and obligations is one who, as a Chinese proverb describes it, has adequate capital "for advance and attack or for retreat and defense." In the same way, the lot of the physically or mentally defective, while unfortunate in the sense that the defects hamper development of the individual and may bring sufferings, may not be marked by social dissatisfaction. As long as they fit into the right categories with regard to the kinship structure, they will be married and otherwise taken care of, in spite of the fact that their ability for fulfilling some of their obligations may be exceedingly limited.

The really miserable individual is he or she who has no place in the kinship structure or who does not live among the members necessary for the successful functioning of the structure, whether because of his or her own fault or because of circumstances beyond his or her control. Such a person will be very much at the mercy of the individuals with whom his lot is cast. A child who has lost his mother may happen to be lucky enough to have a benevolent step-mother. An heirless widow may happen to acquire a dutiful adopted son. On the other hand, the same child and the same widow may have, respectively, a selfish step-mother and a ruthless adopted son—in which case their fate will be terrible. The same thing applies to other individuals in the penumbra. Theoretically the simple principle of substitution or replacement takes care of them. The step-mother substitutes for the lost mother; the adopted son for the unborn son; the concubine is merely fulfilling part of the wife's functions; and so forth. Practically, however, the society is so organized that the welfare of the individual rests almost entirely upon the fixed resources of the kinship structure, and there is very little social pressure to alleviate the destiny of those who are not properly placed within it. People in the penumbra are, therefore, at the complete mercy of human nature which is such that, when self-interest is combined with an absence of social control, it will normally follow courses dictated by temperament, prejudice, and selfishness.

It will be noted that in the penumbra life is harsher on women than on men. Unless the male is caught in infancy by a ruthless step-mother or lacks an heir in his old age, his difficulties are not insurmountable. There are fewer limitations on his efforts for self-improvement than on those of the female. Furthermore, as a review of the foregoing pages will show, most of the circumstances of the penumbra apply to the female rather than to the male.

CHAPTER X

Culture and Personality

WE MAY now ask: What does such a culture mean to the personality of the individual? The answer is not easy. Some inferences, based upon overt behavior, will be made. In this connection two concepts given in Chapter I must be used: basic personality configuration and status personality configuration. The first norm is that common to the entire society bearing a given culture; the second is that which is linked with a certain socially delimited group within the society bearing the given culture.[1]

One of the persistent, but unsettled, questions concerning the formation of personality is whether heredity or culture is more important. For the present, at least, and without minimizing the great potentialities of the work of William Sheldon and others, the answer to this question given by Ralph Linton will seem to be the only workable one. Except in the case "of a few small societies whose members have a homogeneous heredity, where the influence of physiological factors in determining the psychological potentialities of the majority of these members cannot be ruled out, culture must be considered the dominant factor in establishing the basic personality types for various societies and also in establishing the series of status personalities which are characteristic for each society."[2]

[1] Ralph Linton, *The Cultural Background of Personality*, New York, 1945, pp. 128–130. These two concepts are also similar to what two other authors call the "communal component" and the "role component" of personality. (See C. Kluckhohn and O. Mowrer: "Culture and Personality, a Conceptual Scheme," *American Anthropologist*, vol. 46, 1944, pp. 1–29.)
[2] *Ibid.*, pp. 145–146.

AUTHORITY AND COMPETITION

The two outstanding factors in the culture of West Town which appear to have the most bearing on the development of personality are authority and competition.

In all cultures infants are more or less supervised and fed by adults. Therefore we may say that all infants are subject to some authority. But the extent and intensity of the authority, as well as the manner in which this authority is exercised, vary widely. In West Town the mother, or on occasion some other female relative, closely supervises every movement of the infant and freely feeds it whenever it so demands. The father has practically nothing to do with the infant's early care but his role as a disciplinarian becomes more important as the infant grows older.

The father's authority over male and female children functions differently. With the son the disciplinary relationship is direct; discipline over his daughter is applied by his wife, acting as his agent. Should the mother lose control of her daughter or if a serious offense such as adultery is committed, the father will lose no time in taking direct disciplinary measures.

The thing which distinguishes West Town authority from that in many other cultures is, however, that, although it is intense and inclusive, it is far from being a one-sided command-submission pattern. In fact the obligations between the father and son are so mutual, and the power so counterbalanced that the father-son relationship is best described by the term identification. For paternal authority does not originate from the living parents alone, but springs from and is couched in the names of numerous forebears reaching back many generations and reinforced by the utterances and achievements of these glorified personages. The paternal authority does not stop when the younger person has come of age, but is continued as long as the father is alive. The father, while alive, acts as the ancestors' agents. Upon death he has merely become one of the ancestors whose influence remains the most potent factor to control the younger man's life. Then the younger man takes the father's place in the great family continuum.

Thus the son is under ancestral authority; but so is his father. The son is not free to act; but nor is his father. Furthermore, while the son is dependent upon his father, the father is also dependent upon his son. The pattern of father-son identification makes them dependent upon one another not only materially but also socially and after death.

In this way the thing of primary importance in shaping personality is the ancestral authority. The more reliance upon this authority the individual shows, the better adjusted he becomes throughout life. This authority over him and prearrangement for him runs through every aspect of his life and work, including his marriage and means of livelihood. At every turn the individual is confined within this prearranged framework.

Far from being opposed to the drive for competition the pattern of father-son identification actually encourages it. For every individual can add weight and content to this ancestral authority by his achievements. The drive for competition expresses itself not only in the acquisition of wealth but also in ceremonialism, ancestral honor, display of socially approved virtues and power, and various ways of insuring successes in general. Competition operates not only between different clans and different lineages within the same clan but also among different households within the same lineage and different members within the same household. It is largely responsible for the absence of a strong clan organization. Thus, while theoretically all members of a clan derive benefits from a "good" common graveyard, when it comes to burying one's own parents, competition narrows down to a struggle for the best location within the best graveyard.

If we look, however, at the objects of these competitive efforts, we find that they all come within the framework closely defined by parental authority and ancestral tradition. As long as ambition functions within this framework, the individual has every encouragement to get ahead of everyone else. The fortunate are those who are on the right side of the barrier: the unfortunate are those who are not. At this point there is an apparent paradox. Those who fail to do well reflect upon the conduct of their ancestors, and their ancestors share the disgrace of their failing to do well. The ancestors so affected may be those of the entire clan or the more immediate ones of a single lineage. From the point of view of the stranger, the poverty or the misery of certain families reflects upon the ancestors of their entire clan. From the point of view of a clan member, it may merely refer to the immediate forebears of the particular lineage.

Those who have not done well under the ancestors' shadow are unfortunate, but those who are outside the shadow, namely, those in the penumbra, are in much worse circumstances. Everything depends upon whether one is within the shadow or outside, and the insecurity which threatens these unfortunates in West Town culture is much greater than in contemporary American culture. They are entirely at the mercy of the favors or disfavors of the people who act as substitutes for the relatives whose absence causes him or her to be in the penumbra. This insecurity increases the incentives to competitive efforts to get ahead.

These two patterns of behavior, authority and competition, are clearly reflected in West Town religion. I have shown the existence of an elaborate spiritual hierarchy and the place of ancestral spirits within this hierarchy. I have pointed out that this wider hierarchy corresponds to the machinery of government and that the hierarchy of ancestral spirits corresponds to the family and the kinship organization.

Under the jurisdiction of this spiritual hierarchy, highly and the lowly situated spirits are subject to the worldly patterns of submission to authority and competition. There are distinctions between the more fortunate spirits and those less fortunate according to the traditionally defined framework, and there are also unmistakable signs of struggle for personal salvation along the traditionally circumscribed ladder of ascendance. The spirit who had more virtues while alive and the one whose descendants have burned more paper money or performed more elaborate and numerous scripture-reading services for him will have a much better fate than others.

THE BASIC PERSONALITY CONFIGURATION

What is the effect of these cultural forces on the basic personality norm? As far as the overt behavior is concerned, the first outstanding quality is an explicitly submissive attitude toward authority. For the growing West Towner there are very few choices and very few uncertainties. All routes are, so to speak, barred except one, that which follows the foot-steps of his father, his father's father, and the whole line of his more remote ancestors. Along the established path, life is agreeable; all other trails lead to misery and self-destruction. The West Towner tends to be keenly aware of the necessity for orthodoxy. He tends to be apprehensive of any departure from the beaten path.

Within the socially approved framework and under the impetus to glorify his ancestors the individual exhibits a strong drive toward success. This is the second outstanding quality in the basic personality. Nothing would be farther from the truth than to characterize West Towners as being fatalistic. Fate and fatalism they talk about, but believe in only when such a belief happens to be convenient. The average West Towner is no more fatalistic than the early American who prayed to God and kept his powder dry. To the early American, God was a consolation. To the West Towner, fate serves the same function and is a good mechanism to tide over any frustration caused by failure. Furthermore, the West Towners, as do all Chinese, distinguish between "lifelong fate" and "periodic fate." The former is the fate of the individual during his entire lifetime. The latter is his fate during a particular period of time, for the individual may now run into a "favorable periodic fate," and again into an "unfavorable periodic fate." When all signs point to an unfavorable periodic fate, one must be careful to avoid making important transactions or decisions, for a favorable periodic fate will come along later.

In general, the average West Towner, far from being confined by such ideals, will do everything in his power to solve his problems and improve his social and economic position at any time. Even when he has been told by the diviner that according to his lifelong fate he is doomed and even when he has already experienced many reverses, he will still try to do something about it, such as, perhaps, propitiating other gods or performing traditional good deeds. The most striking examples are found in connection with illness which threatens life. As long as the patient is still breathing and the family can finance the projects, no effort is spared and no stone is left unturned by way of finding a cure for the unfortunate person. Various kinds of doctors, various types of spiritualists, and all kinds of gods will be resorted to. But finally, when all efforts have failed and the patient has died, then, and then only, do the family members believe that "medicine can cure diseases, but cannot cure fate."

This is why we must conclude that in spite of his concern with rituals, gods, and other-worldly existence, the West Towner's orientation in life is essentially a worldly and positive one. For him the world of spirits is but a necessary supplement to the world of the living.

This untiring struggle expresses itself, however, within the definite limits of tradition. Both the lines of progress taken and the final objectives desired are well confined within this framework. Money is one objective for any male West Towner. Yet even if it is possible to make money by running a laundry in the community, he will not do it, for laundry work is woman's work and therefore below his dignity. Success in business enterprise is one of the objectives. If the fortune of the family has gone from bad to worse, the family head, although he will not turn a deaf ear to sensible advice on management, will have the sites of his ancestral homestead and graveyard checked by a geomancer. When the question of the next burial comes up within his household, he may even abandon the old site in favor of a more "advantageous" one.

Everyone wants prestige. The West Towner will try to acquire it not only by the acquisition of wealth and power, but also by generous contributions to local prayer meetings, elaborate funerals and other ceremonial displays, building huge but unused family homes, extensive and showy graveyards, and the exhibition of ancestral honors.

The two qualities just analyzed, submission to authority and competition for a superior place in life, lay the foundation of West Town basic personality configuration. Instead of conflicting with each other, they re-enforce and merge into each other. As a matter of fact, the starting point of competition is the household. Brothers, instead of trying to get ahead by independent paths, tend to begin by competing for their father's favor.

In view of this groundwork, certain behavior characteristics become intelligible. The first of these characteristics is the preference for anonymity. The average West Towner wants to compete with other West Towners, achieve success, and show that he has something which the others do not have, but he does not want to prove that it is he as a person with a particular name and better creative ability who is winning the contest. He would much prefer to emphasize the fact that the merit really belongs to his parents and ancestors or is occasioned by fate, either of the lifelong type or of the periodic type. To show that he personally has something which the others have not would be embarrassing to the latter; to pass the merit on to his parents or to his ancestors and fate would not be so embarrassing, because this would assume that his good fortune is something which is evidently beyond the control of the less fortunate.

By the same token, if the average West Towner has to punish or be hostile to someone else he prefers to couch the punishment or the act of hostility in terms of the culprit's offense against ancestors, sex morals, filial piety, or other good customs of the land. This preference motivates all behavior. In refusing to grant a request, a man will give as an excuse not that he cannot grant it, but that his employer does not allow it. The reason he gives for turning down an offer will be, not that he does not like the offer, but that his parents will not let him accept it.

The second characteristic is seemingly a contradiction of the first, the flare for excess. It may seem impossible that people who are so much confined within a framework of tradition and who prefer to "pass the buck" behind the protective wall of the ancestral shadow should be capable of excesses of any sort. Nevertheless, there are many observable excesses in the community. They occur not only in ceremonialism, such as exhibitionistic funerals and weddings, not only in the elaboration of family homes, graveyards, and clan temples, not only in the trouble taken to display honors earned by relatives in the remote past, but often in oppression, cruelty, and lack of calculated economy.

It is not hard to reconcile this trait with the meticulous attitude of submission to authority and conformity to form. Two factors are operative in this connection. The first is excessive parental tutelage, which tends to prevent the growth of economic foresight. This factor is above all responsible for the upper-class West Towners' habits of excessive spending and taking life too easy. The average child in American culture gets used to the idea of having some cash of his or her own very early in life. He is given a periodic allowance, and he has to make ends meet. The West Town child has no such experience. He spends what he can get out of his father, and when cash is short, all he has to do is to go again to the same person. In this way the authority of the father over his children is made firmer than ever. The same infantile attitude is continued in the West Towner's adulthood. A fixed budget seems out of the question because there are so many competitive social obligations which he must fulfill. Everybody tries to be a little more showy in the conventional sense than others, and in due course, his means will be no longer sufficient to meet his ends. When he no longer has a loving father magically to rescue him from his financial difficulties, he will go to someone else, according to custom; for the ends, which have the backing of authority and tradition, cannot be changed, and the ends justify any means. This is at the root of extravagance and official corruption.

However, there are two customs in West Town culture which appear, at least theoretically, to compensate for the lack of economic foresight. One is the custom of family division under the same roof, and the other is the importance of trading.

In a situation in which most members of most families assist in or carry on trading procedures or enterprises an appreciation of monetary values and the ability for rational calculation tend to be sharpened. The youngsters may not be fully aware of all the difficulties which their parents encountered in their struggles, but they are not likely to be entirely out of touch with reality. They may be competent to maintain whatever success their forebears have achieved in life.

The custom of family division under the same roof may exert a greater influence upon the formation of the personality. Without this custom the youngsters would have little opportunity for economic independence or any family responsibility. The emphasis on the big-family ideal tends to delay the partial emergence of the young from the over-all protection of the old. However, the true weight of trading with regard to this partial emergence of the young in West Town culture remains to be ascertained by further investigation. At this point it should be remembered that trading is not engaged in by sons of the rich and that the good effects of family division under the same roof may be nullified by the omnipresent shadow of ancestors.

The second factor bearing on customs which seem excessive is the psychological effect of displacement. In practice this may be implied in several types of oppression and cruelty, such as the cruelty which may be imposed on a slave girl,[3] or on some unfortunate woman who has eloped, but gotten caught, or on those who are in the penumbra, or on those who have no present tie with any kinship group.

Its overt manifestation is as follows. The son has to submit to his father's authority regardless of his own wishes. He must do the same with reference to all those to whom he stands in a similar authority-submission relationship. He has no complaints against the arrangement as such, because his turn will come later, when others will have to submit to his authority.

A woman has to submit to the authority of her father, husband, mother-in-law, and, after the death of her husband, even her sons. She merely waits for her chance to "take it out on" her daughter or daughters-in-law or on the men or women who are not related to her, but happen to be in her way. In West Town it is uncommon to find

[3] We have to distinguish between two types of cruelty. Many Western observers have commented on Chinese callousness. But they have not distinguished intentional cruelty from that which is a result of neglect or of customary indifference to suffering. Intentional cruelty, whether to human beings or to animals, is not encouraged in American culture today, except in special areas where racial antagonism is great. But cruelty which is a result of neglect or customary indifference is common in England and in the United States as in China and in many preliterate parts of the world. The Englishman or the American who is shocked by the sight of Chinese callousness to wounded horses or his method of holding a live chicken has probably never paused to reflect upon the agony of the fox followed by a pack of hounds or the fish tied by the mouth to the side of a vacationer's boat. Lobsters are universally cooked alive wherever they are eaten. It is interesting that the Society for the Prevention of Cruelty to Animals does not even mention such matters. Some members of such societies are probably expert anglers when they go on vacation. In the present connection the terms "oppression" and "cruelty" both refer to acts which are, by and large, committed intentionally.

two men fighting each other with their fists, but it is not at all uncommon to observe women tearing each other's hair and rolling on the ground, one on top of the other. To observe a husband beating his wife or even an older brother punishing his younger sister would make one conclude that women of West Town are unquestionably submissive and that because of their helpless attitude and behavior under such circumstances they deserve sympathy. But given the opportunity to be roused by an outsider, whether the latter be man or a woman, the same "helpless" women will fight most valiantly and to the end. There is no mystery about this phenomenon; it is simply that energy may be so released that could not escape in other ways. The higher incidence of fighting among women is probably explainable by their greater submission to authority. The man who gets a chance to hit an unfortunate girl who has eloped is responding to a similar psychological stimulus. The severity of the cruelty inflicted on such women merely testifies to the intensity of the suppressed wishes which have not found any regular outlet.

The third behavior characteristic closely follows the other two. This is the inability to create or to enter a new and untried path. The individual encounters comparatively little insecurity in life, but neither is he encouraged to make any plans of his own. He does not have to grope for his future, but he is also not equipped to meet new situations. He will certainly possess no means for seriously challenging the existing scheme of things. If and when the existing scheme of things has broken down, he will merely try to build up a new series of schemes in strict accord with the forms and principles defined and delimited by the recognized authority. Within the framework of tradition the individual behaves and works with the greatest of ease; outside the framework the individual is at a loss and puzzled at every turn. Within the framework the individual will manifest benevolence, kindliness, and generosity or excess cruelty, harshness, and cold-bloodedness, according to circumstances. Outside the framework the individual merely becomes bewildered, panicky, and frantically eager to get back into the framework. In other words, within the framework it is comparatively easy for the individual to adjust; outside, the same individual will be hardly capable of adjustment. The individual will see the necessity of alms for the poor and donations for prayer meetings against cholera epidemics. He will recognize the importance of contributions for the establishment of schools and a hospital as long as they can be calculated to increase his spiritual welfare and social prestige. But he is not likely to see that they are needed in terms of a higher percentage of literacy and an improved state of communal health; therefore his very act of charity may nullify its good effects.

Within the framework the individual is fortunate, lucky, and secure; outside, he becomes unfortunate, suffers, and is miserable and insecure. Since the individual has been trained to depend upon this framework for his every movement, it is obvious that only the eccentric will even dream of trying to question or improve it. This fact has been responsible for the misleading observation that China is a country of the golden mean. As seen from the above analysis, this principle has little to do with West Town behavior.

STATUS PERSONALITY CONFIGURATION

Thus far, the behavior characteristics emphasized are those of the basic personality configuration and are stated, except in a few instances, as they apply to the male. What are the characteristics of the status personality configurations? To answer this question it is necessary to give, first of all, a résumé of the statuses recognized in the community.

There are six general categories of paired statuses: (1) upper generation versus lower generation; (2) male versus female; (3) older versus younger; (4) rich versus poor;

(5) high bureaucrats versus low bureaucrats; and (6) bureaucrats or literati versus commoners and illiterates.[4]

Let us examine the characteristics of these groups, which must for present purposes be combined into three broad groups. Generation must be seen together with age. The former usually, though not invariably, coincides with the latter, for there is usually an age difference between two individuals of different generations. The center of generation or age statuses is the father-son relationship. The relative positions of other individuals of different generations or age levels are more or less varied versions of this relationship. Generation and age are practically synonymous with authority and submission. That is, with relation to each other, an individual of the upper generation is older and is authoritative, and the person of the lower generation is younger and is submissive. The one commands; the other obeys. At any given point of time the individual of the upper generation or older in years than another has a higher social worth than the younger. Whether it is true or not, such an individual is regarded as being wiser and better acquainted with life than the other.

Most active Americans dread the idea of retirement. The height of the American male's career is in his early middle age. From that point, he starts to slow down, and his worth becomes less and less, until he comes to a point when he understands or is made to understand that he is completely out of the running. For the American female the turning point comes somewhat sooner.

This is not the case with West Towners. As the foregoing chapters should have made clear, the kinship structure is such that, the worth of the individual is commensurate with his or her age or generation. Except for those in the penumbra, the individual is in a continuous process of transition through which he or she reaches increasingly

---

[4] Needless to say, any one individual usually occupies several of these statuses at any given time. For example, a person may be male, upper generation, older, rich, a bureaucrat at the same time just as another may be male, lower generation, old, poor, and illiterate.

greater security, prestige, and value. The son in West Town culture can surpass his father by making more money and attaining higher degrees and offices than the older man. But the father-son tie identifies his achievements with those of his father, and the usages with regard to generation and age enable his father to outrank him at all times.

From the point of view of personality formation such an arrangement must have significant consequences. Yet apart from the dominance-submission pattern there is little that we can point out as typifying the personality configuration of an individual of the upper generation or one of the lower, or of an older or a young person. This is not hard to explain. Any West Towner is likely to be on both generation levels at most given periods in his lifetime. Unlike his American brothers, who may live in isolated homes without parents or children, the West Towner usually resides among parents, uncles and aunts, sons and daughters-in-law, and other relatives of various generation levels. For this reason the personality of an individual of a certain generation level tends in the course of the lifetime of any West Towner to merge with that of individuals of other generations. The same picture is more or less true in respect to the differences between older and younger persons.

The really important status personality difference occurs (1) between male and female on the one hand, and (2) between the rich or highly placed and the poor or lowly situated on the other (the latter being a combination of categories (4), (5), and (6) given at the beginning of this section).

As far as can be observed, the cultural patterns of submission to authority and encouragement for competition apply to the male as well as to the female. Like the male, the female has to submit to the authority of parents, ancestors, and tradition, but unlike the male she must also submit to the authority of her husband and certain other related males. Like the male, the female freely exhibits a desire for competition, but unlike the male she often competes for a different set of objects. Her competitors may be her husband's concubines or his brother's wives. Her objects may be success in business ventures or the fostering of good behavior in her children. As may be expected, her life is circumscribed by the household environment, and her opportunities in the struggle for a better place in life are much more limited than those of her husband. For example, for the man success or failure in marriage is a matter of fate in the periodic sense; but to his wife, it is a matter of lifelong fate. The husband can transcend fate and look forward to a better period in his life when he may be married to someone better suited to him; his wife has to resign herself passively and accept the unhappiness as one of life's inevitables. What is more, while it is possible as time goes on, for the younger ones to become older, for the sons to become fathers, and, at least theoretically, for the poorer to become richer, there are no means which will enable females to become males.

The result is a female personality configuration which exhibits two distinguishing marks. First, the female is much more limited by fate than the male. For the male, fate is but a temporary retreat; for the female, it is often a permanent shelter. That is partly why West Town women appear to be so much more devoted to religious worship and other spiritual matters than are their husbands and sons. The second distinguishing mark of the personality norm is rather its lack of any sharp distinction from that of the male. In Western Europe and America the ideal type of woman, in the minds of the upper class at least, may be summarized as a graceful ministering angel. She will be personal in her views, kindly, likely to faint at the sight of blood, completely devoted to her love object, and protected in every way. The personality difference between her and her husband or sons is qualitative rather than quantitative.

This is not so in the female personality configuration of West Town, where there is no idea that women have finer sensibilities than men or possess qualities which will magically heal men's wounds. There is no conception of feminine perfection such as that defined by Tolstoy in his criticism of Tchekov's story, "The Darling."

> . . . and it is true not only with regard to birth, nurture, and early education of children. Men cannot do that highest, best work which brings man nearest to God—the work of love, of complete devotion to the loved object, which good women have done, do, and will do so well and so naturally. What would become of the world, what would become of us men if women had not that faculty and did not exercise it? We could get on without women doctors, women telegraph clerks, women lawyers, women scientists, women writers, but life would be a sorry affair without mothers, helpers, friends, comforters, who love in men the best in them, and imperceptibly instill, evoke, and support it.[5]

To West Towners such a statement would be absurd. The West Town male would not even be able to comprehend what special faculty Tolstoy was so desperate about having women exercise. The female in West Town is expected to exhibit about the same general personality characteristics as the male. She differs from the male only in the same sense that a person of one generation or social status differs from someone in another generation or social status. They differ to a certain extent in work and very much in prestige. They also differ in the physiological sense, which makes women ritually unclean. The female is likely to burst into tears or be unreasonable in the same way that petty men or children may be. But these are about the only differences that West Towners recognize in the personalities of the two sexes. If a rough comparison is helpful, we may say that in terms of personality females are regarded as immature males who will never grow up.

The differences in personality configuration between the rich and the poor, or between the "top dog" and the "under dog," are more drastic in nature. They have their roots in the entire family and social organization.

To understand these differences, it will be necessary

[5] Translation by Constance Garnett, London, Chatto and Windus, 1927.

briefly to review once again the objects and methods of education. The objects of the education of the rich and of the poor, it will be seen from a glance at the table given in Chapter VIII, are different in several respects. Their training with regard to a livelihood differs almost completely. The common elements in the activities of the rich are superiority and dominance; both are significantly lacking in those of the poor. The training in social adequacy is similar in both status groups, with the exception of objectives of competition. The activities of the poor are calculated to achieve some degree of financial security. For the rich security is taken for granted, and their activities are aimed at attaining greater power, prestige, and ancestral glory. Therefore, the basic orientation of the poor in competition is economy, while that of the rich is conspicuous waste.

Significant though these differences are, they are not as important as some factors in the methods of education. Apart from the fact that boys emulate their fathers, and girls their mothers, there is no basic sex difference in the technique of education. This is also true of the rich and the poor. The techniques of education are, universally, (1) direct participation (observation, imitation, and conscious instruction) and (2) a system of reward and punishment. There is no sphere of adult life, except that of sex, from which the male child is entirely excluded. In fact, the latter is encouraged to enter adult life as early as he can.

The result is that sons of the West Town rich are as rich and as powerful as their fathers. Sons of the poor are as poor and insignificant as their fathers. The father-son identification and the big-family ideal require that there shall be complete community of interests between the old and the young. Whatever the father has, the sons share, and vice versa, without qualification. Children are, therefore, encouraged to be frugal and hardworking if their parents happen to be poor and to lead the life of wasteful parasites if their parents happen to be wealthy. In fact, the wealthy parents consciously or unconsciously consider their children's leisure and comfort as partly indicative of their own social prestige. The psychological mechanism under-lying father-son identification is thus not unlike that which exists between the husband and the wife in Euro-American culture as graphically pointed out by Thorstein Veblen.[6] It is in the light of these considerations that an apparent contradiction in West Town culture may be understood. We may ask, why is it that while in general West Town children are subject to strict authority, they are neverthe-less free from restraint with regard to food habits?

The answer is twofold: first, West Town parents have little obsession over their children's diet as a matter of principle, but the children's freedom may be drastically cur-tailed as a result of practical necessity. Wealthy children can overeat, but poor children often must tighten their belts. Even the mother's milk may be drastically reduced by malnutrition. From this angle it is obvious that a large number of West Town children are forced to grow up under food restrictions regardless of parental intentions.

Much more significant, I think, is a second point. West Town parents do not merely refrain from imposing restric-tions on their children's feeding habits. Those who have no cause to worry about food take great pleasure in seeing their young ones eat freely. The same is true regarding the spending of money.

Thus, hard as I tried, I did not find that frugality and industry were valued intrinsically; they were but necessary evils under pressure of adverse circumstances.

In most societies, including those of Europe and America, the objectives of the rich and of the poor are different. Take contemporary United States as an example. Most wealthy American industrialists and business men do not care about their ancestral glory, but many of them work for prestige, fame, and power, while the poor merely struggle for their very existence. However, their methods of training their children for life are a far cry from those employed by West Towners. The primary difference lies in the fact that

[6] *The Theory of the Leisure Class*, New York, 1899.

West Towners emphasize direct participation and encourage their children to share in adult life on a full scale, but the Americans, while not excluding direct participation, expect their children to develop under the limitations of childhood and to share in adult life only gradually. Sons of American millionaires have much more limited resources at their disposal than do the sons of wealthy Chinese parents. The absence of the father-son identification and the big-family ideal make most American youngsters realize early that they will have to work for what they want. Sons of West Town rich, on the other hand, tend to have the entire resources of their fathers at their disposal. In fact, the wealthy father feels very proud to be able to say that his son does not have to work at all. If the youngster is in trouble, the older man will do whatever he can to help the young ne'er-do-well. He will usually back the latter up, regardless of the issues involved, to the limit of his ability.

I have no doubt that there are wealthy American parents who give their sons "soft" jobs in their own establishments and pamper them, but there seem to be more that require their sons to go through a strict course of discipline, regardless of their social status.

For this reason sons of the wealthy and the powerful in West Town tend to have wealth and power go to their heads early in life. The degenerating effect of wealth and power on the young is given full play. When the youngsters do not voluntarily react to their surroundings in that way, the people in their environment tend to give them preference because of their fathers' wealth and power and influence their thinking accordingly. Wealth and power, even in the hands of adults who prospered by hard and honest work and have feelings of justice and humanity, if unchecked will be detrimental in the long run. How much more dangerous will they be in the hands of youngsters who have never worked for a single day and who firmly believe that whatever they desire in life will be forthcoming to them simply for the asking or the taking?

Thus, through the same cultural patterns of a strong

father-son tie and the big-family ideal, both of which are integrated under the ancestors' shadow, two different personality configurations are formed. The poor sons share their parents' hard-working habits and receive the training of honest, hard-working men. The rich sons share their parents' power and glamor and begin life in the firm belief that they are destined to command, rule, control, and be supplied with a permanent bed of roses.

Little wonder that the status personality configuration of the poor and the lowly differs strikingly from that among the rich or the highborn. These differences tend to become more pronounced in the younger members of a family one or two generations after its rise to power. The personality configuration of the former status group tends to be submissive, careful, rational, frugal, realistic, industrious, and sincere. The personality configuration of the latter status group tends to be vain, unsympathetic, licentious, impulsive, unrealistic, extravagant, carefree, insincere, and to lack economic and common sense.

Certain qualifications must be attached to this categorization. First, it is extremely difficult to ascertain the exact dividing line between the two status personality configurations, because it is impossible to ascertain the exact line at which West Towners may be divided into rich and poor, or the highly placed and the lowly. There are observable a polarization of behavior at the extremes and numerous intermediate grades. Secondly, it is not asserted that *every* individual who is definitely placed in one or the other group invariably possesses the general personality configuration of his particular status group. A few individuals whose social and economic stations place them without doubt in one status group nevertheless exhibit the general personality characteristics of the other group. Thirdly, the poor and the lowly exhibit the personality characteristics of their status group, not with any great sense of pride, but because of necessity. As soon as they prosper, their sons or at latest their grandsons, will tend to exhibit the personality traits of the other status group, and no one will then have any desire to tell the youngsters to do otherwise.

This difference in personality configuration between the two status groups explains, it seems to me, in large part, why family fortunes tend to rise and fall within a period of two or three generations. The hard-working children of poor parents may not succeed in causing their family fortune to rise at once, but there is at least such a possibility. The easygoing children of rich parents may not bring about their family's immediate downfall, but their parasitic life will probably be the beginning of a downward trend.

It is possible that the customs of general trading and of family division under the same roof may have exerted some beneficial influences on the personality configuration of the status group of the rich, so that it will at least be plausible to expect that the fortunes of West Town big families will hold out longer than elsewhere in China. However, as far as my investigation is concerned, I have discovered no definite evidence for such optimism. Of the four highest-ranking families, only the sons of one show that they will at least be able to maintain the status quo if not to improve matters. The sons of two others show signs of the usual weaknesses. The fourth family does not yet present any consistent picture. Outside of these families, I can point to several loafers whose forebears only one or two generations ago were great names in the community.

SUMMARY

In the preceding chapters I have attempted to describe and analyze West Town culture and its general bearing on the formation and development of personality.

Briefly, the most basic element of the culture is the pattern of a close father-son tie, which is characterized by authority on the part of the parents and filial piety on the part of the son. All other relationships in the family and kinship structure have this tie as their basic point of reference. Coexisting with this tie are five other basic patterns of behavior which are interrelated: (*a*) estrangement between the sexes, (*b*) the big-family ideal, (*c*) education to emulate the old, (*d*) emphasis on the solidarity between living and their dead relatives (ancestor worship), and (*e*) equality among males or females of the same generation.

The characteristic of the close father-son tie plus (*a*) through (*d*) is authority. The characteristic of the sixth basic pattern is competition. Authority stresses difference in status. Competition emphasizes equality in status. This competition is strictly circumscribed by the authority of parents, ancestors, and tradition. These several sources of authority dovetail into and re-enforce each other. They never conflict with one another. They provide the groundwork and the limitation for both the means and the objects of this competition. In such a culture competitors are like the jockeys in a horse race; to win and achieve distinction they have to proceed along a given track toward the same destination. Any branching off along a different track or toward a different destination means total failure.

The lack of security for those within the penumbra, the distinction between men of various statuses as shown by privileges, prestige, and power, and the fluidity of the structure in the long run all go to heighten the drive to competition.

The same forces of authority and competition also operate outside family and kinship groups as represented by: (*a*) holders of various ranks in the bureaucratic hierarchy, (*b*) rich and poor, and (*c*) literati and the illiterate. Competition characterizes the relationship of those who are approximately on the same level, namely, literati, the illiterate, governmental functionaries of similar ranks, and others. Here the competition is essentially circumscribed by the previously-mentioned source of authority. They limit the means and the objectives of the competition in much the same way as they do within family and kinship structures. The lack of security of those low in status, the distinction between various statuses, and the fluidity of the social structure in the long run again go to heighten the drive for competition.

Submission to ancestral authority and competition within a framework determined by this authority thus are the most important elements in the basic personality type of the community. However, this basic type applies to different status groups in different ways. In this connection four status personality types may be distinguished: (*a*) male, (*b*) female, (*c*) rich (or literati or those holding high offices), and (*d*) poor (or illiterates or those in humble circumstances). The basic personality type applies equally to the male and the female. But the female is subject to more authority than is the male, and she is permanently precluded from ever reaching a status equal to that of any male. She is much more limited than is the male in her efforts and in the objectives of competition. The female is subject to the restraints of fate much more than the male.

Between the other two status personality types the differences are more far-reaching in their consequences. Again the basic personality type applies in a general way to both. But the rich and those having a higher status adhere much more to authority, while the poor and those in humble circumstances exhibit more drive for competition within the framework delimited by this authority. The former give their sons carte blanche to be extravagant and carefree, while the latter teach their sons to be frugal, industrious, and calculating. In fact, the matter probably involves a minimum amount of conscious instruction, if any. The young in each status group merely share the life of their elders.

In this way, while authority and competition apply to both groups, the end results tend to be drastically different. The children of the fortunate tend to exhibit many weaknesses which will ultimately bring about the family's downfall, while those of the less fortunate tend to develop qualities of energy and enterprise which are indispensable in the struggle for existence.

These status personality differences are, in my view, responsible for cycles of rise and fall with regard to families. They are, again in my opinion, also at least partially responsible for the cycles of rising and falling dynasties. The fall of dynasties has so far been related by social scientists to two factors: parasitic expansion of the bureaucracy and overpopulation. Without minimizing the importance of either of the two factors, we should not find it difficult to see that the ruler who rules wisely will not aggravate the effects of overpopulation, thus enabling the dynasty to hold out at least longer, while the ruler who is careless and extravagant will bring about its doom much sooner. When the latter performance is repeated over a few generations the downfall of the dynasty is assured.

CHAPTER XI

Wider China

NO ASSUMPTION is made that West Town culture is identical with that in other parts of China. In the preceding chapters we noted some features of this culture which apparently distinguish West Town from other parts of the country, even though our knowledge of the latter is limited. Yet the observations on personality configuration made here may be corroborated by data from a much wider field than West Town. In broad outline they apply to South Village, another Yunnan community I have studied. They apply in Manchuria, where I was born and brought up. They apply to Shanghai, Peking, Taiyan, and a number of large cities, as well as to some backward areas of China in which I have studied, worked, or visited briefly.

Most interesting corroborations have been found in two recently published autobiographies and an old novel. One is *The Daughter of Han*,[1] the other is *My Autobiography*, by China's famed "Christian General."[2] The old novel is entitled *Kuan Ch'ang Heien Hsing Chi* (*Queer Scenes behind the Curtain of Officialdom*).[3]

The "Daughter of Han" started life in urban poverty and struggled through it in the same poverty. She supported herself and her family by being a servant for officials and missionaries and gives fascinating descriptions of life be-

[1] *The Daughter of Han*, being an autobiography of a Chinese working woman, recorded and translated by Ida Pruitt, Yale University Press, 1945.

[2] Feng, Yu-hsiang, *My Autobiography* (in Chinese), Tientsin, 1945.

[3] An old and popular novel, written toward the end of the nineteenth century.

hind the walls of their households. The Christian General started life in rural poverty and struggled through most of it, first as a soldier, then as an officer of low rank. During the first part of his life he maintained direct contact with humble villagers and was a rebel against official corruption, extravagance, and irresponsibility. The old novel has woven together a tremendous body of honorable and dishonorable episodes of the literati and the officials in their efforts to maintain or to better themselves.

In all three works we see both the "rich" and "poor" types of personality configuration in action. Not only the Chinese officials exhibited the characteristics of the rich type of personality configuration, but even missionaries who employed the "Daughter of Han" and who have lived in China for some years showed the same traits and were evidently proud of them. All three works show the very slight importance of women and the complete indifference to the Euro-American conception of the romantic female personality as a motivation for struggles among males.

At the same time, a review of these three works and of my personal observations and experiences during the last thirty years in various parts of China has convinced me that the categories thus far established only begin to define the problem. When and if more intensive inquiries are made, it will be possible to distinguish between many more personality configurations. Even now some other personality configurations may be surmised.

Let us call the kind of personality which we have designated as "poor" Type 1 and that which we have designated as "rich" Type 2. Type 1 configuration is found among the vast majority of China's small farmers, craftsmen, small traders, and other manual workers in cities. Type 2 is found among the literati and among individuals whose fathers are wealthy because they are powerful.[4]

---

[4] This sentence probably needs some explanation. In a capitalist society, such as the United States, wealth comes by way of creative efforts, commercial and industrial enterprises. Wealth is the founda-

In imperial times this type was most numerous among the descendants and close relatives of emperors, princes, and high officials. The royal descendants usually grew up among court favorites and eunuchs who were only too anxious to please their masters by demonstrating and abusing their masters' power and prestige. The descendants of high officials, provincial governors, militarists, and lesser persons of one kind or another, either in imperial times or in Republican days, grew up among their fathers' lieutenants and bodyguards in the same way that princes grew up among court favorites and eunuchs. These people do not exhibit the personality characteristics of the "rich" merely in West Town. Because of their birth into greater power and wealth, the disastrous effects of their behavior tend to be much more intensive and extensive. It is only common sense that, given the same qualities, people in higher places have a much greater potentiality for good or for evil.

Besides these two types there appear a number of others, the definition of which will be clarified by more intensive investigation. There is a kind of personality configuration which we may classify as Type 3. This is found among persons whose fathers are well-to-do and on whom rests the chief hope of keeping the family property intact (*shou yeh*). Some of these fathers purposely encourage their sons to smoke opium as a means of keeping them at home. Sons who have grown up in such circumstances tend to exhibit some of the characteristics of Type 1, in that they are submissive and careful, but they differ from people of Type 1 in that they are not necessarily industrious, frugal, rational, and sincere. In fact, most of them will have no ability or desire to work. They tend also to exhibit some of the characteristics of Type 2, being insincere and pos-

---

tion of power. In a society like that of China, where industrial and commercial activities are maintained on tiny profits and a very low standard of living, the chief way to acquire wealth was and is by becoming a high official. Being in power, one is then in a position to swing matters to self-advantage at the expense of the people and the nation. Power is therefore the origin of wealth.

sibly licentious, but they differ from people of Type 2 especially in having a sense of realism in social and legal matters. For example, many individuals with bureaucratic connections or aspirations will go to great lengths in litigation or other methods of revenge to get the better of an opponent on points worth less than the expenses incurred. A person of Type 3 is more likely to refrain from such steps by reflecting on the dangers of making unnecessary enemies.

Type 4 configuration is found among some people whose fathers are powerful and wealthy, but who nevertheless fail to exhibit the personality characteristics of Type 2. Instead they show great intelligence, rationality, sincerity, industry, foresight, and initiative. Some of them become great leaders. One of the best examples is provided by Marquess Cheng Kuo-fan and his descendants. The Marquess was largely responsible for pacification of the Tai Ping Rebellion in the middle of the nineteenth century. His power and prestige were great, and his wealth, considerable. His son made outstanding contributions in foreign relations, and his grandchildren are today public figures in the fields of education and social welfare.

On the reverse side, there is Type 5. This is found among a number of people whose fathers are poor and may be hardworking peasants or craftsmen, but who, nevertheless, fail to exhibit the personality characteristics of Type 1. Instead, they show all the signs of the degenerate drunkard and habitual gambler known in American culture. One of the best examples is the husband of the Daughter of Han.[5] Being poor and lowly, he was not able to ruin a nation, but he did his best to make his family miserable. He not only failed to support his family, but he stole whatever money his wife made. He not only failed to educate his children, but he sold his daughter for payment of his gambling debts. In other words, he exhibited many personality characteristics similar to those of Type 2.

[5] *The Daughter of Han, op. cit.*

PROBABLE PERSONALITY CONFIGURATIONS IN CHINA

Type	Social origin	Characteristics	Numerical ranking
1	Father is poor and of a lowly status	Submissive, careful, realistic, rational, frugal, industrious, and sincere	1 (Vast majority of Chinese)
2	Father is rich and powerful; has a very high status	Vain, excessively touchy about prestige, unsympathetic, licentious, impulsive, unrealistic, lacks economic and common sense, extravagant, carefree, insincere, and boastful	3
3	Father is well-to-do, but not very highly situated in the official hierarchy	Submissive, careful, possibly lazy, insincere, and licentious; realistic in the sphere of social and legal life, but not in economic matters	2
4	Father is rich and powerful; has a very high status	Rational, sincere, industrious, far-sighted, and full of initiative	5
5	Father is poor and lowly, but may be hardworking	Lazy, degenerate, unrealistic, lacks economic and common sense, carefree and insincere	4

The exact mechanisms which produce Type 4 and Type 5 are not very clear at this point. It is possible that heredity plays some important part. I do know, however, that Marquess Cheng was not only a believer in strict discipline but also maintained close personal supervision over his children. His collected letters to his sons and grandsons have now become one of the outstanding modern classics, both from the literary point of view and from the point of view of the principles they embodied and warmly elaborated.[6]

In connection with Type 5, it is interesting to observe that all villagers and townspeople whom I have come into contact with in various parts of China were aware of the evil of spoiling children. They told innumerable anecdotes and tales about the disasters which had befallen such parents. The following proverb circulated widely in North China:

> Spoiling your sons is equal to killing them.

Whether Marquess Cheng's descendants turned out so well due to his close supervision and whether some of the children of the poor turned out to be rascals due to their parental overindulgence are questions to be investigated. On a common sense plane, the relationship in each case appears to be reasonable.

From the point of view of the entire population the number of Chinese who approximate Type 1 is the vast majority. The number of Chinese who approximate one or another of the other types is, by comparison, small. Of the smaller groups, the numerical strength of Type 3 is probably the largest; that of Type 2 comes next; that of Type 5 is smaller than either Type 2 or Type 3, while that of

---

[6] Just compare the trouble Marquess Cheng took over his descendants, as seen through his family letters, and the relationship Chia Cheng maintained with his son Pao-Yu, the hero of *The Dream of Red Chamber*. Chia Cheng also was a believer in strict discipline. His son feared him so much that he shivered whenever they met. Yet Chia Cheng had practically no contact with his son except on special occasions. Once the son's licentious behavior led to the suicide of a young maid. Chia Cheng then came home and ordered Pao-Yu to be beaten almost to death. At most other times Pao-Yu carried on in his usual manner with his female cousins, homosexuals, and the numerous young maids without any interference at all.

Type 4 is the smallest. Types 1, 3, and 5 are to be found among the masses, while Types 2 and 4 are the rulers.

Apparently there have been three fortunate features in the situation which have, I believe, served as brakes against, or at least partially compensated for, the ill effects of Types 2, 3, and 5. The first feature is that Type 1 approximates the personality configuration of the vast majority of Chinese. The second feature is the occasional existence of Type 4 among the rulers. The third feature is that women were more segregated and restricted in the families which produced Types 2, 3, and 4 than in those which produced Type 1.[7] As a result, the degenerating effects of wealth and power did not reach girls to the same extent as they did boys, if at all. Thus, the personality configuration of the female of all classes tended to remain constant and closer to Type 1 than to the other types.

It is to be pointed out again that all five types of personality configuration postulated here are products of the same father-son identification under the big-family ideal. Their differences are, as far as the present inquiry is concerned, due largely to three factors: the economic and power factors are largely responsible for the contrast between Types 1 and 2; at least superficially, discipline seems to be responsible for the contrast between Types 4 and 5. The first contrast shows that an increase in economic welfare of the country without a change in the technique of home education would be undesirable, because it would increase the proportion of Type 2. On the other hand, the second contrast shows that if our inferences are correct even under the same father-son identification and big-family ideal, a stricter and closer parental supervision can at least avoid the pitfalls of Types 2 and 5. However, this combination is very hard to achieve, since under the conditions of wealth and power such strict discipline and supervision are contradictory to the basic emphases inherent

[7] Because families which had high social aspirations adhered to external signs of tradition much more than did others.

in the father-son identification and the big-family ideal. All fathers want their sons to be great sons. Yet few highly placed fathers can enjoy the idea of having their sons divorced from their own wealth and power; nor can they tolerate having others look upon their sons without full regard to their own wealth and power. The social convention says that to do so is to slight their sons, and to slight their sons is to slight the fathers. Thus, highly situated fathers, while worrying about being slighted, forget or ignore the degenerating effects of wealth and power on the younger generation. For this reason we must expect to find comparatively few representatives of Type 4.

With western contacts and the establishment of the Republic, a number of new factors have come into play. The significance of some of these new factors in terms of the present thesis remains to be seen. Some general remarks, however, may be made here. First, the old examinations system has been abolished. In imperial times, although a degree like *chin shih* (third examination) did not automatically entitle the holder to any office, the possession of such a degree was the absolute prerequisite especially for higher bureaucratic posts, and they were checks to family and other influences. The system having been abolished, there is a less definite standard for promotion and demotion. A powerful minister could put his daughter virtually in charge of a most important government bank, and a provincial war lord could give his son almost any office to which he aspired. These would not have been possible before the Republic.

From this point of view, we may expect a higher degree of continuity in family prominence. However, a review of *Who's Who in China*[8] over a period of twenty years has revealed little evidence to support this expectation. The time is, of course, too short to tell. Most entries in the volumes of *Who's Who in China* examined also concern

[8] Published by *China Weekly Review,* Shanghai, 1915 to 1936.

only government officials and educationalists. It is probable that many men who made good in other walks of life have been left out.[9] But probably a more important reason is that even if they are given paternal encouragement and every conceivable opportunity, individuals with a personality configuration of Type 2 will find it difficult to hold their own once their fathers (who are their blind supporters) have passed out of the picture. That is why, I think, few sons of war lords in the last thirty years have succeeded in achieving the same degree of prominence or notoriety as their fathers had, in spite of the fact that most war lords have dynastic ambitions.

The second factor which has become operative since western contacts and the coming of the Republic is a change, or the possibility of change, in family behavior. The items which are most important to the present thesis are: the big-family ideal, father-son identification, and sex inequality. In all three cases the changes affect the educated or wealthier classes much more than others.

The change in the big-family ideal has been the subject of much writing, but elsewhere I have shown that as far as the existing evidence goes the shift is still largely a matter of verbal preference rather than actual. While there are data showing discontent among students with the age-old cultural emphasis, all inquiries have also revealed that, whether in rural or urban areas today, families among the

---

[9] Formerly the vast majority of the ambitious aspired to become members of the literati and then of the bureaucracy. The multitude of other occupations had simply no comparison in prestige and remuneration. For a comparison of the reward of bureaucrats and other workers see F. L. K. Hsu, "A Closer View of China's Problems," *Far Eastern Quarterly,* November–December, 1946, pp. 50–57. A limited growth of industrialization and a more extensive development of modern commerce in connection with Western products have given rise to a new middle class, with a structure and dignity of its own. In imperial times sons of high officials would be bureaucrats or idle members of the long-gown class at home. The instances are not numerous, but in the last several decades we have seen men from a literati or bureaucratic background turning to commerce, banking, or industrial enterprises.

wealthier, and presumably the better educated, classes as a whole are still larger than among others and that the joint family type, consisting of parents, their unmarried children, their two or more married sons, sons' wives and children, and sometimes a fourth or fifth generation still prevails among the largest groups.[10]

The father-son relationship is being more drastically modified. There is good evidence that this relationship tends to be less a matter of authority and submission and more a matter of companionship and intimacy. It remains a subject for investigation to determine how far the father-son relationship can be modified without seriously affecting the big-family ideal. For the present there is little evidence to show that the long-established pattern of father-son identification has been appreciably altered.

However, some changes in the relationship between the sexes have added a new element to this father-son identification. Sex inequality is becoming less popular in many ways. Before the modern Chinese law, men and women who are educated enough to resort to it are practically equal. Freedom of choice in marriage has become the most acute and the most popularly recognized point of difference between the generations. At home the educated modern Chinese wife is gaining in authority and influence with relation to both her husband and her sons.[11] There is definite

[10] F. L. K. Hsu, "The Changing Chinese Family," in Ruth N. Anshen, ed., *The Role of the Family in Contemporary Society,* New York, Harper and Brothers, 1948. Science of Culture Series, Vol. V.

[11] Surveying the newspaper *Chung Nan Pao,* published in Tientsin during the years 1945 and 1946, I have found the question of parental interference in marital choice the most recurrent subject raised by young men and women who wrote letters to the editor. Miss Lang has found that among 482 male and 428 female students investigated, only 2 men and 3 women answered that they would let their parents choose mates for them (Olga Lang, *Chinese Family and Society,* New Haven, Yale University Press, 1946, p. 288). Yet elsewhere she has found that "many parents even in . . . relatively advanced [modern] circles still insist on their old privileges and . . . not all the children fight for their rights" (*ibid.,* pp. 122–124). Miss Lang also has some data on the improved position of the educated modern wife (*ibid.,* pp. 212–214).

evidence to show that, while the father tends to become an intimate companion of his sons, he is coming also to share a similar intimacy and companionship with his daughters.[12] This, plus the fact that there is a definite tendency toward change in the husband-wife relationship, has meant the broadening of the traditional father-son identification. At least temporarily, this identification may include the daughter and even the wife.

This has given rise to a situation which has enabled some women whose fathers or husbands happened to be wealthy because they are powerful to exhibit the personality characteristics approximating Type 2 and, occasionally, Type 4. With greater freedom and wider scope for action, women can do much more damage as well as more good than before.[13]

The field investigation of which the present book is a result was carried out without the aid of psychological techniques. It was carried out by one anthropologist who relied only upon his own training in social observation and common sense. Because of this lack of means for probing into deeper layers of the mind, the correlations between personality and culture thus far attempted are necessarily comparatively simple and obvious. Had the present author been able to utilize, for example, the Rorschach Test along with his field work, the inquiry might have been pushed further and the results might have proved more definitive.

[12] Miss Lang has obtained some interesting results on this matter (see *op. cit.*, pp. 300, 309). Her Table XIV shows that among both male and female college students investigated the number of those who questioned paternal authority is practically even with those who submitted to such authority. Miss Lang's arrangement of Table XIII is unusual. Even so, it shows an increase in companionship and intimacy between the modernized father and his children as compared with the old-fashioned father and his children.

[13] It will, of course, be erroneous to argue that therefore sex inequality has been a good thing. To uphold such an argument is like proposing that we shall only find peace and happiness by returning to the age of the caveman.

The writings of Oberholzer and Hallowell are a convincing testimony to the potency of this technique.[14]

The present volume must, therefore, be regarded as an attempt to blaze the trail, in expectation of more intensive and extensive research in a practically virgin field.

[14] For an excellent summary and exposition see A. Irving Hallowell, "The Research Technique in the Study of Personality and Culture," *American Anthropologist,* XLVII (April–June, 1945), 195–210.

Kinship, Personality, and Social Mobility in China

WHILE DOING the research for this book, and since its original publication, I have been intrigued by the rise and fall of Chinese dynasties. I attempted to link that over-all political cycle with the principles underlying Chinese family, kinship, religion, and personality formation through a microscopic study of one community. Prominence of family lines among the Chinese people as a whole also seemed to be highly impermanent.

The rise and fall of a ruling dynasty was a more complex affair than those of a single prominent family. No simple equivalence between the two is scientifically defensible. However, we are not precluded from seeing at least the latter as in some ways related to the former.

My principal conclusion was that the concatenation of forces favored a recurrent reduction in ability and achievement motivation on the part of the sons of the rich and well placed—therefore they or their sons would fail to live up to their ancestors' shadow, thus unavoidably making room for the children of the poor and less well placed. A family and kinship system which would seem to protect the continuation of the social status of its descendants has built in its very system forces which favored the reverse trend, thus providing the traditional Chinese society with a remarkable degree of social mobility.

One objective measure of support for this conclusion was sought in a study of the kinship links among Chinese who achieved prominence through various ages. Two sources of data were resorted to: the first covers those Chinese who reached national prominence, and the second covers those who were not so prominent but nevertheless became important for local areas (districts). From both sets of data the major conclusion of this study, that social mobility was high in China, was borne out. These analyses were originally given in Appendix IV "A Study of Family Prominence."

Since publication of *Under the Ancestors' Shadow* the results of a number of different studies point in the same direction and lend further support to my conclusion. First, biographies from four more districts (mentioned in Appendix IV in the original edition of the book but not discussed) were analyzed in much greater detail and the results support the same conclusion. This analysis was published in a paper entitled "Social Mobility in China" in the *American Sociological Review* (Vol. XIV, No. 6, Dec. 1949, pp. 764–771), and is now included here as a new "Appendix V: More Evidence on Social Mobility in China." In this new appendix I refer to a study by Edward A. Kracke, Jr., entitled "Family vs Merit in Chinese Civil Service Examinations Under the Empire,"[1] which was published just before *Under the Ancestors' Shadow* and was not known to me when I completed my analysis of the data for Appendix V. Kracke's results support the same conclusion, although his sources of data are entirely different from mine.

More evidences of a remarkable degree of social mobility in traditional Chinese society came to light with the publication of *The Ladder of Success in Imperial China* by Ping-ti Ho[2], Robert Marsh's *The Mandarins: The Circulation of Elites in China, 1600–1900*[3], Wolfram Eberhard's *Social Mobility in China*[4] and a collection of shorter

[1] *Harvard Journal of Asiatic Studies*, Sept. 1947, Vol. 10, No. 2, pp. 103–123.
[2] Subtitled "Aspects of Social Mobility, 1368–1911," New York, Columbia University Press, 1962.
[3] Glencoe, Free Press, 1961.
[4] Leiden, E. J. Brill, 1962.

papers entitled *The Chinese Civil Service: Career Open to Talent?* edited by Johanna M. Menzel[5].

While the sources of data of Ho, Marsh, and Eberhard all came from written documents, Ho and Marsh concentrated on members of the bureaucracy (or elites who were prominent enough to figure in national lists), and Eberhard took certain clans and analyzed by way of actual genealogies the social status of every male member in each clan, thus giving us some idea regarding the fates not only of those individuals who achieved national prominence of some sort but also those who were less notable. The data used by the first two scholars (Ho and Marsh) are similar to those of Chiang Liang-fu which we used in the first part of our original Appendix IV to *Under the Ancestors' Shadow,* while the data used by the last of the three scholars (Eberhard) are in line with those used in our original Appendix IV as well as the new Appendix V. The booklet edited by Menzel contains published papers by Ho, Marsh, and Kracke, as well as by nine other scholars.

It is interesting that all of these more recent published works support the general conclusions reached in our Appendices IV and V. That is to say, whether we look at the national scene or the local arena, social mobility in Chinese society was remarkable. Marsh concludes that in "the Ch'ing bureaucracy the rule of seniority and other norms operated in such a way as to equalize the chances for advancement of officials from family backgrounds as disparate in privilege as official families and commoner families".[6] Ho demonstrates a great deal of regional differences and differences between periods in mobility, but concludes that "there seems to have been a remarkable continuity in the social mobility pattern between Sung and Ming times" and that "modern students without preconceived theories

[5] Boston, D. C. Heath and Co., 1963.
[6] Menzel, *op. cit.,* p. 55 (Reprint of Marsh, Robert M., "Bureaucratic Constraints on Nepotism in the Ch'ing Period," *Journal of Asian Studies,* 1960, XIX, pp. 118–132).

or prejudice would perhaps rather agree with François Quesnay, a typical eighteenth-century French philosophe, who . . . believed with basically valid reason that by and large the Chinese ruling class was recruited on the basis of individual merit."[7]

Furthermore, wherever a quantitative picture is available, the results are similar. Kracke's study of the two extant Sung *chin-shih* (second highest imperial degree) lists shows that candidates from non-official families constituted 56.3% of the total of the class of A.D. 1148 and 57.9% of the class of A.D. 1256.[8] Ho's roughly corresponding data from the Ming dynasty (A.D. 1371–1610) yield the average figure of 50%.[9] These agree with our average derived from figures given in Appendices IV and V of this book, that "roughly 50 per cent of the local prominents in any district studied came from unknown origin." It is highly significant that the mobility rates among the nationally prominent and among the locally notable should agree with each other to this extent.

Ho, the historian, explains this remarkable mobility in two different and apparently contradictory ways. On the one hand he gives great weight to the Imperial Examination as a mechanism for humble people to rise:

> In fact, the examination system's long history of thirteen centuries is a most eloquent testimonial to its usefulness as a channel of mobility and as a socially and politically stabilizing factor. . . . The constantly changing social composition of the bureaucracy was well nigh impossible because academic success and official appointment owed not so much to blood as to intelligence, assiduity, and perseverance.[10]

[7] Menzel, *op cit.*, p. 32 (Reprint of Ho, Ping-ti, "The Examination System and Social Mobility in China, 1368–1911." Proceedings of the 1959 *Annual Meeting of the American Ethnological Society*, pp. 60–65).

[8] Menzel, *op. cit.*, p. 5 (Reprint of "Family Vs Merit in the Chinese Civil Service Examinations during the Empire," *op. cit.*).

[9] Ho, *op. cit.*, 1962, p. 114.

[10] Ho, in Menzel, *op. cit.*, p. 32.

On the other hand he sees the absence of primogeniture as having a major role in the failure of prominent men's descendants to live up to their ancestors' shadow:

> But by far the most important reason for the failure of the bureaucracy to be a self-perpetuating body was the absence of primogeniture and the inevitable process of progressive dilution of family property by the typically Chinese clan and family system. This causal relationship is nowhere more succinctly and piercingly pointed out than by Ke Shou-li, one of the famous censor-generals of the sixteenth century, who, on the occasion of donating some 1,000 *mu* of land as his clan's inalienable common property, remarked: "When the ancient clan system of which primogeniture formed a hard core can no longer be revived, the empire can have no hereditary families, the imperial court can have no hereditary ministers."[11]

The question may be asked, if "intelligence, assiduity, and perseverance" figured so largely in success in the examinations and bureaucracy, what happened to the "intelligence, assiduity, and perseverance" of the descendants of those families which were already so prominent? Lack of primogeniture could progressively reduce their wealth, but how would it reduce their "intelligence, assiduity and perseverance"? Furthermore, the same inheritance rule prevailed among all families, high or low. If lack of primogeniture dissipated the wealth of the already prominent families, would it not have dissipated that of the lowly placed families even more?

In his later and fuller treatment of the subject, Ho augments this position somewhat and states that *any one of the following five factors* could have been instrumental in the long-range downward mobility of high-status families (italics mine):

> . . . failure to provide children with a proper education, the competitive nature of the examination system which was based in the main on merit rather than on family status, the limited *yin* privilege of high officials, the mode of life and cultural expressions of the leisured class, and

[11] Ho, *ibid.*, pp. 32–33.

the progressive dilution of wealth due to the absence of primogeniture.[12]

However, upon closer scrutiny, we find that his last two factors led to dilution of wealth (the extravagance of the leisured class and lack of primogeniture) that would apply to all families, official or non-official; his third factor which led to dilution and reduction of rank (the limited *yin* privilege of high officials) would actually favor high official families and be a disadvantage to the commoners (because those who could inherit at least some rank by *yin* were in the last analysis better off than others who were not touched by the privilege in the first place); and his second factor (the competitive nature of the examination system) simply opened the door to all. Contrary to Ho's view, we find none of these four factors (singly, as Ho would have it) to be a sufficient or even a significant cause for the downward mobility trend of the prominent families, if success in the examinations and bureaucracy were greatly determined by "intelligence, assiduity and perseverance." In fact, at least one, if not two, of his factors would work in favor of prominent families against the commoner families.

The one factor truly crucial in this situation is the first one mentioned by Ho, namely, the "human environment," or the "failure" on the part of prominent families "to provide children with a proper education." Ho has given us some details as to what he means either by way of statements of past observers or data from actual case histories. For example, Yeh Tsu-chi, a "noted scholar of the late Yuan and early Ming periods" generalized as follows:

> If the ancestor's wealth and honor were first obtained by serious studies, the descendants, being accustomed to a life of ease, are bound to look down upon studies. If a family acquired its fortune through hard work and frugality, its descendants, with a fortune at their disposal, generally forget about diligence and thrift. This is the basic reason why there are so many declining and declined families. May this be a warning to all of us![13]

[12] Ho, *op. cit.*, 1962, p. 165.
[13] Ho, *op. cit.*, 1962, p. 142.

Other writers were more specific and the following is a good sample of a case history (in this instance of Wang Ao [1450–1524], a famous prime minister and leading man of letters):

> Wang Ao's son Wang Yen-che was by nature extravagant. He built a huge mansion in which to house his collection of female entertainers and concubines. When his children went out they were followed by tens of servants of both sexes, all in resplendent attire. His jewels, curios, ancient bronzes, porcelains, calligraphic specimens, and paintings were worth hundreds of thousands of taels. At a New Year's Eve banquet he invariably hung up a lantern made of pearls. All wine cups were ancient and made of jade. When he returned home, his sedan chair was first placed in front of the middle gate. After the gate was opened, it was carried inward by buxom female servants. He was usually surrounded by some twenty concubines, each of whom was waited upon by two maids. Everybody got drunk. When sufficiently stimulated, he rubbed women's shoulders and retired to an inner chamber, with an orchestra leading the way. In the chamber he drank once more until he fell asleep.[14]

Here Ho has indeed put his finger on the single most basic factor for downward mobility of the official families not only from the facts he presented but also in terms of our analysis of the family, kinship and personality formation in one Chinese local community. However, our position differs from that of Ho in certain important respects. For example, what Ho states in general terms as "failure to provide children with a proper education" is rooted in what we discovered to be father-son identification—a feature that is at the core of the Chinese kinship system. This identification means that, as I described it in the body of the book, "whatever the one is, the other is; and whatever the one has, the other has."[15] "The result is that sons of West Town rich are as rich and as powerful as their fathers. Sons of the poor are as poor and insignificant as their

[14] Ho, *ibid.*, pp. 144–145.
[15] See above, p. 63.

fathers."[16] We then went on to ascertain the differential consequences of the same pattern of father-son identification among sons of the rich and those of the poor, and demonstrated how these differential consequences might be instrumental in or at least heavily contributory to the long-range fall of the rich and rise of the poor.[17]

When this is understood, we shall be able to see why the same pattern of father-son identification worked differently in the bureaucratic families and among the non-bureaucratic ones. The sons of the prominent people, being identified in the public eye with their illustrious fathers and accustomed to a protected and pampered life of luxuries, extravagancies, concubines, and power over other human beings, simply had a drastically different kind of educational experience from the sons of the commoners, who were identified similarly with their lowly situated fathers and had a life of hardship and perseverance and among whom advancement as a whole could not be achieved except by the dint of hard work.

When this is understood we shall also be able to see some of the inadequacies in Ho's interpretation even where he is on the right trail and points to the "human environment" as a factor for downward mobility. We noted some of his facts which support his characterization of this factor as the "failure to provide children with a proper education." However, after having identified this factor so positively, he seems to reverse himself and says:

> Even without noticeable depravity or evidence of being spoiled, descendants of distinguished officials might still sink if they were not studious or were otherwise inept.[18]

[16] See p. 277.

[17] Since publication of *Under the Ancestors' Shadow* further work on Chinese kinship in a comparative context (as compared and contrasted with American, Hindu and certain African systems) has led me to replace the term "father-son identification" with the concept of "dominance of the father-son relationship," (as contrasted to "dominance of the husband-wife relationship," "dominance of the mother-son relationship," etc.). (For a fuller statement of this new development, see Francis L. K. Hsu: "The Effect of Dominant Kinship Relationships on Kin and Non-Kin Behavior: A Hypothesis," *American Anthropologist*, 1965, Vol. 67, pp. 638–661.)

[18] Ho, *op. cit.*, 1962, p. 146.

Ho then goes on to relate the case of a famous early Ming prime minister, Huang Huai (A.D. 1367–1449), who was known for his "prudence, foresight and power to analyze all sides of a problem," but whose descendants less than one hundred years later became "so impoverished that . . . they sold even the stone tablets of their ancestral graves."[19]

Furthermore not only was there no evidence for "failure" on the part of the elder "to provide their children with a proper education," but on the contrary, according to Ho, the elder most probably gave his children excellent education. Ho relates:

> Since from 1427 on he (Prime Minister Huang Huai) enjoyed twenty-two years of retirement in his ancestral home . . . it is unlikely that he should have neglected the proper education of his descendants as many of his colleagues did.[20]

There is an obvious contradiction here. Ho presents the case of Huang Huai in support of his contention that "failure" on the part of prominent elders "to provide their children with proper education" was the cause for downward mobility. (But this was not offered as support of any other of his "causes" such as lack of primogeniture.) And yet, the Huang Huai case turns out in Ho's own estimate to be opposite to his thesis.

We suggest that the contradiction is not due to the facts but to Ho's failure to appreciate the central importance of father-son identification in the Chinese kinship system and the manner in which it works to affect the educational processes of the young. As I explain in Chapter X:

> For this reason sons of the wealthy and the powerful in West Town tend to have wealth and power go to their heads early in life. The degenerating effect of wealth and power on the young is given full play. When the youngsters do not voluntarily react to their surroundings in that way, the people in their environment tend to give them preference because of their fathers' wealth and power and

[19] Ho, *ibid.*, p. 146.
[20] Ho, *ibid.*, p. 146.

influence their thinking accordingly. Wealth and power, even in the hands of adults who prospered by hard and honest work and have feelings of justice and humility, if unchecked will be detrimental in the long run. How much more dangerous will they be in the hands of youngsters who have never worked for a single day and who firmly believe that whatever they desire in life will be forthcoming to them simply for the asking or the taking?[21]

Because of this failure to understand the true meaning of father-son identification, Ho thinks that since Huang Huai had over twenty years' retirement in his home town, he certainly would not have neglected the proper education of his descendants. The pattern of father-son identification operated in such a way that the education of the sons of the prominent fathers was likely to be literally taken out of the elders' hands, as we explained above, even if the latter had time and wished to make it "proper." It is in this way we can understand why, though Prime Minister Huang Huai had ample time to provide proper education for his descendants, the latter still turned out so badly. Chances were that, in view of the prominence of his status, the pattern of father-son identification defeated Huang's hopes and intentions.

Seen in a world-wide perspective, no empire or dynasty has had an uninterrupted existence.[22] The founders of empires or dynasties are everywhere more role-oriented than status-oriented, while the inheritors of empires of dynasties tend to be more status-oriented than role-oriented. But at the same time it is also indubitably true that some empires or dynasties have lasted longer than others. Similarly, while the prominence of a family line in no society is known to last forever continuously, some prominent family lines have lasted longer than others, presumably involving also a similar shift in role-status orientation.

The continuation of an empire or dynasty, by virtue of the fact that it involves a much larger number of people,

[21] See p. 279.
[22] Raoul Naroll, "Imperial Cycle and World Order," *Proceedings, Fourth Peace Research Conference,* Forthcoming.

must be affected by many more factors and therefore is a more complicated matter than that of continuation of prominence of single family lines. For example, once having militarily and politically consolidated itself, the ruling regime, even without primogeniture, could have generated or cultivated a bureaucracy or military establishment whose own continued existence depends upon its continued loyalty to the ruling regime however incompetent. This is not likely to be the case for single prominent family lines.

However, compared with other societies, notably premodern Europe, Chinese dynasties lasted much longer along hereditary lines. This in spite of the lack of the notion of a permanent and divine legitimacy to rule and the prevalence of the notion of Mandate of Heaven which provided for the replacement of an incompetent dynasty by a new and more efficient one. On the other hand, the conspicuously noticeable fact was that prominence of family lines among the Chinese people had a much shorter existence than their counterparts in Europe, in spite of all the elaborate designs and factors favoring continuation of family prominence as described in the body of the book.

Our guess is that the high social mobility among the elite made it possible for the able and ambitious among the common people to rise, thus reducing the pressure for rebellion against the political regime, which enabled the latter to continue much longer than its counterparts elsewhere. In this, the Chinese family and kinship system, which promoted an inward-looking or centripetal tendency on the part of the individual, was helpful. It discouraged the individual Chinese from spilling permanently out of his kinship group and local area, though it also augmented his incentives for fattening the latter at the expense of the larger society.

At the outset of this essay we noted that in spite of their ambitious intentions and drastic measures, even the Communist government in China today cannot achieve the changes too easily or too speedily or effect innovations without reference to the old patterns. Each subsequent step for change is likely to enjoy a greater chance of success than the step preceding it, provided that the general direction of the successive steps remains constant. Many readers will undoubtedly have entertained the notion that the direction of change since 1949 differs greatly from that which went on for a whole century before it. This is not correct. Ever since the coming of the West, the major concerns of an economically impoverished, politically chaotic and militarily prostrate China were nationalism and industrialization. These have been the objectives of the Communist government, the Nationalist government, and reformers and well-wishers of China before them, including foreign missionaries. The missionaries attempted to woo Chinese children away from their parents and traditional ways through Bible classes and churches and Christian schools. Daniel Kulp II, onetime missionary professor of sociology in the University of Shanghai, where the author received his college education, expressed the opinion in a still useful monograph on a South China village that Chinese ancestors have hung a millstone over the young.[23] The Nationalist government did the same, by making Dr. Sun Yat-Sen's Three Peoples' Principles required curriculum in all schools and colleges with its Three Peoples' Principles Youth Corps, through exhortation to college graduates to serve in villages, and by initiating Generalissimo Chiang's New Life Movement. At the core of these attempted changes by the missionaries, the Nationalists and the Communists was and is the notion that the Chinese people must be weaned from their kinship ties and must substitute for them a higher or larger form of loyalty: loyalty to a more universal cause, to a party leader, or to the national state.

To the extent that each of these waves of innovation has achieved any results at all, it must have shaken the Chinese family and kinship system. The Communist efforts so far are not only more drastic than those which went before

---

[23] Daniel H. Kulp, *Country Life in South China* (The Sociology of Familism; Phoenix Village, Kwangtung, China), New York, Columbia University, Bureau of Publications, 1925.

but, by the very fact that they were preceded by other efforts in the same direction, are likely as a result to be more effective. Under the influences of missionary schools and the National Government, some young men and women quietly deviated from the ways of their ancestors. But under the stronger hand of the Communist government some young men and women have openly denounced their parents. In each instance the Chinese who took positive and militant action in the new direction were a minority. But the differing actions of the two minorities indicate something of the differing intensities of the changes desired and promoted.

How has this affected the pattern of father-son identification and its related picture of social mobility in China? Unfortunately we have yet no solid evidence which enables us to deal with either question except inferentially.

Robert C. North, in his study of *Kuomintang and Chinese Communist Elites,* concludes that "a major portion of the elite of both movements came from quite similar high social strata and responded to similar Western and native influences during their years of growth and education. . . . In both parties, the leaders have been drawn most frequently from a relatively thin upper layer of the Chinese population. In both parties these men were often the sons of landlords, merchants, scholars, or officials, and they usually came from parts of China where Western influence has first penetrated and where the penetration itself was most vigorous. All of them had higher education, and most of them had studies abroad. . . . Despite plebian protestations of the Communists, the relatively smaller mass of proletarians have continued to enjoy only limited access to the elite. . . . About half of the Communist elite (was) drawn from upper-class and middle-class families, and another quarter from the prosperous section of the peasantry."[24]

These findings support our analysis that the changes in

[24] Robert C. North, *Kuomintang and Chinese Communist Elites,* Stanford, Stanford University Press, 1952, pp. 46–48.

China since the middle of the nineteenth century have been in the same general direction, whether under Communist or non-Communist leadership, and that this general direction was determined by Western pressure and Western penetration. In terms of the "thinness" of the layer of the population which assumed leadership under both major parties in modern China, North's findings also dovetail the conclusion of Ho, that, "in our long-range retrospect. . . . it may be suggested that the amount of social mobility began to become truly substantial in the Sung, reached its maximum in the greater part of the Ming, started to level off after the late sixteenth century, and continued its downward trend until the final abolition of the examination system in 1905."[25] It is probable that this gradual diminution of opportunities for the poor and humble continued well into the assumption of power by the Communists, which is why the elite of both the modern Kuomintang and the Communist parties, by and large, came from the "upper-class and middle-class families and . . . from the prosperous section of the peasantry."

Ho attributes this reduction of room at the top largely to the "changing economic factor," that the "rapid growth of population" disrupted the old "population-land balance."[26] This undoubtedly was an old and recurrent factor of importance in Chinese history. We acknowledged it in Chapter II of this book along with the other recurrent ailment, that of increased bureaucratic corruption. However, I think that, at least since the forcible coming of the West into China from the 1840s onward and especially since the fall of the Manchu dynasty, this reduction was even more related to forcible opening of China by foreign forces, foreign-instigated and -supported civil wars, and foreign privileges all of which affected the native mechanism for social mobility. For example, the deposed Manchu boy emperor Pu Yi Aisin Gioro would not have been able to keep much of the imperial wealth as he did, with which he

[25] Ho, in Menzel, *op. cit.,* p. 32.
[26] Ho, *op. cit.,* 1962, p. 220.

was able to finance various warlords and foreign swindlers for the purpose of restoring his dynasty's control over the country, except for the safety of Peking's Legation Quarters or Tsientsin's Japanese Concession.[27] Had there been no such protective foreign presence, he and his deranked nobles would probably have met with the same tragic fate at the hands of China's new rulers that the Ming descendants met at the hands of Pu Yi's ancestors when they first conquered China. From his description of himself and what we know about his incompetence through other sources it is obvious that Pu Yi exhibited few of the personality characteristics necessary for founding a dynasty or regaining a lost one. But he was not only able to work all his incompetent machinations but was made puppet emperor of "Manchukuo" under the Japanese.[28]

Similarly, though most officials were given to corruption of some form or other through the last twenty centuries of Chinese history, they or their immediate descendants were subject to severe punishment and confiscation if they went too far, or after the passing of their favorite emperor, or after the loss of power of their highly placed backer in the government. They could not have escaped to a foreign concession, or deposited their loot in foreign banks, or invested it in American stocks as scores of them did since 1842 and especially after 1911.

[27] See Pu Yi, Aisin Gioro, *From Emperor to Citizen* (the autobiography of Aisin Gioro Pu Yi). Peking, Foreign Language Press, 2 vols., 1964.

[28] Another fascinating and informative autobiography is that of General Ts'ai T'ing Kai, who commanded the famous 19th Route Army that successfully defended Shanghai against Japanese invasion in 1932: *Autobiography of Ts'ai T'ing-Kai* or *Ts'ai T'ing-Kai Tzu Chuan*, 1946, Hongkong, Tzu Yu Hsun K'an She. 2 vols. In Chinese. General Ts'ai came from very humble origins, his family being small tenant farmers. He decided that the only way he could get ahead was to join the army. He did so well in this that he rose to become general through very many hard battles against bandits and in various civil wars. After he became a famous general and wealthy, he found that his sons did not turn out well. He actually blamed the conditions of life of a prominent and wealthy man for the unsatisfactory conduct and lack of achievement motivation on the part of his children.

Finally when going abroad for education became the fashion it was mostly the sons of the wealthy and the prominent who were most able to take immediate advantage of it. In modern Chinese parlance, studying in Japan was popularly known as "silver-gilding" and studying in Europe or America, "gold-gilding." These silver- or gold-gilded sons of the prominent needed not fall even if they did little or no real academic work abroad or received their diplomas from no more than correspondence schools or some other third-rate new world college. They automatically enjoyed more social prestige and had much better chances for high positions than stay-at-homes because they were riding on a popular tide in which the psychological need for some kind of Westernization was paramount.

In other words, the traditional forces in Chinese society and culture which made for social mobility were greatly overshadowed by factors extraneous to them, so that the incompetent sons of prominent men did not have to compete with those of commoners on any kind of equal ground such as the Imperial Examination System provided before. In the same way the traditional forces in Chinese society and culture which made for the rise and fall of ruling dynasties were also greatly altered by factors extraneous to them, so that very corrupt regimes could have a much longer life than before because they had foreign backers with enormous economic aid and especially superior weapons. Some changes did occur in the family and kinship system, but these did not alter the pattern of father-son identification to reduce its degenerative effect on the sons of prominent men to any significant extent. However, the abolition of the examination system, the general yearning for and nondiscriminate prestige accorded "gold-gilded" students made it much less possible for the incompetents to be replaced. This could not but create general frustration on the part of the poor and the humble who hoped and actively strived to rise. This hope and striving were always, according to our analysis in the following pages, part of the Chinese family and kinship system, for one of its two major values was competition. The wealthy and highly placed competed for greater displays in ceremony in conspicuous consumption while the poor and lowly competed for a place in the sun.

Ho hypothesizes that this downward trend of opportunities for the poor and humble since the late sixteenth century may be related to internal unrest.

> For a nation so used to a "Horatio Alger" sort of social myth . . . the steadily shrinking opportunity-structure for the poor and humble must have engendered a great deal of social frustration. It is worth speculating, therefore, whether the persistent downward trend (among the commoners) has had anything to do with social unrest and revolutions that have characterized nineteenth and twentieth-century China.[29]

This indeed is an interesting line of thought worth speculating about. Following it can we not see a link between the recent rise of the Red Guards in mainland China and the fact that, up to now, the Communist elite, like its Nationalist counterpart, mostly came from "a relatively thin, upper layer" of the population? Movements similar to that of the Red Guards are not new in China, but its appearance again at this time is specially interesting. It has been reported that the Red Guards enjoy the blessing of Mao and his reputed successor, Lin Piao, because the aged leaders fear the sagging of the momentum of the revolution and that the general population might then either settle back in its ancient ways or develop capitalist tendencies. I have every reason to think there is some truth in this. However, while a few leaders can stir up some kind of movement, they cannot hope to drum up widespread enthusiasm for it and sustain it, unless it is also an outlet for some real and general dissatisfaction. Can we not see the Red Guards movement as an expression and a demand for greater social mobility than what the modern Chinese society, under Western impact and circumstances beyond its control, has been able to provide? Furthermore, can we

[29] Ho, *ibid.*, p. 33.

not see the Red Guards' reported wild attempts to divest China of signs of Western influence as based upon some sort of realization on their part of one of the origins of their frustrations?

So far in this essay we have concentrated on the mechanism for social mobility inherent in the Chinese family and kinship system, and shown how external changes have largely nullified the effect of that mechanism and the possible consequences. But we must be aware of the fact that revolutionary movements, each one more radical than its predecessor, cannot but have a profound effect on the family and kinship system itself so that the age-old pattern of father-son identification is not likely to continue functioning as before.

A perusal of Jan Myrdal's *Report from a Chinese Village*,[30] containing the verbatim short autobiographies of about thirty active men and women in the northern Shensi village of Liu Ling with little or no commentary by the visitor, reveals that men and women who formerly were in dire circumstances and who had no hope of rising on the social or economic ladder before the Communist Revolution are now in some position of local importance. This could have been biased by Myrdal's selection of his biographies, but viewing the picture of the village as a whole, there did not seem to be many other persons of substance who had been overlooked. Some of these active men and women or some of their sons and daughters will surely seek to rise by going to schools and universities, and joining party organizations. They are likely to swell the ranks of rectification or protest movements such as the Red Guards, unless they find regular channels into which their aspirations for social mobility can be translated into reality without severe obstruction.

An elite drawn from "a relatively thin upper layer" of the population helped to usher in the Communist Revolution. The revolution they helped to usher in may have

[30] New York, Pantheon Books, 1965.

awakened so many more common people than before that the elite is in danger of being swept aside by the rising tide of aspirations. In this process the underdogs enjoy the advantage that for the last twenty centuries Chinese society has not known absolute barriers for upward social mobility. With new laws, new social structure, new political ideology, and new values of interpersonal behavior, which reinforce even more powerfully the forces which began to undermine traditional Chinese family and kinship systems over a century ago, the pattern of father-son identification, the age-old mechanism for social mobility, will be weakened (though not easily eliminated). How far the traditional pattern can adapt itself to the new demands, and how the two will combine to reach a new synthesis or equilibrium are matters that time alone will tell.

The Distribution of Living Quarters in Three Households

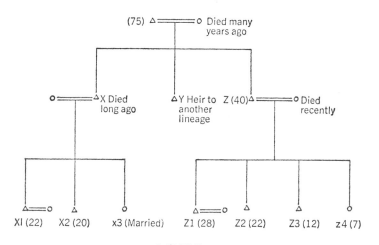

C FAMILY

FIGURE 18

IN THE C family the old father (75) lives in 1B1. X's widow lives in D, which is above 1B2, on the second floor. X1 and wife live in 1B2. X2, when at home, lives with his mother in the room just above 1B2. Z is usually in Kunming; before his wife died, they lived in 2B1. Z1 and wife live in 2B2. z4 lives with Z1 and wife in the same room. Z3 lives in the room of X's widow. Before her marriage x3 lived in the same room with her old grandfather, who was then in 1B2. Before his marriage X1 lived with his mother who was then in 1B1. After X1's marriage his mother gave up 1B1 and moved to D on the second floor. The old grandfather then changed from his original room 1B2 to 1B1. The reason for this change from 1B2 to 1B1 is that his bedroom could not be located below that of his daughter-in-law (X's widow). All members of Z's branch use kitchen Y, while all of X's branch use kitchen X. The toilet is shared by all, but X and children use one pig sty, while Z and children possess the other.

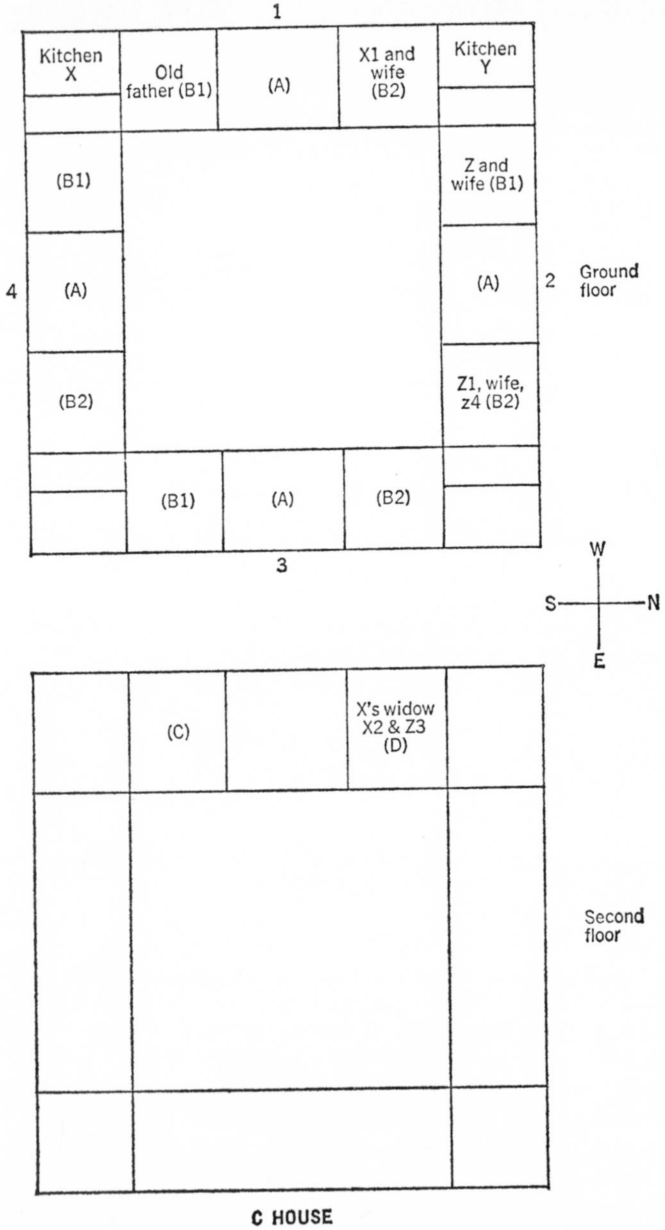

FIGURE 19

Room symbols in this and the next two "house" diagrams
are identical with those employed in Figs. 2, 3, and 4.

Wings 3 and 4 were normally unoccupied, and at the time of
investigation they were rented to tenants.

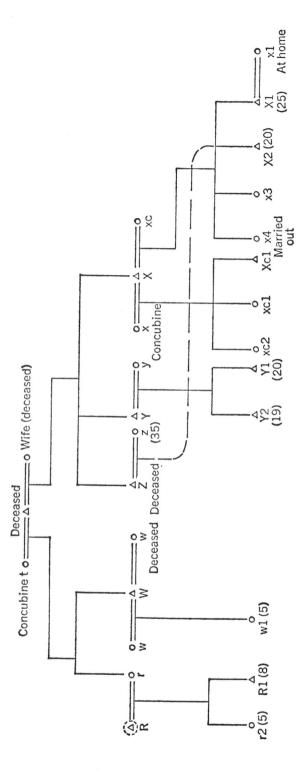

Y FAMILY

FIGURE 20

R is separated from r, X, his concubine x, and their three children, xc1, xc2, and Xc1, live in Kunming. Y2 is in the refugee college; Y1 is in the army, place unknown. W and w live in Kunming. X2, adopted son of Z, is studying in a Kunming school. X1 is working in Chungking.

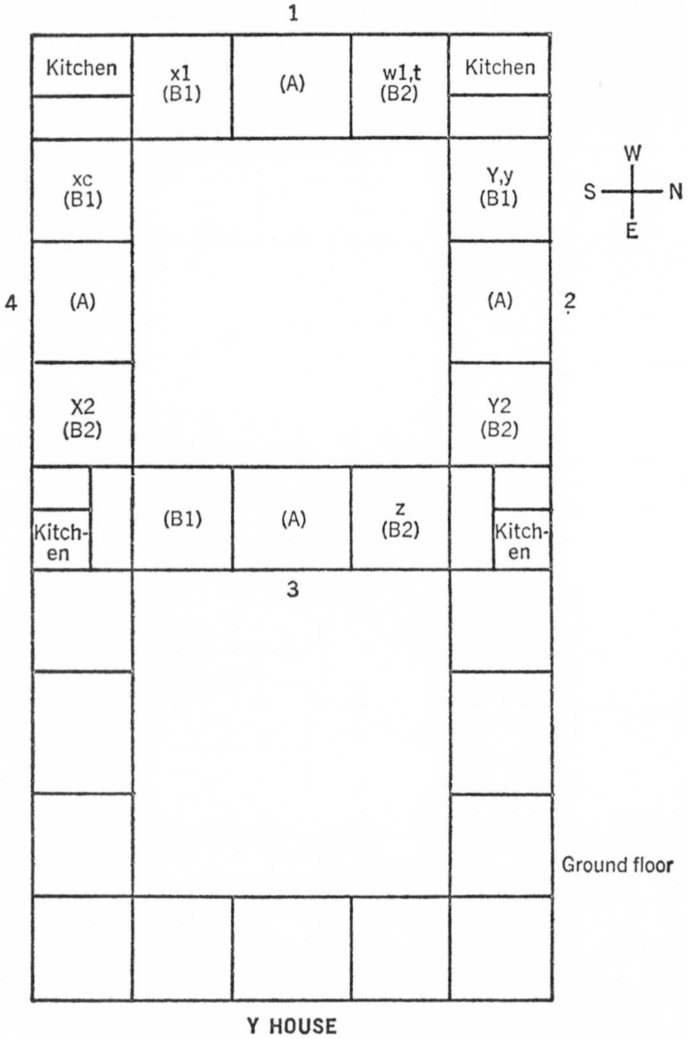

1

| Kitchen | x1 (B1) | (A) | w1,t (B2) | Kitchen |

xc (B1)

Y,y (B1)

4

(A)

(A)

2

X2 (B2)

Y2 (B2)

Kitchen

(B1)

(A)

z (B2)

Kitchen

3

W
S —— N
E

Ground floor

Y HOUSE

FIGURE 21

r, R, and r2 sleep in the little room above the kitchen, between 4B1 and 1B1.

A second example is the house of Y family.

In this house the three wings in the lower courtyard were normally unoccupied; at the time of this investigation they were rented to tenants. xc's bedroom is in 4B1. Her younger son, X2, though adopted by z to continue the line of Z, lives in 4B2 when he comes home from school.

Just above room 1A is the family shrine to which all go for worship. On the right-hand side of the shrine are two looms, on which r and t work all the time partially to support themselves. r and t also have a loom in t's bedroom. The second-floor rooms in the other wings are used for purposes of storage and usually are badly neglected. 3B1 and 3A are also left empty. r, R1, and r2 live in the second floor room just above the kitchen between 1B1 and 4B1.

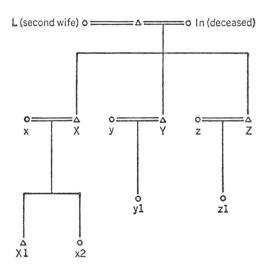

Ch FAMILY

FIGURE 22

A third illustration refers to the Ch family. This is a smaller house.

There are three sons in the family. The second son, Y, has married a Burmese wife. He and his wife and daughter live and work in Mandalay, Burma, permanently. Each of the brothers at home occupies one wing of the house. X, being the eldest, has the west wing, which houses the family shrine, and Z has the other wing. The family talks of building a third wing on the southern side when and if Y and his wife return. It will be seen that X and L appear twice in the house plan. This is due to the fact that although they each have a room with their wives, they do not sleep in the same rooms with their wives. The father and son prefer to occupy a bachelor room by themselves on the second floor. This is a custom which is prevalent not only in West Town but also in the whole of rural Yunnan.

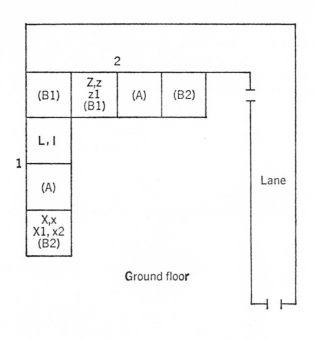

Ground floor

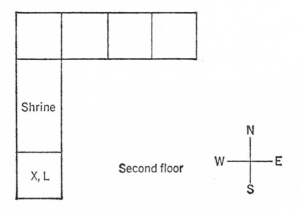

Second floor

Ch HOUSE

FIGURE 23

Cases of Concubinage

FIVE CASES IN WHICH THE WIFE HAS GIVEN BIRTH TO NO
SONS

C. S. Y.   Wife has no son. Husband used to be trader in
Hankow and Hongkong; had seen Peiping. Concubine from Pao Shan, a town 300 kilometers to the
southwest on the Burma Road. Concubine gave
birth to three sons. Concubine used to accompany
him to Hankow and Hongkong.

M. T. T.   Wife has no son. Husband is about 45; Concubine
is about 20. She disliked him and had affairs with
other men. Later she went to Kunming and divorced him. She left her two sons with him.

M. T. T.'s
cousin   Wife has no son. Concubine gave birth to a son.

Li   He is now dead. Wife has no son. Concubine gave
birth to a son and a daughter.

Y. C. Y.   He is about 40 years of age. Wife gave him no
children, so he got a concubine, after which his
wife chased him out of the old home in Pin Chuan.
She took charge of the old family property. Family
has a big house in West Town. He does trading.
Concubine has no son yet (several years after marriage). He expressed to me that he had not developed his trading on a large scale outside West
Town because he has no son, and must stay at
home and concentrate on getting a son.

SIX CASES IN WHICH THE WIFE HAS GIVEN BIRTH TO ONE OR
MORE SONS

C. S. Y.'s   Wife has 2 or 3 sons. Concubine has one son. He
brother   and his two female companions lived in Kunming.

Y   He is now dead. Wife (deceased) gave birth to 3
sons. Concubine (still living) gave birth to a son
and a daughter.

Y's son   Shopkeeper in Kunming. Wife has given birth to
2 sons and 2 daughters, all married. Concubine who
stays with him in Kunming has so far given birth
to a son and 2 daughters. She is still young.

C. N. T.   One of the richest men in West Town. Wife has
given birth to a son, who is married and very pro-
lific. The concubine is about the same age as his
daughter-in-law and has so far given birth to two
children.

Ya   Old man of 73. First wife (now dead) gave birth
to 4 sons and 3 daughters, all of whom are married
and have children. Second wife (now divorced for
some obscure reason) gave birth to a daughter who
has a *zou mei* husband, and both live with the family. It is said that a few years ago the old man went
to Pao Shan and cohabited with a widow on a clandestine basis. The sons were worried. The old man
then asked them to get him a girl. They bought a
concubine for him from Pao Shan. She was 16
when first married to him, and has so far given
birth to a daughter.

Li, T. T.   He is a man of about 45, who was once wealthy.
He now trades tobacco for a living. His wife is 38.
She gave birth to one son and two daughters. The
son is seventeen. Both the son and one of the
daughters are engaged. His concubine has no off-
spring. She is a native of Ko Chin, a town many
miles to the southwest. His wife and children live
in one house: he and his concubine live in another.

APPENDIX III

Size and Distribution of Households

HOUSEHOLDS		DIVIDED FAMILIES	
Size of household	Number of households	Size of families	Number of families
2	2	1	1
3	1	2	6
4	2	3	6
5	5	4	10
6	6	5	15
7	4	6	16
8	2	7	7
9	3	8	3
10	4	9	4
11	2	10	2
12	3	11	1
13	2	12	1
14	1	394	72
16	1		
17	1		
21	1		
23	1		
32	1		
394	42		

Average 9.38 persons per unit   Average 5.47 persons per family

APPENDIX IV

A Study of Family Prominence

FROM Professor Chiang Liang-fu's book *Native Places and Dates of Birth and Death of Noted Men in Various Dynasties*[1] all individuals who bore 30 clan names are here listed. These include five of the commonest clan names in the country; they are borne by the largest number of individuals. Together they make up a total of 3,787 individuals, or about one third of the names given in that volume. Of these, the native places of 2,897, or 76 percent of the total, are available. The following two tables reveal some surprising facts.

In the first table, column 3, is given the number of any two or more individuals who share the same birthplace, but were born either less than 15 or more than 60 years apart. For example, Li Shen and Li Tien were born in the same place, Shu Yieh. But the former was born in A.D. 1109, while the latter was born in A.D. 174.

Column 5 of the same table gives the number of individuals whose only relationship with each other was the common clan name. Each of them had a different birthplace.

From the point of view of our present thesis, Column 4 of this table is the most important. It gives the number of any two or more individuals who share the same birthplace and who were born within the 15 to 60 years range. For example, Li Hung-jui was born in A.D. 1761 and died in A.D. 1818, while Li Yien-Chang was born in A.D. 1794 and died in A.D. 1836. Since they were both born in Hou Kuan, they are regarded, for our present purposes, as being lineally related (that is to say, they are assumed to be either father-son or grandfather-grandson). In instances which involve more than two individuals a slight change of procedure is allowed. For example, Li Liang-chin was born in A.D. 722 and Li Cho was born in A.D. 730. They were born less than 15 years apart and therefore should

[1] The book contains some mistakes in dates, duplications, and undue omissions. These mistakes are corrected wherever possible in our tabulation. But no exhaustive effort has been made in this respect. The material is here given as evidence for whatever it is worth.

RELATIONSHIP AMONG NOTED INDIVIDUALS BY AGE AND BIRTH PLACE

	1	2		3		4		5	
Clan	Number of Noted Individuals Recorded	Number Whose Birthplaces Are Known	Percentage of Those Whose Birthplaces Are Known (Column 2 divided by column 1)	Number Who Shared Birthplaces but Were Not Born within 15-60 Years Range	Percentage of Those Who Shared Birthplaces but Were Not Born within 15-60 Years Range (Column 3 divided by column 2)	Number with Same Birthplace and Born within 15-60 Years Range	Percentage of Those with Same Birthplace and Born within 15-60 Years Range (Column 4 divided by column 2)	Number Not Born in Same Place	Percentage of Those Not Born in Same Place (Column 5 divided by column 2)
Li	481	332	69	92	27.7	72	21.6	168	50
Wang	540	439	81	113	25	161	36.6	165	37
Chang	408	322	80	93	28.5	70	21.5	162	50
Chao	157	157	100	42	26.6	45	28.7	70	44.5
Wu	191	113	40	23	20	2	1.8	88	78
Hsieh	44	35	79.5	1	2.8	13	37	21	60
Wen	33	27	81.8	15	55.5	12	44	0	0
Hwang	131	110	84	21	19	31	28	58	52.7
Hsu	35	27	77	6	22	0	0	21	77.7
Wei	53	44	83	2	4.5	20	45	22	50
Tung	37	27	72.9	5	18.5	10	37	12	44

Ho	69	56	81	6	10.7	19	33.9	31	55
Wong	76	68	89.5	17	25	29	42.6	22	32
Tang	64	43	67	2	4.6	6	14	35	81
Ting	38	25	65.8	1	4	6	24	18	72
K'ung	41	31	75.6	4	12.9	23	74	4	12.9
Sun	116	88	75.9	15	17	21	23.9	52	59
Hsü	154	122	79	28	22.9	33	27	61	50
Chu	133	98	73.7	25	25.5	30	30.6	43	43.9
Sung	80	41	51	9	21.9	5	12	27	65.9
Kao	90	56	62	14	25	12	21.4	30	53.5
Loo	99	81	81.8	24	29.6	33	40.7	24	29.6
Shen	89	76	85	9	11.8	43	56.5	24	31.5
Kung	19	15	78.9	2	13	4	26.6	9	60
Liang	57	40	70	9	22.5	7	17.5	24	60
Ch'ui	62	45	72.5	9	20	12	26.6	24	53
Koo	71	57	80	18	31.5	23	40	16	28
Fang	53	41	77	5	12	21	51	15	36.5
Kuo	70	49	70	8	16	9	18	32	65
Chen	296	229	77	74	31.9	56	24.5	100	43.6
TOTAL	3,787	2,897	76	693	24	816	28	1,378	48

be assumed to be not lineally related. However, from the same place, Lung Hsi, were also four other individuals, two of whom were born in A.D. 668 (Li Wu-lu) and A.D. 767 (Li Yuan-su). This fact alters the picture. Li Liang-chin (A.D. 722) could not be the father of Li Cho (A.D. 730), but either of them might be the son of Li Wu-lu (A.D. 668) or the father of Li Yuan-su (A.D. 767). For this reason Li Liang-chin and Li Cho, although born less than 15 years apart, were both included in this column.

It is obvious that the number of prominent individuals in these clans who were actually father and son or grandfather and grandson must be smaller than the figures given in Column 4. The surprising thing is that, even after allowing for this and for other liberal benefits of the doubt (for example, even individuals born in the same place and within 15 to 60 years of one another might not be lineally related at all), the number of individuals in this column is very small. It averages about 28 percent of the total number of individuals whose birthplaces are on the record.

The second table goes a step farther. It shows to what extent family prominence was continuous. The numbers following each clan name indicate the frequency of such continuity in the individual clans. For example, following the clan name of Wang the number 24 means that among the prominent Wangs, there were 24 instances in which two individuals were born within 15 to 60 years of each other. Where three individuals are concerned, the age difference involved may be much larger than the 15 to 60 range. For example, the number 13 in the next column means that there were 13 instances in which three individuals are assumed to be lineally related to one another, but that the total age difference among any three individuals may be within or without the 15 to 60 year range. An actual example will clarify this point. Wang Yu-cheng (born A.D. 1706), Wang Fu (born A.D. 1747), and Wang Yun (born A.D. 1760) constitute one of the 13 instances; but Wang Yen-chiu (born A.D. 868), Wang Chu-na (born A.D. 900), and Wang Hsi-yuan (born A.D. 961) also constitute one of the 13 instances. It will be noted that the age difference among the first three is within the 15–60 range, but that among the second three it is larger than that range. As long as Wang Yen-chiu and Wang Chu-na were born within sixty years of each other, and Wang Chu-na and Wang Hsi-yuan were born within sixty years of each other, all three are thereby considered lineally "related."

The result is as obvious as it is surprising. In the vast majority of these cases only two or three individuals are found to be so related in age. Under the definition employed in the present experiment, this means that in all thirty clans family prominence was continued not more than two or at most three generations at a time. After a regression the family might rise again at a later date. In the case of the Wu clan, we can find only one instance in which prominence continued for two generations. None of the prominent names of the Hsu clan are, by our definition, related. One extraordinary exception is found in the Wang clan. In this case there is one instance in which family prominence continued over a period of nearly five hundred years (the first individual was born A.D. 185 and died A.D. 269; the last, or the 39th, individual was born A.D. 645 and died A.D. 728).

The facts given thus far may prove what by our definition they are supposed to prove, namely, that prominence did not last over two or three generations in the vast majority of families. However, there is one serious objection to this position. Throughout the last thousand or more years the number of Chinese who have reached positions of some prominence must be much larger than the total figure given by Professor Chiang. There must be many individuals who were not prominent enough to be included in this volume, but whose achievements were such that they could not be regarded as representing a decline in the prominence of their family as a whole. From this point of view the facts given in the tables may not prove that family prominence was shortlived. This objection is met by an analysis of the biographies contained in the histories of the following districts (hsien chih): Chin Hsien, Chen Hai, Tse Hsi, Ting Hai, (all four are located in Chekiang Province), Tan Tu, Kiang Hing (both are located in Kiangsu Province), and Nan Pi (Hopei Province). District histories are found in most districts. These histories are compiled and revised from time to time by the local people, usually following the appearance of some particularly prominent or wealthy individual in the community. The larger ones run into fifty or a hundred volumes. The smaller have ten or more volumes. Without exception all such district histories contain, amongst other things, a large number of biographies of noted local men who lived during the last one thousand or more years. Some district histories give the biographies of local men who were bureaucrats only. Others include biographies of all those who were bureaucrats and of all those who exhibited such qualities as filial piety, loyalty, community spirit, and skill in the literary art even though they failed to pass any of the imperial examinations. In a number of instances men belonging to several generations within the same family were prominent enough to be given

Instances of Continued Prominence

(By clan and by number of individuals born in same place within 15–60 year range)

Clan	Individuals												
	2	3	4	5	6	7	8	9	10	11	12	14	39
Wang	24	13	1	1	3	..	1	..	..	..	..	..	1
Li	15	7	1	1	2	..	..	..	..	..	..	..	..
Chang	17	5	1	2	..	1	..	..	..	..	..	..	..
Chao	9	2	2	1	..	..	1	..	..	..	..	..	..
Wu	1	..	..	..	..	..	..	..	..	..	..	..	..
Wong	4	3	..	..	2	..	..	..	..	..	..	..	..
Hsieh	1	..	..	..	..	..	..	..	..	1	..	..	..
T'ang	3	..	..	..	..	..	..	..	..	..	..	..	..
Hsu	0	..	..	..	..	..	..	..	..	..	..	..	..
Wei	8	2	..	..	1	..	..	..	..	..	..	..	..
Ho	6	1	1	..	..	..	..	..	..	..	..	..	..
Tung	2	2	..	..	..	..	..	..	..	..	..	..	..
Wen	..	..	..	..	..	..	..	..	..	..	1	..	..

Name																	
Chen	11	5	2	.	1	1	1	.	.	.	.	.	.	.	.	.	.
K'ung	1	4	1	1	1	.	.	.	.	.	.	.	.	.	.	.	.
Hsü	9	5	.	.	.	.	.	.	.	.	.	.	.	.	.	.	.
Sun	5	1	.	.	.	.	1	.	.	.	.	.	.	.	.	.	.
Ting	3	.	.	.	.	.	.	.	.	.	.	.	.	.	.	.	.
Chu	8	3	.	1	1	.	.	.	.	.	.	.	.	.	.	.	.
Kung	2	.	.	.	.	.	.	.	.	.	.	.	.	.	.	.	.
Shen	4	4	1	1	1	.	.	.	.	.	.	.	1	.	.	.	.
Kuo	3	1	.	.	.	.	.	.	.	.	.	.	.	.	.	.	.
Fang	4	1	1	.	1	.	.	.	.	.	.	.	.	.	.	.	.
Ku	6	1	.	.	.	1	1	.	.	.	.	.	.	.	.	.	.
Ch'ui	1	2	1	.	.	.	.	.	.	.	.	.	.	.	.	.	.
Kao	3	2	.	.	.	.	.	.	.	.	.	.	.	.	.	.	.
Loo	2	1	1	1	.	1	.	1	.	.	.	.	.	.	.	.	.
Liang	.	1	1	.	.	.	.	.	.	.	.	.	.	.	.	.	.
Sung	1	1	.	.	.	.	.	.	.	.	.	.	.	.	.	.	.

separate biographies. All those who did not have separate biographies, but who were in any way noted in the community were given a brief or lengthy mention in the biographies of their kinsmen, such as fathers, sons, or brothers. Analysis of these histories has revealed the extent to which prominence was lineally continuous. The results of the entire study will be published *in extenso* later. Data from three of the district histories are summarized in the two tables below. So far as can be ascertained from a general survey of the histories from all the other districts mentioned previously, these figures would seem to be typical.

SOCIAL MOBILITY IN THREE DISTRICTS

District	Total number of biographies	Biographies whose subjects are related	
Chen Hai	334	142	42%
Tse Hsi	739	359	48.5%
Chin Hsien	1,109	693	62%

The first table shows to what extent prominent individuals of each locality reproduced among themselves. The individuals counted under "Biographies Whose Subjects Are Related" include not only the prominent individuals who were fathers and sons or grandfathers and grandsons but also those who were brothers and patrilineal cousins. The percentages given are self-explanatory. They show that in these districts those who became prominent were as likely to be of unknown origin as to have come of prominent kin groups.

The next table gives us a more specific picture. It is arranged more or less in the same way as the table on pages 330–331, except that it is based upon district and not clans. Like that table it shows to what extent family prominence was continuous, but unlike the former because in it the continuity is actual and not inferred. Continuity is counted in two ways. In the vast majority of cases it was unbroken throughout the number of generations recorded. In a small number of cases the continuity was broken by the intermission of one generation. If the father was prominent, the son was unknown, and the grandson was again prominent the case is counted as representing prominence lasting throughout two generations. If the intermission lasted two or more generations, the case is excluded. In a still smaller number of cases the family was prominent for a few

Family Prominence in Three Districts

Number of Generations Through Which Prominence Lasted	CHEN HAI DISTRICT		TSE HSI DISTRICT		CHIN DISTRICT	
	Persons Having Separate Biographies Only [a]	Persons Having Separate Biographies and Mention in Kinsmen's Biographies	Persons Having Separate Biographies Only [a]	Persons Having Separate Biographies and Mention in Kinsmen's Biographies	Persons Having Separate Biographies Only [a]	Persons Having Separate Biographies and Mention in Kinsmen's Biographies
2	15 } 24 82.7%	38 } 48 84%	69 } 89 93.6%	122 } 166 80%	100 } 138 92%	170 } 249 74.7%
3	9	10	20	44	38	79
4	3	7	3	9	6	30
5	2	3	3	5	3	26
6	..	..	..	3	3	14
7	..	..	..	2	..	5
8	..	..	..	..	..	7
9	..	..	..	..	..	2
Total	29	58	95	185	150	333

[a] Including a number of instances in which the continuation of the prominence is interrupted by one generation.

generations, then became unknown for several generations, and then became prominent again for a few generations. Such a family is counted as two instances of continuity.

The results shown by the present table are remarkably similar to those tabulated on pages 330–331. In all three districts about 80 percent of all instances of continued prominence lasted only two to three generations.

APPENDIX V*

More Evidence on Social Mobility in China

I. THE PROBLEM

Not much is scientifically known about social mobility in China. Most people who discuss the subject, including some serious students, have been impressed by the great imperial examination system which has functioned in China for over a thousand years, which was a model for the development of the civil service examination systems in the West,[1] and which served to build a great empire the administrators of which were chosen by ability and talent.[2]

A number of scholars adhere to a more or less opposite view. This group, though comparatively small, is gaining in importance. The outstanding student among this camp is K. A. Wittfogel, who has up to date presented the only body of quantitative data on the subject. The major observation of this student is that the imperial examination system, far from encouraging vertical mobility, was very much undercut by the *Yin* privilege, through which the son of an official could enter the bureaucracy without having anything to do with the examination system.[3]

The purpose of this paper is to show that the *Yin* privilege notwithstanding, there is substantial evidence in support of the former view, namely that a fairly high degree of social mobility existed in Chinese society during the last thousand years. This will be done by showing that (1) in the majority of cases

* Reprinted from *American Sociological Review*, XIV, No. 6, 1949.

[1] Ssu-yu, Teng, "China's Examination System and the West," in H. F. MacNair, *China*, Berkeley, 1946, pp. 441–451.

[2] E. R. Hughes, *The Invasion of China by the Western World*, London, 1937, p. 132, and S. W. Williams, *The Middle Kingdom*, New York, 1899, Vol. I, pp. 562–565.

[3] K. A. Wittfogel, "Public Office in the Liao Dynasty and the Chinese Examination System," *Harvard Journal of Asiatic Studies*, Vol. 10, No. 1, 1947, pp. 13–40.

prominence (chiefly bureaucratic, but also social, economic or literary, as will be made clear below) did not last over one generation; and (2) that of the families which did maintain themselves a little longer, the vast majority did not last over two generations. These facts have led me to the tentative conclusion that there was a considerable degree of vertical social mobility in China, since with no evidence for any drastic reduction of the opportunities of prominence, the families which fell would in the normal course of events be replaced by others which rose.

II. ANALYSIS OF MATERIAL FROM DISTRICT HISTORIES

The material to be presented here represents a partial report of a wider study which is still in progress.[4] The basic data are taken from the biographies contained in Chinese district histories. District histories (sometimes called District Gazeteers) are a well-known documentary source to students on China. The vast majority of the nearly two thousand districts in China have such histories. Some of these documents consist of five to ten volumes; others run into thirty, or fifty, or more. Each set of district histories, amongst other things, contains a large or small number of biographies of male natives of the district who have, for one reason or another, achieved some prominence. These histories have been in existence for various lengths of time. Some, like those for Changsha, were first composed in 1871; others, like those for Nan Pi of Hopei province, were made only less than twenty years ago. The ones which began many centuries ago have as a rule been rewritten or recomposed several times by effort of natives of the districts who had reached some social and political height. Many additions of material, including many new biographies, have usually been made with each fresh effort at rewriting or recomposing the district history.

In connection with the local biographies I am first of all concerned with two things: (1) Some men rated individual biographies, others did not; and (2) some men, though not biographees,[5] were mentioned in the biographies of their fa-

[4] This work is under the sponsorship of The Committee on Research of the Graduate School of Northwestern University. The basic data used in the present analysis were extracted from the district histories by Mr. Yuan Liang, of the University of Chicago.

[5] The term "biographee" signifies in this paper the person whom the biographer writes about in any given biography.

thers, brothers, uncles, patrilineal cousins, or other family members, while others were not. For purposes of this study those men who were mentioned in other people's biographies are regarded as having achieved some degree of *prominence* over those whose names were not mentioned in any biography; and those men who rated individual biographies themselves are regarded as having achieved a higher degree of *prominence* over those who were merely mentioned in some biographies. Since the composers of most district histories appear to spare little effort in identifying the ancestry or progeny of all their biographees, particularly the more prominent ones, the assumption is not absurd that those immediate ancestors and descendants of biographees who were in any way notable would rate separate biographies or be mentioned in their kinsmen's biographies; and that, conversely, those immediate ancestors or descendants who did not rate as individual biographees, nor were mentioned in their kinsmen's biographies, were probably not prominent at all.

Data from four major district histories will be presented here. These are: Chang Sha (Hunan); T'ai An (Shantung); Wu Hsien (Kiangsu); and Sian (Shensi). These four are chosen for presentation here because they represent four widely separated areas and also because of their relative importance in different periods of Chinese history. The data are analyzed in the following ways:

1. First the data are arranged to reveal the proportion of those in which only the prominent man himself is mentioned as compared to those biographies which are related to one another by lineal relationship, or in each of which other lineal ancestors (such as father) or descendants (such as son) are also mentioned by name. For example, the biography of H. C. Ou of Changsha made no mention of anyone except himself and his achievements; on the other hand the biography of C. Y. Fan of Wu Hsien, Kiangsu, contained some references to his sons, his grandsons and his great-grandsons by name and by achievements. Furthermore, each of Fan's four sons and one of his grandsons rated a separate biography in the same district history. (See Figure 24)

2. Secondly, those biographies which contain references to the biographee's lineal ancestors or descendants by name and by achievements, or which are tied up to each other by lineal relationship, are then analyzed to reveal the number of generations through which prominence lasted. For example, in the biography of M. S. Teng of Wu Hsien, Kiangsu, only his son Hsiu, is mentioned. This is then entered into the results as *one instance* in which family prominence lasted two generations.

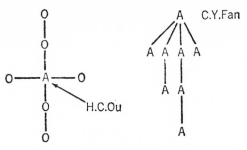

FIGURE 24

In Figures 24 through 28, A represents a biographee or his kins-men who have been mentioned in his biography, or who rated separate biographies. O represents a person whose existence is assumed but who is not a biographee nor mentioned in any biography.

The same would be true if the son were a separate biographee. If the sons of Mr. Teng's son were mentioned, or if Mr. Teng's father were mentioned in the same biography or in a different biography, the case would then be entered into the results as *one instance* in which family prominence lasted three genera-tions. (See Figure 25)

FIGURE 25

However, three other circumstances are of importance here. For example, Mr. C. C. Pan of Wu Hsien, Kiangsu, not only has a son who is a separate biographee but also two brothers, C. D. and C. T., who are also separate biographees. Further-more C. T. has one son who is named in C. T.'s biography, while C. D. has a son and a grandson who are also separate biographees. In this case we have three separate lines of con-tinued prominence and accordingly the data are entered in the results as two instances in which family prominence continued for two generations and one in which it continued for three generations. (See Figure 26a)

A different condition prevails in the aforementioned case of C. Y. Fan of Wu Hsien, Kiangsu. The biographies men-tioned that Fan had one "seventh generation grandson," named

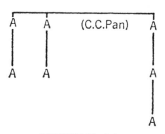

FIGURE 26a

Pang Cheh who had a son Wen Ying. In addition the biographies also mentioned two other groups of Fan's descendants: 1. a "seventeenth generation descendant," Yun Lin and his son P. Ying: and 2. a "twenty-third generation" descendant Lai Chung and his son Hwa. All three cases are entered into the results as three instances in which family prominence was continued for two generations.

The third condition concerns a rule of thumb. If a father is a biographee or mentioned in a biography, the son is not but the grandson again is, then the case is entered as an instance of continued prominence lasting *two generations*. But if the prominence is interrupted by more than one generation the prominence is considered discontinued. (See Figure 26b)

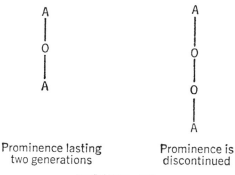

Prominence lasting
two generations

Prominence is
discontinued

FIGURE 26b

3. When the prominence is interrupted by more than one generation the classification of the prominent descendants who came later on will depend upon whether the sons and grandsons of the latter continued the prominence or not. If the descendants mentioned after an interruption of more than one generation had no prominent sons or grandsons they are merely noted in a separate category. In this category are also included prominent brothers, nephews or patrilineal cousins, whose chil-

dren are not biographees or mentioned in the biographies. (See Figure 27)

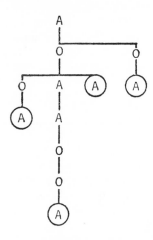

FIGURE 27
The individuals in circles are grouped together and are then added to the total number of individuals among whom prominence continued for two or more generations.

4. Fourthly the data are arranged to reveal the number of individuals who are related to each other (brothers, cousins, uncles and nephews, great-grandfathers and great-grandchildren) but among whom no continued prominence according to the above rules is found. (See Figure 28)

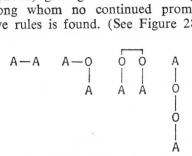

FIGURE 28

5. Lastly the data are analyzed to show the kinds of achievements by the biographees and others who are mentioned in the biographies. Five kinds of achievements are found: (1) being a member of the bureaucracy; (2) having received one or more imperial degrees; (3) being locally known for exemplary conduct, according to Confucian and other traditional ethics, such as filial piety, harmony among brothers, charity toward the public, etc.; (4) having become wealthy through commerce; and (5) being well-known for distinctions in art, poetry, literature or knowledge of sacred scriptures.

The results of the analysis are given in the following table. (See table)

A number of observations may be made on this table. First, the number of biographees among whom prominence continued for two or more generations is consistently lower in every district than the number of biographees among whom prominence did not continue after one generation. (The percentages in Analysis III are always smaller than those in Analysis IV). This result agrees substantially with my previous study of three district histories from Chekiang Province. (Chin Hsien was the exception, in which case Analysis III would have been 62 per cent and Analysis IV, 38 per cent).[6] This would seem to suggest that in these districts those who became prominent were more likely to be of unknown origin than to have come from prominent kin groups.

When we employ "being mentioned in a biography" as a criterion of prominence we find the picture changes slightly. The order is reversed so that the number of prominents in some districts "among whom prominence continued for two or more generations" became larger than those among whom prominence failed to so continue. (Some percentages in Analysis V are larger than those in Analysis VI.) The tendency for the former to increase is consistent, although the rate of increase, governed by some unknown factors, is not. The general reversal of the numerical strength of the two groups indicates that, within the frame of reference of the present paper, more descendants of prominent individuals achieved moderate prominence. Expressing the same thing differently, it means that, if we lower the criterion of prominence we find a higher incidence of inbreeding among prominents. However, in every district, even with the lowered standard of prominence, "fresh blood" seems apparently to appear to the extent of 35 to 80 per cent of all cases involved in the various districts.

Next let us consider the length of continued prominence. As explained in the beginning of the paper, in each district the number of instances of continued prominence is registered. The instances are then arranged in sequences to show through how many generations they lasted. In this section of the analysis no distinction is made between biographees and those who are merely mentioned in biographies. Two things emerge at once: (1) In all districts the incidence of prominence lasting two generations is much higher than that lasting three or more generations; and (2) in all districts the incidence of prominence lasting two or three generations constitutes 80 per cent or more of the whole. This again agrees very well with my previously obtained results in three districts of Chekiang Province. In the

---

[6] See table on p. 334 in Appendix IV.

TABLE

Analysis \ Locality	Chang Sha	Sian	Tai An	Wu Hsien
I. Total no. of biographies	1,382	1,212	1,855	880
II. Total no. of prominent individuals	2,360	1,789	1,911	1,296
III. No. of biographies among whom prominence continued for two or more generations	609 or 43%	361 or 28.8%	324 or 17.4%	365 or 41.5%
IV. No. of biographies among whom prominence did not continue after one generation	773 or 57%	851 or 71.2%	1,531 or 82.6%	515 or 58.5%
V. No. of all prominent individuals among whom prominence continued for two or more generations	1,549 or 65%	883 or 49%	376 or 20%	755 or 58.0%
VI. No. of all prominent individuals among whom prominence did not continue after one generation	811 or 35%	906 or 51%	1,535 or 80%	541 or 42%
VII. Total number of instances of continued prominence	511	273	142	217
VIII. Number of generations through which prominence lasted among all — Two generations	237 or 46%	197 or 72%	94 or 66%	142 or 65%
Three generations	176 or 34%	46 or 16%	36 or 25%	45 or 21%
Four generations	88 or 17%	17 or 6%	9 or 6.3%	16 or 7%
Five and over	3%	6%	2.7%	7%
IX. Number of prominent individuals who are related to the prominent lineages singly (included in V)	20 (about 1.2% of V or 2.4% of VI)	41 (4.6% of V or 4.2% of VI)	7 (1.9% of V or 0.4% of VI)	203 (26.8% of V or 39% of VI)
X. No. of prominent individuals who are not related to prominent lineages but are related to each other singly (included in VI)	70 (4.2% of V or 8.5% of VI)	107 (12.1% of V or 11.8% of VI)	18 (4.8% of V or 11.6% of VI)	58 (7.6% of V or 10.7% of VI)

XI. Kinds of distinction achieved by all among whom prominence lasted for two or more generations

	Locality	Chang Sha (Total XI:1,549)	Sian (XI:883)	Tai An (XI:376)	Wu Hsien (XI:755)
Biographies	A*	507 or 83%	311 or 86%	267 or 82%	252 or 69%
	B	9 or 1.5%	None	14 or 4.6%	10 or 3%
	C	61 or 10% (Total 609)	23 or 6.3% (Total 361)	19 or 5.8% (Total 324)	45 or 13% (Total 365)
	D	None	None	None	None
	E	4 or 0.7%	13 or 3.7%	9 or 2.7%	38 or 10%
	F	28 or 4.6%	14 or 4%	15 or 4.9%	20 or 5%
Non-biographies	A	777 or 83%	422 or 81%	19 or 37%	228 or 58%
	B	81 or 8.7%	18 or 3%	18 or 35%	22 or 6%
	C	72 or 7.6% (Total 940)	70 or 13.8% (Total 522)	10 or 19% (Total 52)	94 or 24% (Total 390)
	D	None	None	None	1 or 0.2%
	E	7 or 0.5%	10 or 2%	4 or 7%	43 or 11%
	F	3 or 0.2%	2 or 0.2%	1 or 2%	2 or 0.8%

XII. Kinds of distinction achieved by all among whom prominence did not last after one generation

	Locality	(Total XII:811)	(XII:906)	(XII:1,535)	(XII:541)
Biographies	A	312 or 40%	494 or 58%	622 or 41%	221 or 43%
	B	72 or 9%	15 or 2%	646 or 42%	16 or 3%
	C	270 or 35% (Total 773)	277 or 27% (Total 851)	189 or 12% (Total 1,531)	171 or 33% (Total 515)
	D	None	None	None	None
	E	20 or 2%	68 or 8%	19 or 1.2%	88 or 17%
	F	99 or 14%	47 or 5%	59 or 3.8%	19 or 4%
Non-biographies	A	15 or 39%	30 or 54%	None	8 or 30%
	B	17 or 44% (Total 38)	2 or 3.6% (Total 55)	None (Total 4)	None (Total 26)
	F	6 or 17%	23 or 42%	4 or 100%	18 or 17%

* Key to letters: A. Being member of the bureaucracy, or holder of any official title. B. Holders of imperial degrees. C. Exemplary conduct. D. Wealth through commerce. E. Distinctions in art, literature, calligraphy, poetry or sacred scriptures. F. Combinations of the above.

three Chekiang districts analyzed, the incidence of prominence lasting two to three generations constituted 75 to 94 per cent of the whole.[7]

Two questions must be answered here. One question is, granted that prominence did not last along lineal family lines, what about individuals who became prominent because they had prominent cousins, uncles, nephews, or great-great-grandfathers? If the number of such individuals is large, does it then not mean a high degree of inbreeding among prominents?

In answering the question we must look for two kinds of facts. First, the number of prominent individuals who are related to members of prominent lineages (i.e., lineages in which prominence was continued for two or more generations) as cousins, great-great-grandfathers, nephews, etc. In three of the four district histories the number of such individuals is so small (ranging from 7 to 20) that they would be of no significant consequence to the main observations, however they are handled. Only Wu Hsien of Kiangsu province has a much larger number (203) which would make a quarter of all Wu Hsien prominents among whom prominence continued for two or more generations. However, all of these numbers, large or small, were included in the computation of the percentage of individuals among whom prominence continued for two or more generations. (That is to say, the numbers for each district contained in Analysis V include the numbers contained in Analysis IX for that district.) The addition of these numbers made no difference to our major conclusion. For example, in the case of Wu Hsien, even after adding the very large number of 230 to the total of "prominent individuals among whom prominence continued for two or more generations" (Analysis V), the size of the latter category is still well within the range set by districts.

A second kind of facts consists of the number of prominent individuals whose prominence was not continued lineally, but whose cousins, uncles, or brothers were prominent; the prominence of the latter was also not continued lineally. (See Figure 28.) The percentages occupied by these prominents in each district are again so small (ranging in number from 18 to 107) that they would not have made any difference, one way or the other, to the major thesis of this paper.

To sum up: the purpose of this paper is to elucidate by quantitative data the extent of vertical social mobility in Chinese society. With specifically defined criteria for the term prominence and a particular set of documentary material, it has been demonstrated that roughly 50 per cent of the local prominents in any district studied came from unknown origin and that

[7] See table on p. 335 in Appendix IV.

roughly 80 per cent of the descendants beyond the grandson generation of the local prominents also became unknown.

This picture of rapid change of family fortune within a few generations is very striking, especially where class is usually determined by position in the bureaucracy, and where the position in bureaucracy depended very much upon family influence. The latter being the case, one would expect family prominence to continue, for obvious reasons. Even from the present analysis, the strength of family influence in bureaucracy is evident. For example, if we examine the biographees among whom prominence lasted for two or more generations, we find in three out of four districts over 80 per cent of them distinguished themselves by position in bureaucracy. (See Table, Analysis XI). On the other hand, of the biographees among whom prominence did not last more than one generation, only about 50 per cent were bureaucrats. (See Table, Analysis XII). These facts suggest that distinctions in bureaucracy had better chances of being continued along kinship lines than others. Nevertheless, taking the data as a whole, the singular thing is that, in spite of the importance of family influence, the picture of discontinued prominence emerges more vividly through this analysis than otherwise.

But here a further question arises. There is an American saying, "From shirt sleeves to shirt sleeves in three generations." Would such a saying not suggest that prominence also fails to last along lineal lines in the United States as well? While one cannot at present express a definite opinion on the subject, one must reject any close comparison between the two societies in this respect due to a basic reason. In American life an individual may achieve social prominence in a variety of ways. It has been said that the diaper service, which is now a nation-wide American industry, was started by a group of enterprising University of Chicago students during the depression. In China, on the other hand, the path of social ascension has been very narrow. Of 7,359 prominent individuals involved in 5,331 histories from four widely separated districts, only one individual was marked as distinguished due to "wealth through commerce." (See Table, Analysis XI, Wu Hsien). Practically all cases of prominence in all districts were based upon (1) position in bureaucracy; (2) imperial degrees or honors; (3) distinction in literature, poetry, art, etc.; and (4) exemplary conduct following Confucian principles. The largest percentage of any group of prominents was based upon position in bureaucracy.

This being the case, the term prominence may be defined for China as we have done it here with some actual correspondence to the class structure of the society, but it becomes much more complicated if applied to the United States. Is the machine-tool-shop-owner-son of an American small town politician less prominent than his father? Where vertical mobility is complicated by so much horizontal mobility, there are as yet neither the necessary criteria nor the relevant data for drawing definite conclusions on comparative social mobility in the United States and in China.

III. FURTHER OBSERVATIONS

This picture of a fairly frequent vertical social mobility agrees with my observations in several communities as well as in the wider Chinese national scene in general. For example, whether it is the North China village in which I was born, the Manchurian town in which I spent the latter part of my youth, or the two Southwest communities at which I stopped as a field worker, I found it easy to acquire knowledge about the present downcast conditions of members of families which only a few years ago, or one or two generations back, had still been prosperous.

This fall of many prosperous families does not seem to have much to do with the argument advanced by H. T. Fei in an article on *Peasant and Gentry*[8] namely, that powerful families have a tendency to lower their fertility, so that they die out. The only evidence that Fei gave was his own family. Yet even *a priori,* the fact that concubinage and better nutrition are the prerogatives of the well-to-do will deprive Fei's argument of plausibility. Also when we look at the numerous descendants of such well known men as Yuan Shih-Kai, Li Yuan-Hung, Chang Cho-lin, Li Hung-Chang, Cheng Kuo-Fan, and many others, we shall find fertility has rather little to do with the fall of families. The rich and well situated do reproduce, but their descendants tend to fail the standards set by their forebears.

The rather drastic difference between the conclusion offered here and that of Dr. Wittfogel, which was referred to at the beginning of this paper, is obvious. In Dr. Wittfogel's article already mentioned, he presented a quantitative statement on the social origin of "111 leading officials" (mostly prime ministers) of T'ang dynasty and "153 biographies of officials of different rank who lived during the dynasty's middle period when T'ang

[8] H. T. Fei, "Peasant and Gentry," *American Journal of Sociology,* July, 1946.

institutions were in full flower."[9] Upon analysis he found 77.5 per cent of the 111 leading officials reached their rank by way of examinations; 16.2 per cent no record; while only 6.3 per cent by way of their father's position. Among the 153 officials of different rank the picture is much less clear. Here 27.4 per cent reached officialdom by way of examination; 60.8 per cent no record; while 11.8 per cent by way of *yin*, that is, their father's position. Dr. Wittfogel's observation is:[10]

> The number of officials in the second category who benefited from the *Yin* privilege is impressive; it is even more impressive when seen in relation to the number of degrees recorded: 18 to 42.

It is hard to see how data such as these convey any impressiveness of the *Yin* privilege. No information is given as to how the 153 officials were selected; nor what proportion of the 153 formed of the total number from which the smaller number were selected. Lastly, it is also hard to see any scientific value in any quantitative statement of which 60 per cent of the data is unknown.

Of course, Dr. Wittfogel was discussing an early period of Chinese society and the material presented here from the district histories refer mainly to later periods, especially Ming and Ching dynasties. Secondly, it is probable that, with more of his monumental work coming to light, some of the present difficulties will be resolved.

After completion of this paper I discovered, to my surprise and satisfaction, that a conclusion similar to mine was reached by Dr. E. A. Kracke, Jr. in an article entitled "Family vs. Merit in Chinese Civil Service Examinations Under the Empire."[11] Dr. Kracke's sources—two lists of civil service graduates dated 1148 and 1256—were entirely different from mine, but he came to the same general conclusion.

[9] K. A. Wittfogel, *op. cit.*, pp. 26–27.
[10] *Ibid.*, p. 27.
[11] *Harvard Journal of Asiatic Studies*, Sept. 1947, Vol. 10, No. 2, pp. 103–123.

Short Bibliography for Further Reading

A. THE TOTAL NUMBER OF WORKS IN ENGLISH on Chinese community or village life is very small. Some of these appeared before the publication of *Under the Ancestors' Shadow* and others after it. Those on China before the Communist Revolution are as follows:

Fei, H. T.
1939 *Peasant Life in China*, London, G. Routledge & Sons. This is a study of Kai Hsien Kung, a village on the Yangtze River in Eastern China. Its special focus is on family, kinship, and the economic life of the peasants.

Fei, H. T. and Chang, Chih–I
1945 *Earthbound China* (A Study of Rural Economy in Yunnan). Chicago, University of Chicago Press. This is a study of family finances, consumption, land tenure, population movement, organization of commerce and industry in three villages in Western Yunnan, all situated within 100 miles west or southwest of Kunming, the provincial capital of Yunnan and the China terminus of the Burma Road. These three are about 200 miles east of West Town, which is the subject of *Under the Ancestors' Shadow*.

Freedman, Maurice
1965 *Lineage Organization in Southeastern China.* London, Athlone Press. This is not a localized community study, but a restatement, in terms of social anthropology, of the rural social structure in the specified area. The author has made use of a wide variety of data on village communities published in books and articles.

Freedman, Maurice
  1966 *Chinese Lineage and Society: Fukien and Kwangtung*. London, Athlone Press. This is a further analysis of kinship and clan in southeastern China. In doing so, the author has made use of scattered and unpublished data, particularly those concerning the Chinese in Kowloon and the New Territories which are part of the British Colony of Hongkong.

Fried, Morton H.
  1953 *Fabric of Chinese Society* (A Study of the Social Life of a Chinese County Seat). New York, Praeger. This is an anthropological study of Ch'u Hsien, in Eastern China. It deals with family, kinship and non-kinship ties and how they bear on Chinese life.

Gallin, Bernard
  1966 *Hsin Hsing, Taiwan: A Chinese Village in Change*. Berkeley and Los Angeles, University of California Press. This is the only book length report in English so far of a village in Taiwan, for nearly fifty years a Japanese colony and since 1945 under the Nationalist Government. Besides tribal peoples who still maintain their tribal identities, a majority of the population in the island were Chinese from Fukien province across the Taiwan straits who found their new home several centuries ago.

Hsu, Francis L. K.
  1952 *Religion, Science and Human Crises* (A Study of China in Transition and Its Implication for the West). London, Routledge and Kegan Paul. This is an analysis of what traditional measures people of West Town (which life is the subject of *Under the Ancestors' Shadow*) took to ward off a terrible cholera epidemic, what explanations they gave for the epidemic, how they reacted to modern medicine and hygienic ideas when these were made available to them and in what way all

these were related to the social organization and age-old values.

Gamble, Sidney D.
1954 *Ting Hsien, A North China Rural Community.* New York, Institute of Pacific Relations. This is a study of the social survey type rather than an integrated anthropological work. Ting Hsien, in Hopei province, North China, was the best known center of the famous "Rural Reconstruction Movement" under the National government before Japan invaded China in 1937.

Kulp, Daniel H.
1925 *Country Life in South China.* New York, Teachers College, Columbia University Bureau of Publications. This is a study of Phoenix Village in Kwangtung province, of which Canton is the capital, in South China. The work emphasizes family, kinship, ancestor worship and other religious practices.

Osgood, Cornelius
1963 *Village Life in Old China* (A Community Study of Kao Yao, Yunnan). New York, Ronald Press. This community is only a few miles southwest of Kunming, the provincial capital. This is an important record of life (family, economic activities, leadership, life cycle, and religion) in China before the Communist Revolution, when she was under Japanese aggression. By this time China's railways, industrial centers and coastal cities were mostly in Japanese hands, but life in Yunnan villages was not yet touched very much.

Yang, Martin C.
1945 *A Chinese Village.* New York, Columbia University Press. This is an analysis of life in Taitou, a village in Shantung Peninsula, in North China, by a scholar who was raised in it. Its focus is the family, kinship, religion, and certain other aspects of the communal life.

B. STUDIES OF THE VILLAGE COMMUNITY ON MAINLAND CHINA SINCE 1949 are even rarer than those before it. Many journalistic and travel logs have appeared. Many of these are valuable in one way or another. However, only the following five books are works of research in given localities:

Crook, Isabel and David
1959   *Revolution in a Chinese Village: Ten Mile Inn.* London, Routledge and Kegan Paul. The work was actually done about 1947 or 1948, when the Kuomintang was still in power in the major part of China, and engaged in a life and death struggle with the Communists. This village is located normally in northwestern Honan province, but at this time it was included in a regional administrative area under Communist control.

Crook, Isabel and David
1966   *The First Years of Yangyi Commune.* New York, Humanities Press. This may be called "Ten Mile Inn Revisited" after about ten years, except that the village is now more fully seen as part of Yangyi Commune. The Crooks, who teach English at the Foreign Languages Institute in Peking, report the many changes that have been brought about in the village on the formal level.

Myrdal, Jan
1965   *Report from a Chinese Village* (translation from the Swedish by Maurice Michael), New York, Pantheon Books. This is a collection of about thirty verbatim autobiographies of nearly all the active men and women in a northern Shensi village during one month in 1962. The author was assisted by his wife, Gun Kessle, who is an artist and photographer. They lived and moved freely among the villagers with a government-appointed interpreter.

Yang, C. K.
1959   *A Chinese Village in Early Communist Transi-*

tion. This is the village of Nanching in a suburban area near Canton in South China. The field work was done from 1948 to 1951. It deals with the changing relation of the village to the greater national community under the centralized Communist rule.

C. TWO BOOKS IN ENGLISH ON THE CHINESE FAMILY IN MODERN TIMES may be of interest to show the same trends of change before and after 1949. These studies do not concentrate on any one locality:

Lang, Olga
1946   *Chinese Family and Society.* New Haven, Yale University Press. This is a sociological analysis based upon many questionnaires, field observations, and written sources. It presents data and discussions on family organization, family types, romance and marriage, clan, conjugal relationships, childhood and old age, and friendship.

Yang, C. K.
1959   *The Chinese Family in the Communist Revolution.* Cambridge, Harvard University Press. Using the concepts of structure and function, the author analyzes the shift in the form of marriage and divorce, the alteration of age and sex as criteria for family status and authority, the reduction of functions of the family and disorganization of the clan, and the waning of ancestor worship as he personally saw it in the early days of the Communist Revolution.

D. IN ADDITION TO COMMUNITY STUDIES, a number of autobiographies (either self-written or dictated to someone else) may assist the reader to obtain an intimate glimpse of Chinese life. Some of these autobiographies are remarkable in the extent to which they reveal the bearing of kinship and a kinship oriented personality formation. In particular the reader will find the following three works of interest:

Chiang, Yee

1963   *A Chinese Childhood*. New York, W. W. Norton. This is a book by an eminent artist of international repute about his early life in central China. He confirms many of the details in *Under the Ancestors' Shadow*. His family was financially comfortable and scholarly, but not prominent in the bureaucracy.

Pruitt, Ida

1945   *A Daughter of Han*. New Haven, Yale University Press. This is an autobiography of an old woman servant who told her life story to Miss Pruitt, who was born in North China of American missionary parents. The book includes fascinating details of the servant's struggle for livelihood and her observations of the homes and personalities of different employers including Western missionaries.

Pu Yi, Aisin-Gioro

1964   *From Emperor to Citizen* (The Autobiography of Aisin-Gioro Pu Yi). Peking, Foreign Language Press, two volumes. Pu Yi was the last Manchu emperor and was deposed when he was five. Later he was made the puppet emperor of the Japanese sponsored "Manchukuo," captured by Soviet Russian forces, appeared in the post-World War II war criminal trials in Tokyo after Japan's defeat, imprisoned in mainland China for a number of years during which he went through self-examination and thought reform, has now remarried and is working as an ordinary citizen. The book contains many details of court intrigues, of machinations of Chinese militarists and foreign powers (chiefly Japan), and social and political conditions of China since 1911. But of special interest here is how the forces of kinship among the highly placed bore on the personality characteristics of their chief product. Pu Yi seems to be remarkably conscious of the factors which figured largely in his variegated long career.

Index

Abortion, 110, 253

Acculturation, of Western tribes, 18

Adler, Alfred, 249

Adoption, 75–76, 254–55

Age: authority of, 116–17, 119, 131; concern over burial, 131–33; and generation, 273–74, 282; prerogatives of, in housing, 54, in rituals, 190

Agriculture, 65–66

Ancestor(s): authority of, 262–65; as basis of education, 200, 243; communal worship of, 18, 167–77, 185, 200, 244–46, 282; festivals to, Ch'ing Ming, 23, 132, 180, 7th Moon, 23; filial piety, 56–63, 147, 162–63, 167, 171, 186, 208–9, 329, 340, 345; and genealogical records, 78, 109, 126, 184–85, 232–37; and graveyards, 40–50, 179–83; offerings to, 118, 179–91, 202–3; "shadow of," 8; shrines, family, to, 31, 40, 183 ff.; as source of prestige, 37, 41, 46, 53; temples, clan, 41, 50–53, 167–69, 186–92, 195–97. *See also* Big-family

ideal; Kinship system; Spirits

Ancestor festival, 184–92

Anti-Semitism, xii

Anwhei province, 17

Apparition (*hsien sheng*), 135

Apprentice system, 219

Arensberg, C. M., 64

Authority, 131, 246, 273–74; of aged, 116–17, 119, 131; ancestral, 262–65; in development of personality, 8, 12, 262–65, 281–83; division under same roof, 248–50; parental, 262–63, 268 ff., "safety valves," 248–50; psychological effects, 12, 270–71; sexes, differences in, 274–75; submission to, 52, 265, 268 ff.

Barrenness, of women, 75–76, 105, 253–55, 322

"Basic personality configuration," 10–11, 13, 261, 265–72. *See also* Behavior characteristics

Behavior characteristics, 267–72; anonymity, preference for, 267–68; excesses, 268–71; idealized from classical-literary world, 163; initiative, lack of, 271–72